MEANING IN ENGLISH

DATE DUE

-2. NOV. 1999		
13. NOV. 2001		
27. NOV. 2001		
21 JUN 2013		
GAYLORD		PRINTED IN U.S.A.

Also by Lesley Jeffries and published by Macmillan

THE LANGUAGE OF TWENTIETH-CENTURY POETRY

Meaning in English

An Introduction to Language Study

Lesley Jeffries

First published 1998 by
MACMILLAN PRESS LTD
Houndmills, Basingstoke, Hampshire RG21 6XS
and London
Companies and representatives
throughout the world

ISBN 0–333–73946–9 hardcover
ISBN 0–333–65916–3 paperback

A catalogue record for this book is available
from the British Library.

This book is printed on paper suitable for recycling and
made from fully managed and sustained forest sources.

10 9 8 7 6 5 4 3 2 1
07 06 05 04 03 02 01 00 99 98

Typeset by Forewords, Oxford/Longworth Editorial Services
Longworth, Oxfordshire.

Printed in Hong Kong

Published in the United States of America 1998 by
ST. MARTIN'S PRESS, INC.,
Scholarly and Reference Division,
175 Fifth Avenue, New York, N.Y. 10010

ISBN 0–312–21379–4 cloth
ISBN 0–312–21380–8 paperback

Contents

Preface   ix

Phonetic Symbols   xi

1 Introduction   1
 1.1 'Look at it Like This'   1
 1.2 'I Mean What I Say'   12
 1.3 The Power of the Sign   16
 1.4 Pinning the Butterfly?   27
 1.5 Is it All in the Words?   29
 1.6 The Scope of the Book   34

2 Sounds and Meaning   37
 2.1 Beauty in the Ear of the Hearer?   37
 2.2 'Her Voice Betrayed Her'   48
 2.3 Shouting and Squealing   54
 2.4 Rhythm and Music   63

3 Words and Meaning   71
 3.1 Empty Words   71
 3.2 The Smallest Units of Meaning   79
 3.3 Analysing Word Meaning   87
 3.4 Meaningful Relationships   98
 3.5 You Know a Word by its Reputation   108
 3.6 Multiple Meanings   114

4 Structure and Meaning   121
 4.1 Words in Combinations   121
 4.2 'Naming' and 'Doing' Words   129
 4.3 Subject – Verb – Object   136
 4.4 Information and Sentences   141
 4.5 Locating Meaning in Sentences   147

5   Textual Meaning   157
     5.1   Connections   157
     5.2   Speaking or Acting?   166
     5.3   Answering Back   170
     5.4   Whose Turn Next?   176
     5.5   Storytelling and Persuasion   187

6   Contextual Meaning   197
     6.1   Style and Manners in Interaction   197
     6.2   When, Where, Who, Why and How?   207
     6.3   Whose Meaning is it Anyway?   215
     6.4   Ideologies, Common Sense and Texts   222

7   Meaning and Reality   229
     7.1   The Whorfian Hypothesis   229
     7.2   Meaning and Literature   236
     7.3   Negotiating Meaning   240
     7.4   Chickens and Eggs   246

Further Reading   253

Glossary   257

Index   265

To Ella Jeffries,
my lovely daughter

Preface

This book is aimed at students and interested 'lay readers' who have not yet acquired a large technical vocabulary in linguistics, but who want, or need, to be able to make accurate and sophisticated assessments of how particular texts in the English language manage to create meaning. Although it is inevitable that advanced study of the English language will eventually require some level of technical competence, it is also true that many introductory books lose sight of the goal in their anxiety to train students in the formal analysis of texts. Here, the reader is taken gently through the 'levels' of language, and introduced to how each level creates meaning as well as how the layers interact in producing meaning. Although the style remains accessible throughout, the book does not avoid the issues raised by adopting particular theories of language and it opens and closes by discussing the role of theories and models themselves in helping us understand human linguistic behaviour.

Much of the material included here has been gestating for a long time and has been used as course material with students at the University of Leeds and the University of Huddersfield. I would like to thank all the students at these institutions who contributed in countless ways to the development of my thoughts. Some of the examples and ideas relating to lexical field analysis and componential analysis were developed whilst I was working as a researcher in the OUP lexical research unit at the University of Leeds. Tony Cowie, Joanna Channell, Penny Willis and Rosie Sansome should share any credit for the good aspects of this part of the work. More recently, I have unashamedly used colleagues from Huddersfield in trying out ideas and looking for examples or references. Those who have helped me to avoid more mistakes than I would otherwise make include Glynis Ridley, Hugh Robertson, Gordon Byers, Liz Holt and Cathy MacGregor. I would also like to thank my colleagues for their support in covering my teaching during the sabbatical semester in which much of this book was written. Those friends who have unwittingly supplied 'living' examples include my children, Sam and Ella, and Lynette Hunter and Peter Sansom. Credit should go to Dave Webb for his technical expertise, particularly in last-minute printing problems. Dave, Sam and Ella should also be thanked for the equal amounts of encouragement and nagging that helped me to finish this piece of work. All the faults remain my own.

Phonetic Symbols

There are a small number of phonetic symbols used in this book to indicate sounds more accurately than is possible by orthography. Those symbols which might be unfamiliar to the reader or might have different phonetic value to normal, are represented here.

Consonants

- /θ/   as in *thigh*
- /ð/   as in *thy*
- /ʃ/   as in *ship*
- /ʒ/   as in *leisure* (this consonant does not occur initially in English words)
- /tʃ/   as in *cheep*
- /dʒ/   as in *jeep*
- /j/   as in *young*
- /ŋ/   as in *sing* (this consonant does not occur initially in English words)

Vowels

The written vowels have many different pronunciations in English. For the sake of consistency, the following symbols (relating to an RP accent) are used here:

- /ɪ/   as in *bit*
- /iː/   as in *feet*
- /e/   as in *bed*
- /æ/   as in *bad*
- /ɑː/   as in *bath*
- /ʌ/   as in *cup*
- /ɒ/   as in *stop*
- /ɔː/   as in *four*
- /ʊ/   as in *foot*

Phonetic Symbols

/uː/   as in *food*
/ə/   as in unstressed *the*
/ɜː/   as in *heard*
/aɪ/   as in *bright*
/eɪ/   as in *fate*
/aʊ/   as in *found*
/əʊ/   as in *load*
/eə/   as in *fair*
/iə/   as in *fear*
/ʊə/   as in *poor*

1

Introduction

1.1 'Look at it Like This'

The main aim of this book is to enable the reader to find ways of talking about meanings in language, particularly in relation to English. Meaning is fundamental to human society and language is one of the primary ways of conveying meaning. However, meaning is not a simple phenomenon and even the previous sentence could be seen as over-simplifying the relationship between meaning and language. It implies, after all, that meanings are there first, and that language comes later, as a straightforward representation of these prior meanings.

In order to analyse any phenomenon, natural or human-made, we need to simplify it to a certain extent. Imagine you are a zoologist on an expedition and you have just discovered a new species of guinea-pig. There are 300 of them and you only have two days to make notes about them before travelling back to your laboratory where you will try to work out whether they all belong to the same species, or whether there is actually a cluster of related species. You will not waste time and effort describing features of each individual creature, such as the fact that one of them has a brown spot just above his tail, while another has a brown spot higher up on his back. This method would give you 300 different descriptions and will not begin to make an analysis of the sub-groups of guinea-pigs. What you *will* be interested in, however, is whether a sizeable group of them has the brown spot whilst another group has black noses.

If we simply look at the complex phenomena to be described and describe them in every detail, without any generalisations, we will end up with a description that is just as complex as the phenomenon being described. Such a description is not very useful.

To avoid this problem, scientists and social scientists create 'models' to describe the data they have available. Models are usually rather like metaphors, because they use one thing to describe another. Some simple examples of models/metaphors that we use in everyday life are the following:

> A heart is like a pump.
> The brain is like a computer.
> The seasons/months are like a circle.

It is interesting to speculate on what other models could be used to describe these ideas. If our society did not have pumps, we might use the analogy of canal locks to describe the way in which blood moves from one chamber to the other in the heart. Some of us can just remember the world before computers and presumably in those days we had other ways of modelling the brain; perhaps as a filing cabinet full of information? It is difficult, nowadays, to imagine the brain functioning in any other way. Such a close match between a concept and its model has both advantages and disadvantages which will be discussed shortly.

It is clear from the examples above that some models are a better fit than others; they describe the data more exactly. If we consider the usual circular models used to describe seasons and months, we see that there are some occasions when human beings prefer one model to another for psychological reasons, rather than because they fit the data.

There is one obvious problem with the circular model of the seasons; it implies that each year's cycle blends into the other with no forward motion to represent time. If we made our circle move forward, like a wheel, it would be much closer to matching the data. After all, the evidence is there; we all get older each year! A similar problem occurs with the weekly and monthly cycles as well.

Even the proposed new, improved model of a forward-moving wheel has some problems, however. The smooth transition from one season to the next does not allow us to represent the two identifiable points in the year that stand out from the circle. These are the summer solstice (the longest day of the year) and the winter solstice (the shortest day of the year). Another model of the seasons suggests itself at this stage, since a 'wave-form' diagram (see Figure 1.1)

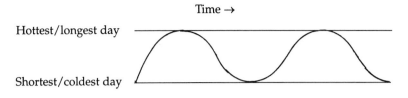

Figure 1.1

allows for high-points and low-points as well as forward motion (time) and smooth transitions (the curves of the wave).

Despite these improvements on the more common circular model, it might be suggested that such a model will never catch on. There are at least two possible reasons. First, it may be too complex for our usual human needs. Secondly, we may wish to avoid remembering the time axis (i.e. our mortality) and concentrate on the renewal of yearly cycles which may be satisfactorily served by the circular model.

If we return to the model mentioned earlier where the brain is seen as being like a computer, we can see how even very well-matched models may cause problems. The closer a model's fit, the more likely it is that people will forget that it is only a model. There is evidence, for example, that the human brain does not work as methodically as computers. When a computer has a problem (such as a chess move) to work out, it will be programmed to go through all the possible solutions one by one in some kind of order. Because it can perform calculations very quickly indeed, it appears to work like a human brain. However, the brain will sometimes make leaps thereby avoiding going doggedly through hundreds of possible answers – and so far scientists have not been able to replicate this on a computer. The danger of taking models too far is that they may restrict our imagination just at the point when what we really need is a new – or adapted – model.

All of the features of popular or scientific models also apply to models of language description: all models have limitations. Sometimes a simpler model is needed, even though it is less accurate than other options. At other times, in order to get the most accurate description of very complex data, we may need a number of different models.

Let us return to the idea of meaning and language which was

criticised in the first paragraph of this section. It was implied there that meaning was a kind of 'invisible, unclothed being', waiting for the clothes of language to allow it to be seen. This assumes that meaning and language are in a simple relationship where language reflects some 'given' reality. Much of the rest of this book will challenge this model.

One of the most commonly discussed models of language is where all linguistic elements (e.g. words or phrases) are seen as being like beads on a string, each following the other in sequential order. This model picks up the inevitable linearity of language, where words have no option but to follow each other and cannot occur simultaneously:

Although it is important to recognise the linearity of language, there are other aspects of language which this model ignores. One of the problems is that there are clearly restrictions on the occurrence of words and these restrictions are not always caused by the adjacent word. For example, the pronoun (*she*) in the following sentence has female gender because the Subject (*his mother*) is female, not because it occurs next to *room* or *looked*:

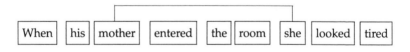

There is, to extend our model a little, an extra piece of string tying together *mother* and *she*.

If we are looking for a general model of meaning in English, we will probably be disappointed. There are so many levels at which meaning operates, and even using the word *level* is to take for granted another model of language which is often used (see Table 1.1). Many introductory textbooks on linguistics use this model of the levels of language, or something similar. And you could go on building up sentences into texts and discourses. In fact, the 'layers' or 'levels' model of language has been very influential in the way that research has been carried out into language. Linguists tended,

Table 1.1

Units at each level	Level of language
Sounds which combine to make ↓	**Phonology**
Morphemes, which combine to make ↓	**Morphology**
Words, which combine to make ↓	**Lexis**
Phrases, which combine to make ↓	**Syntax**
Clauses, which combine to make ↓	**Syntax**
Sentences, which combine to make ↓	**Syntax**
Texts	**Discourse**

until recently, to see themselves as belonging to one or other of the layers. You were either a phonologist or a syntactician, a morphologist or a discourse analyst.

The outcome of this anecdote is, perhaps, inevitable: whilst much very good work was done *within* the levels, very little research covered the overlaps and correspondences *between* levels. What is more, this model has no place at all for meaning. In linguistics, meaning is often called 'semantics' as if it were really another level although it has no position in the levels model because meaning occurs at all the other levels, as we shall see in Chapters 2–5. Chapters 6 and 7 will show that meaning occurs additionally at the overlaps between linguistic material and other kinds of symbolic system, such as body language.

There have been other general models of language proposed. They are usually developments from the levels model and just one of the most influential will be mentioned here. In the 1960s and 1970s, Noam Chomsky (1965) caused a revolution in linguistics by suggesting that language was not just an arrangement of items of different sizes (from sounds to sentences), but that rather like a factory production line, the raw materials of language (sounds, words, etc.) were then processed into the final form (syntax) and interpreted by a series of semantic rules to produce meaning. The model retained the same basic elements, but suggested a dynamic relationship between them and managed to introduce meaning into the model for the first time. Chomsky's model had a great deal of influence in linguistics, particularly in the United States, though increasingly people have become dissatisfied with all early models of language because they seemed largely to ignore the contribution of context to meaning.

One final point about the danger of taking models too far will be made with reference to social/political models of human organisation. Some models can be associated with a number of different visual representations, and the choice of one or other of these representations can subtly influence the way the model develops. For example, there are two ways of representing hierarchical models: as a triangle and as a series of finer and finer grids. In the triangle, the 'top' of the triangle represents the most important and rarest position, whilst the base represents the least important and most common position. In the grid representation, the 'top' of the hierarchy is represented by the largest square whilst the lower levels are represented by increasingly smaller squares. This model emphasises the inclusiveness of the different levels in a hierarchy, rather than their importance.

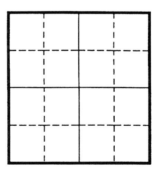

We will see in Chapter 3 that hierarchical models are useful for describing the relationship between words with overlapping meanings. However, if we use two non-linguistic examples for a moment, we can see that hierarchies have changed from symbolising greater inclusiveness to representing levels of importance in human society.

In many democracies, for example, there is one person who is seen as being at the top of the hierarchy, i.e. at the top of the triangle.

In Britain this is the Prime Minister. If we look at the hierarchy from a vantage point above Britain, using the grids as our model, we see that rather than being the most important person in the country, the Prime Minister is simply symbolic of the most inclusive category. In other words she or he is the representative of all the people while Members of Parliament are representative of the people in their constituency, local councillors are representative of all the people in their ward and so on. A similar perspective can be used for looking at the Roman Catholic church, with the Pope not at the pinnacle of a triangle, but as the largest category. Bishops and parish priests would represent progressively smaller categories and the individual people would be the smallest categories of all.

Activity: models and hierarchies

Models
What visual or conceptual models does your society use to structure the following areas of life? You may wish to use diagrams or drawings rather than words for this exercise. You might also think of alternative models, whether or not they are equally recognised by your community.

families
human life (i.e. from birth to death)
luck (good and bad)
history

Discussion
We often think of families in terms of generations, with ancestral trees showing relationships between siblings and married people as closer than, for example, cousins, aunts and uncles. We tend to choose to see these trees as having more branches in later generations:

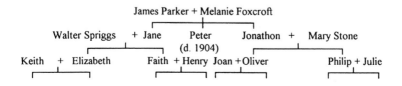

Anyone who has ever tried following their family tree backwards will know that pictures of families like this one are very far from telling the whole story. In order to make this diagram of an invented family, I had to kill off Peter without any spouse or children, because there was not enough room, or the extra dimension needed, to show his life developing. Similarly, I only allowed Jane and Jonathon two children each, to make the picture manageable. If you are Joan, and you are interested in your own ancestors, you might decide to follow a different line of enquiry, turning the triangular branching structure on its head and ignoring anyone who was not a direct ancestor of yours. For simplicity's sake, I have only included first names in the following model:

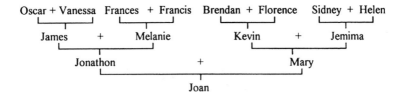

You can see that these models of family relationships are inevitably partial since the true picture of all relationships in a family would be too complicated to represent on flat paper. All models we use are like this in being partial, however cleverly they seem to fit the data. Notice, however, that being less complex than the data does not make them 'wrong'. There is nothing about the two family trees above that is untrue, they are simply two ways of looking at the same family, or data. Nevertheless, there may be political or social reasons why you might prefer one or other trees and thus there may be issues of acceptability for different models. Notice, incidentally, that we use up (i.e. toward the top of the paper) to indicate the past in these models and down to indicate the progress of time.

For the life of human beings from birth to death, we tend to use models that emphasise the repetitive nature of the process. Thus although each individual person only lives a linear life once, barring beliefs about reincarnation and the afterlife. We do not, however, often represent lives as a time line in the following way, although it conforms quite closely to the 'truth':

birth – school – job – marriage – children – grandchildren – retirement – death

Much more often, we use metaphorical models connecting life with the perceived cyclical nature of other time-related phenomena such as the seasons. So we talk in terms of people being in their springtime or of the autumn of someone's life. The model emphasises not the linearity of each individual life, but the continuity of life between generations.

Other cyclical models include the popular view of 'history repeating itself', though an optimistic vision of human 'progress' might argue for a more linear model. Alternatively, the fluctuating patterns of history between peace and war, poverty and riches and so on, might lead us to suggest a model more like a pendulum, where the furthest swing of the pendulum is one of the extremes on a number of measures:

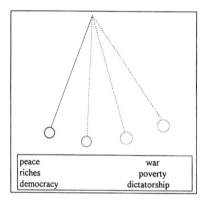

peace	war
riches	poverty
democracy	dictatorship

It is very important for understanding linguistic description to be aware that any categorisations that you are asked to use are models in all of the senses discussed in this section. They are therefore likely to be true, but partial, pictures of the particular aspect of language being described. They are also likely to be just one of a number of alternative ways of perceiving the data.

Hierarchies
How can the following areas usefully be categorised into a hierarchical model? Note the problems that arise in your attempts to categorise neatly and with no overlaps. Do you need a 'ragbag' or miscellaneous category? Are some areas more difficult to fit into this model than others? What alternative model might suit them better?

the animal kingdom
vehicles
furniture
texts (e.g. for library classification)

Discussion

Although hierarchical models are only one option, in practice they are often used to categorise the world around us. The most famous hierarchy of all is the division of the animal kingdom into phyla and species (and lots of levels in between) that we are taught in biology classrooms. This classification works very well, although there are always some individuals that do not fit neatly into the categories which suit most of the material. Thus aquatic mammals like dolphins and whales are unusual in their category since they live in water, and flightless birds like penguins cause a problem for the bird category which could otherwise be defined by flying. Vehicles, at first sight, are more suited to a hierarchical classification:

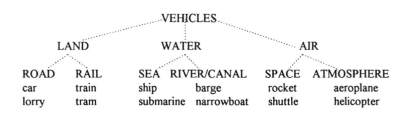

	VEHICLES				
LAND		WATER		AIR	
ROAD	RAIL	SEA	RIVER/CANAL	SPACE	ATMOSPHERE
car	train	ship	barge	rocket	aeroplane
lorry	tram	submarine	narrowboat	shuttle	helicopter

There are other vehicles that would fit into this model very well, but as with all classifications, there are some that are very hard to place. The cruiser, for example, might be used mostly on rivers, but it can also venture onto the sea. We might also find certain important characteristics that cut across the categories of this hierarchy. The significance of such characteristics might depend on context. Thus a governmental inquiry into public (i.e. fare-paying) transport will group together vehicles not on the basis of the medium they travel on or through but on their ability to accept passengers.

Classifying texts into a hierarchical structure would run into difficulty much more quickly. As all librarians know, no classi-ficatory system makes all the connections that are important to the user. The use of 'keywords' to supplement the information implicit in the categorisation of a text is one way of overcoming the shortfall caused by hierarchical structures. There is a sense in which the physical space in a library is a rigid hierarchy. You have to decide the main categories such as science, technology, literature and so on. These categories will then be broken down in turn into smaller areas. Everybody accepts, however, that there will be connections between books that are shelved far apart, which can only be shown on the catalogue by their possession of the same 'keywords'.

The development of sophisticated computers has enabled us to work increasingly in terms of databases. The model for these cross-classified bodies of material is much more difficult to represent on two-dimensional paper, since there are as many dimensions as the material needs which can be built into the database. However, there is some intuitive satisfaction in a model that, although it cannot 'look' at all of the data at any one time, can call up subsets of the data, using different criteria. Thus businesses will use databases to store all the information they have available on their customers or clients, and can search the information in a number of ways, according to need. Thus you may wish to find all the customers living in a particular area and use the postcode to sort them. Alternatively, you may wish to contact all the clients who used your service in a particular month and again the database can be searched from a different angle.

This model is intuitively satisfying too. It seems to mimic the way in which we seek and find words from our memories in a number of ways. We will sometimes make a mistake in confusing words that have similar pronunciations, such as *pinnacle* and *spinnaker*. Or we may get words confused because they have similar, but not identical meanings, such as *summit* and *pinnacle*. It appears that we store words mentally in a number of different ways and that mistakes in our retrieval illustrate this.

Whilst these interesting examples alert us to the social dangers of building too many assumptions on our models, for now the reader should simply remember that all descriptions of meaning in the remainder of this book are simply one way (often the best so far available) of looking at the complex data of meaning.

1.2 'I Mean What I Say'

Why do we sometimes use the odd expression, *I mean what I say?* It
implies that normally we say things we do not, in fact, mean. It is
perhaps most often heard coming from frustrated parents who have
made too many empty threats to their naughty children: *If you kick
Judith once more I'll take you straight home and you'll miss the biscuits. I
mean what I say!* In the face of worsening behaviour, the parents find
they have to emphasise their intention to carry out the threat. It is a
strange feature of communication between parents and children that
it is often precisely when you do not intend to go through with such
a threat that this expression is used. One of the conclusions that we
should draw about language from this picture of parenthood is that
speakers of English instinctively know that there is a difference in
many cases between what we say and what we mean.

We talk about what people 'literally' mean quite often. Many
examples like the following can be overheard on buses and in shops
on any day:

> *I'm literally head-over-heels in love with him.*
> *She's literally turned over a new leaf.*

What amuses us about these examples is that being 'head-over-heels
in love' and 'turning over a new leaf' are metaphors. And the
defining feature of metaphors is that they are *literally* not true! If we
really took to doing forward rolls when we fell in love, there would
be more neck injuries reported at hospitals.

So it seems that in everyday speech we use the word 'literally'
rather loosely to emphasise the honesty and appropriateness of our
statements rather than to point out the literal truth of the words we
say. If there is a useful distinction to be made between literal and
non-literal meanings, it is because so much of the language we use
is metaphorical, inferential, misleading or downright untruthful.

Many of the things we say are intended to be understood by
applying rules of interpretation which are agreed, usually tacitly, by
a community. When something is clearly impossible on a literal
reading (like turning over leaves all the time), we look for a way in
which the utterance might be symbolically relevant or provide some
kind of analogy for the event actually referred to. Thus it becomes

established that turning over leaves means to make a fresh start, and being head-over-heels in love means to feel that your life and emotions are in a state of turmoil. If an utterance seems inappropriate or too simple for the situation we may look instead for implications that could be carried indirectly by the words used.

To illustrate this inferential type of non-literal meaning, let us consider the well-known example of polite requests made at a dinner-table. If the salt/butter/wine is out of reach from where you are sitting, prevailing ideas about manners would presumably cause you to conquer your desire to reach out across the table in front of adjacent diners. Instead you would use an expression like one of these:

> *Pass the salt please John.*
> *Is that the butter up your end Cathy?*
> *Can you reach the wine Diane?*

Only the first of these literally means what it says, asking directly for an action to take place. The others have the same message (often called 'illocutionary force') which looks like a request for information but is in fact a request for action.

It is not only language specialists who can see this gap between apparent and actual meanings of utterances. It is sometimes thought witty to use the distinction as a way of teasing or ridiculing the politeness of the speaker:

> *Yes, I can reach the wine, thanks!*

The reverse of this kind of inference sometimes occurs when a speaker tries to mislead the audience by making them draw conclusions that are not correct. I heard recently of a nine-year-old being teased by his friends who told him: *Your ball has gone under the hut*. Being a sophisticated user of English, he drew the conclusion that his ball had rolled under the outside classroom and was now out of reach. In fact his ball had rolled under the classroom and out the other side! The teasing was based partly on the child's world experience in which balls often roll under the hut, never to appear. But the joy of the child who related this event to me was the realisation that language had power. By exploiting the ambiguity of the preposition *under* which has both a positional and a directional meaning, he could say something that was literally true and at the same time cause his hearer to understand something untrue.

Not all misleading is as harmless as this example. The lives of people in politics or the law, for example, are often full of decisions about how to make people draw the right inferences about their political party, their client accused of crime or their witnesses. On a more personal level we often use true but irrelevant statements to mislead those around us. *I love you* may be quite truthfully said to avert an otherwise difficult discussion about family finances when the speaker has been on an extravagant shopping spree. In some circumstances the same phrase might be true, but have a silent condition attached: *I love you . . . (but not necessarily for ever).* It should be clear from these examples that misleading without actually lying is just one facet of the non-literal uses of the English language.

Misleading has become a very powerful tool in legal and political debates precisely because it is so difficult to identify, being a non-literal use of language. Lying itself is linguistically much more straightforward than misleading is, because the speaker/writer intends the hearer/reader to interpret the utterance literally, even though it is not literally true. For example, the use of *I love you* when it is not even temporarily true is an example of lying. Similarly with the kinds of untruthful statements which often confront parents and teachers: *It wasn't me!, I wasn't anywhere near him, She started it.*

There are a number of linguistic levels on which the distinction between literal and actual meaning works. Two examples are given here to indicate the range of linguistic choices that can be used non-literally. At the level of vocabulary choice we may exploit the less central (even optional) parts of a word's meaning in certain contexts. This may result in the connotations of a word becoming the most important feature of meaning.

For example, when we say *He was a real father to me*, we are categorically denying that the person in question is, in fact, our biological male parent. Instead, we are emphasising common, though not obligatory, aspects of the connotation of the word *father* which include caring, being responsible, providing for material needs. Notice, also, how the grammatical context alerts us to this peripheral meaning of the word. Instead of the usual possessive pronoun *my* which indicates an exclusive relationship between child and father, we have the indefinite article *a*. This choice strongly indicates the possibility that there are other people in a similar relationship to the speaker, so it cannot mean male biological parent here.

If we take the denial of central features of meaning even further, we could conceivably deny the gender of the word *father*: *She was both mother and father to me.* Such a deliberate mismatch of gender leads us to conclude that the use of *father* here is intended to highlight the social rather than the biological features of fatherhood.

The second example of non-literal use of language operates at the level of the discourse, the interaction between participants in a conversation. Similar to the ball rolling under, but not staying under the 'hut' in my earlier example, here the listener chooses not to 'read' the implication which is intended. The example comes from the first of a series of books about a boy called Jennings who attends one of the minor public schools in the England of the 1950s. Whilst they are old-fashioned books far from the experience of many children in the late twentieth century, they retain their appeal by displaying a sense of humour appropriate, for instance, to the teasing boys of my earlier example.

In the episode in question, Jennings is given a punishment by a teacher who is not very good at controlling the children in his class.* The punishment is to go and put his head under the tap in the cloakroom. When Jennings returns with dry hair, he is questioned and innocently replies that the teacher didn't tell him to turn the tap on!

The appreciation of this joke for a child of nine or ten years old is twofold; all children enjoy stories that reverse the power relationship between adults and children and this incident also makes them realise that some triumphs are possible which involve neither physical violence nor lying, these two instincts having been labelled morally unacceptable very early in their lives. Instead they can see that much of what is powerful in discourse is what is left unsaid – or what is left uninterpreted.

Exercise: literal/non-literal meaning

Practice recognising non-literal meaning in everyday sentences. Describe a context in which the following excerpts could occur for (a) a literal interpretation and (b) a non-literal interpretation. Note

---

*This episode can be found in *Jennings Goes to School* (1952).

that some of your contexts may have to be rather unlikely to accommodate the literal meanings!

> *I'm up to my eyes in it.*
> *She was dead on her feet.*
> *Can you see the light at the end of the tunnel?*
> *My head is spinning.*
> *They're under starters orders.*

Discussion

It is very difficult to think of a real situation when you would say *I'm up to my eyes in something*, and mean it. If you were literally steeped in water, earth or leaves, you would be unable to speak. Notice, then, that the third-person version, *he's up to his eyes in the swimming pool*, sounds a more acceptable, if unlikely, sentence. This phrase is most often used when you are overwhelmed by something and feel unable to cope. Thus*: I'm up to my eyes in work,* or if you have a very large harvest from the vegetable patch, it could be *I'm up to my eyes in marrow/potatoes/runner beans*. Many idiomatic expressions like this are only really available as non-literal meanings, although some which have been transferred from special fields may still have both literal and non-literal uses. The last example here is a case in point. The opening sentence of a horse racing commentary will often include the phrase *they're under starter's orders* and yet we may come across it in other contexts where there is no one called a *starter*, but it will be applied to the beginning of a process. Imagine a large family meal where the children start tucking in rapidly while the adults are still waiting for everyone to assemble. You might use the phrase sarcastically to imply that the children should have waited, since it is not a race.

We will be returning to the role of the audience in creating meaning a number of times in later chapters, but a more pressing need is to establish some of the features of human language as a symbolic system.

1.3 The Power of the Sign

One feature of human language that is often mentioned in introductory books on linguistics is the fact that it is an 'arbitrary' system of representation. As we shall see, not all aspects of meaning in English are completely arbitrary, but it is generally true that there is very little 'natural' connection between the words we use and the things they refer to.

Language is not the only symbolic system human beings use, although it is probably the most complex one and is used for a wide variety of purposes. In order to understand the properties of symbolic systems it is useful to start by analysing a simpler, non-linguistic system such as colour symbolism.

It takes very little thought to realise that we use colour symbolically in many areas of life. The meaning of colours varies according to the culture, but even within cultures some colours have a number of meanings. I was talking recently to a cycling campaigner who had just been discussing the virtues of the bicycle over the car as an independent form of transport with a group of 9–11 year olds. The campaigner said *children are much greener now than when I was young*. For a moment I thought he meant that the children were *green* meaning 'naïve' or 'innocent'. Then I realised that he sounded impressed and that he meant *green* as in 'environmentally aware'.

These examples are really uses of the word *green*, rather than the colour itself, but green is also used as a symbolic colour to express:

GO   (traffic lights)
environmentalism   (the Green Party)
open country, parks, etc.   (on maps)

The reader may think of other examples to add to this list. Before we look more closely at what arbitrary symbolism means, let us consider other colours and their meanings.

There are a number of colours that are used to symbolise political parties in Britain. Red is the adopted colour of the Labour Party, but it is also seen as the colour of communism and one notices that as the Labour Party increasingly tries to dissociate itself from unattractive images of socialism, it has toned down its red by using both red and yellow in its campaigning. The Conservative Party in Britain uses blue as its symbolic colour.

We might ask ourselves whether these political uses of colour are completely arbitrary, or whether there is some more intrinsic connection between the colours and the political ideas they summarise. Arbitrary signs are more specifically known as 'symbols', whilst those that represent their referent directly (usually, but not necessarily by means of visual resemblance) are known as 'icons'. The green of environmental politics, for example, is clearly iconic since it is based on the natural colour of much of the plant world. There is some evidence that the red of socialism was first used by Bolshevik communists to symbolise the blood of the revolution that was necessary to overthrow the old order. However, even if this historical reasoning is accurate, there seems to be very little of the 'blood' connotation left in the red of the Labour Party. The blue of British Conservatism however, may be largely arbitrary, i.e. symbolic, although its distance from red on the spectrum is probably one reason for its choice. It has the effect of placing Conservative politics in opposition to those of the red parties. It would be unusual for two parties with very different policies to choose colours that were closely related, such as purple and red. The traditional connection between the Conservative Party and the aristocracy may be a historical cause of the choice of blue, since *blue blood* has connections with royalty. Nevertheless, there does not seem to be any meaningful connection between blue and Conservatism which is relevant today.

We are now beginning to see the model of language first proposed by de Saussure and taken up with great enthusiasm not only by linguists, but also by literary critics, psychologists and sociologists. De Saussure suggested that human language was founded on a three-way relationship between items in the world (referent), concepts relating to groups of these items (signified), and the symbol used to name these concepts (signifier). In these terms, the individual chairs in the world constitute the referents, the concept of what it is to be a 'chair' is the signified, and the word *chair* or *silla* or *chaise* is the signifier.*

Later we will look at how far this model of meaning (known as semiotics or semiology) fits the facts of the English language. We should note here, however, that the model seems to be making a very clear dividing line between the meaning and its representation

*De Saussure distinguishes between 'signifier', which is the physical symbol related to the signified, and 'sign', which he takes to be the indivisible combination of signified and signifier. In practice, many writers on semiotics have found it convenient to use the term 'sign' to refer to the physical manifestation of a signified and in the remainder of this book I will use sign to refer, in this way, to words and pictorial representations.

in language, almost as though language were simply a question of naming concepts. This model of meaning has already been criticised in the previous section as being far too simple.

In addition to the symbolic (arbitrary) and the iconic (motivated by resemblance) connection between sign and signified, there is a third type of relationship between a sign and its referent. This is known as an 'index' and refers to signs which have some connection other than resemblance to their referent. If on a motorway we see a sign showing a knife and fork, it does not indicate that if you stop at the next services you can get a knife and fork! Rather it indicates the availability of food, which is usually to be found in the company of cutlery. The picture *is* iconic of a knife and fork, but its real meaning is indexical: motivated but not resembling its referent.

We can compare colour and picture symbolism with that of language. If there is no obvious reason why pink is often seen as a feminine colour and blue as masculine, then it is even harder to provide a reason why the English speaker should call a chair a *chair* and a table a *table*, while speakers of Spanish call them *silla* and *mesa* respectively. It is no more than an agreement between members of the English-speaking community that when they wish to refer to the idea of 'chair', they will use the sounds /tʃeə/ (in some accents, including RP) or the letters 'c-h-a-i-r'.

In order to introduce slightly more complexity into the semiotic model, we need to consider what kinds of relationships there are between signs. De Saussure's model of language, in addition to proposing the nature of the relationship between language and the world, also stressed the importance of the relationship between the items of the language, the signs.

The notion of 'system' was central to de Saussure's view of the structure of language. The term 'system' was intended to demonstrate that signs (words, etc.) do not exist independently of each other, but are mutually defining. So, for example, the word *chair* would have to change its range of reference if the English language lost one of the other words referring to objects for sitting on, such as *stool*.

Within these general systems (and sub-systems) of signs, there are a number of specific kinds of relationship between signs which will be explored in detail in Chapter 3. For now, we will consider two dimensions along which signs may relate to each other. These two most important relationships are between signs that can replace each other (a paradigmatic relationship) and between signs that can occur alongside each other (a syntagmatic relationship). To start simply our first examples will be non-linguistic.

Let us use an area of human activity which is pleasant to think about at any time of year, namely holidays. If you decide that you will go on holiday, there are a number of related decisions you will have to make. You need to decide who to go with, when to go, where to go, how to get there, where to stay when you arrive and how long to stay. Depending on who you are, some of these decisions might have been made by default. Perhaps you are the mother of two small children and there is no way you can freely decide to take off with a couple of women friends!. You may have so little money that the Bahamas and Greek islands are out of the question. Assuming you have a free choice, you can put together a holiday for yourself by answering the questions posed above.

In making each of these decisions, you have chosen a single item from a number of possibilities. I could have chosen Skye or Shetland, Corsica or Malta, or any other holiday destination. The list from which an item is chosen is known as a 'paradigm'. Other paradigms form the basis of choice for all of the other decisions needed for this holiday. So from the paradigm of accommodation I could have chosen a hotel, a bed-and-breakfast establishment or a campsite. From the paradigm of travelling companions I could have chosen a group of friends, my parents or going alone.

The other relationship between signs is called a 'syntagmatic' relationship. This relationship does not involve choosing between alternatives, but creates a combination of signs by making a number of choices. The series of holiday choices, taken together, form such a combination which is sometimes called a 'syntagma'. Notice that there are often restrictions which operate between the paradigmatic choices. If you are going to Japan, for example, you probably do not have the choice of spending your holiday on a canal boat. If you want to travel by train, you will probably not go to China (from England anyway) unless you have at least a month's holiday.

These restrictions on the kinds of combinations that are possible are like a very simple grammar. The grammar of a language is much more complex, of course, but it operates in the same way. In a clause made up of Subject, Verb and Object, for example, you have to choose a verb that can be followed by an Object, so you will not choose *fall* or *be*. More specifically, you might choose a verb that requires a certain kind of Object. There are verbs which usually require inanimate and concrete Objects such as *break* or *mend*. The paradigmatic choice of the verb in a sentence like 'Freda broke the vase' has put a general restriction on the kind of Object that is likely to appear.

The syntagmatic restrictions on English range from grammatical ones, which result in very strange structures when they are broken, to restrictions of meaning, which result in strange ideas rather than strange structures. If we first of all break a few grammatical rules, we might end up with:

The a long waited John to in happy.

The restrictions which have been broken in this sentence include at least the following:

- Only one article [the, a(n)] can occur in a Noun Phrase.
- The past tense of verbs in English is not normally used as a noun (*waited*).
- Or, if you assume that *waited* is really the verb, then it is not normally followed by an Object (*John*).
- Or, if *John* is the head noun, with *waited* as a premodifer, then there seems to be no verb in this structure.
- The prepositions *to* and *in* cannot occur together in this order.
- Adjectives are not usually turned into mass nouns (*happy*).

At the other end of the scale, there are semantic or meaning-related restrictions which when broken are much less disruptive than grammatical ones. For example, the following sentences were created by a class of students playing a version of the old parlour game called 'Consequences' where everyone writes down a word on a strip of paper, folds it over and passes it to the next person to add another word in ignorance of what is already on the paper. The rules of this grammatical version of the game would stipulate, for example, that the writers should add a noun, or verb, or whatever is appropriate to the grammatical context.

The round rain must have read her giraffe in Irene's car.
Under the bedclothes the pretty elephant would dance the best spider.

Some of these broken restrictions seem more disastrous than others. It is, for example, easier to make an informed guess as to the meaning of *round rain* than how you would *read* a *giraffe*. Nevertheless, the interesting feature of broken semantic restrictions is that as long as a sentence makes grammatical sense, human beings try very hard to interpret it, often assuming that some of the combinations are new ideas or activities, such as a new dance known as the *spider*.

Many of the features of meaning in English to be investigated in the later chapters of this volume will involve either paradigmatic or syntagmatic relationships between linguistic elements such as words or phrases. The arbitrariness of many of the signs of English will be explored as well as the extent to which there is at times a more intrinsic relationship between the English language and meaning.

Before we move on to consider the nature of linguistic investigations into meaning, it will be useful to introduce another term and concept that arose out of de Saussure's work and was the foundation for the linguistic and literary theory known as Structuralism. This concept is most easily illustrated by the term 'system', which refers to any group of signs that has interconnecting relationships. In linguistic terms, this would include, for example, the system of pronouns in English (*she, he, you*, etc.), the auxiliary verb system (*have, be, do, will, could*, etc.) and the system of conjunctions (*and, but, or*). These groups of linguistic signs share two essential properties:

- They are closed groups. In other words there is very little or no change of membership.
- The members are mutually defining. This means that it is part of the meaning of any member of the group that it is *not* any of the other members.

Let us use the pronoun system to illustrate these properties. The pronouns in English between them cover all the possibilities for referring to people or things without naming them. The Subject pronouns, for example, allow us to identify ourselves by *I* (singular) or *we* (plural). We can identify individual females by *she* and males by *he*. Larger groups of people can be referred to by *they* and you can indicate the person or people you are talking to by using *you*. Things can be referred to by *it* (singular) and *they* (plural). Although this works quite adequately, you will be aware, particularly if you speak a foreign language, that the same area of meaning could have been 'divided up' in a number of other ways. For example, English cannot refer by pronouns to an exclusively female group of people since *they* covers both single-sex and mixed groups. Other languages, such as Spanish, can distinguish all-female groups (*ellas*), though the word for all-male groups is the same as mixed sex groups (*ellos*). Similarly, we cannot distinguish in English between inclusive and exclusive *we*, the former including the addressee, and the latter excluding the addressee:

> *You, me and the children – we're all going.* (inclusive)
> *Him, me and the children – we're all going.* (exclusive)

Changes in systems like the pronouns are very rare and take place very slowly. English has largely lost the pronoun *thee* in the last century or so, although it remains in Church usage and in some regional dialects. What happens when a pronoun is added or lost is that the other pronouns have either to lose a part of their meaning to accommodate an extra member of the group or they have to cover a wider range of meanings. Since *thee* has been dropped in most dialects and registers, *you* has had to take over the 'intimate second person' meaning formerly covered by *thee*. The meaning of *you* is no longer narrowly 'formal and respectful second person' and can cover a wider area including all second-person references.

The current meanings of members of the pronoun system in English include reference to the other members. So, for example, *he* means **male, singular, subject pronoun** and at the same time it means *not* **female, plural, object or possessive pronoun**. The significance of this relationship is perhaps clearer if we contrast it with the relationship between members of the noun class of words. It is not so obviously part of the meaning of *house* that it does not mean *tulip* or *bed*. If I introduce a new name to describe a flower that has just been discovered, it will have no impact on the meaning of *bed* or *house* and not much impact on the more closely related *tulip*.

Activity: systems and signs, design features of language

Arbitrariness
Pick three colours from the list below and think of as many different

instances of these colours having a meaning in the world around you as you can.

red, blue, yellow, black, white, green, orange, purple

Now you have a list of possible symbolic uses of colour, consider whether you think these meanings are arbitrary or in some sense motivated by the physical reality being described.

Discussion
Red is a very common colour of warning and it seems likely that there is a good reason for this: human blood is red and the sight of blood is a warning of injury. We therefore find that road signs which constitute a warning have a border of red and the red traffic light also indicates a warning to stop. These are therefore motivated, rather than arbitrary uses of the colour. Similarly, the use of red on hot taps seems to be linked physically to the fact that high temperatures seem to move toward the red end of the spectrum, whereas blue (for the cold tap) is naturally linked with cold. The significance of blue used as the colour of water on maps may be less than obvious to people who live in Britain, but it is true that water looks blue in response to clear skies and sunlight. Similarly, green is used to signify land on maps and this is clearly not arbitrary. Black (mourning, death and evil) and white (purity of soul and cleanliness) are not so obviously motivated signs. Whilst we in Northern Europe may feel that there is a deep-seated connection between black and death, other cultures make different connections which make the link seem more conventional than natural. Thus in Africa many communities link white with death and would no more wrap their babies in white than we dress them in black. Similarly, Hindu wedding ceremonies feature a bride dressed in red, just as symbolic of purity (and passion?) as the white wedding dresses of certain Christian wedding rites.

Systems
You are going to invent a new language, with only three 'words' – or signs – in it! You can choose one of the areas below, which will be the whole area of meaning that your language will cover:

birds, household utensils, clothes, shops, family members, food

Now choose your type of signs. They can be either completely arbitrary symbols, such as numbers (1, 2, 3), they could be colours, or they could be some kind of pictorial signs such as a square, rectangle and circle – or something more motivated and complicated if you wish!

You should now divide your field into three categories and 'name' them in your new language. Think about whether your signs are motivated or completely arbitrary. For example, you may decide to allocate colours to each category on the basis of the dominant colour in that category, or you may allocate them irrespective of this feature. Make sure that you have included all the members of your original field in one or other of your three categories. The final stage is to add a fourth sign to your language; another colour, number, picture-sign, etc. In doing so, note how you rearrange your categories to accommodate the new sign.

Discussion
The first stage probably found you wondering how to divide such a large category into only three sections! You may have tried a few different groupings, such as the following:

Birds: garden birds, birds of prey, 'exotic' birds
moorland birds, mountain birds, water birds
Shops: food, clothes, miscellaneous
household, hobby, food

Categorisations are never completely adequate because there are always some items that do not fit as well as the rest, or one category that is the 'ragbag' or miscellaneous category. What you notice about the idea of the system is that the words are not only significant in relation to the world they refer to. They also have a relationship with each other. The term system, then, refers to this interdependence between the items in a system – in this case the items are words. So when you add another sign to your language of three 'words', you find that you have to change the meaning of the existing signs in order to 'make room' for the new one. This may be achieved by splitting a large category into two, so that, for example, water birds are divided between land and sea water, or household is divided between house and garden. Another possibility is that all the existing categories will be affected and the new category will 'skim off' a little from each. So the bird categories might all yield up their migrating members as a separate category, whilst retaining the original three categories, each similar in meaning to before, but minus any migrating members. Language operates in much the same way, though it is more complicated, of course. Most of the signs of language are arbitrary and yet they form part of overlapping systems where the signs together contribute each others' definition.

Icon, index and symbol

Look at the signs below and consider whether you think that they are (a) iconic, (b) indexical or (c) symbolic. Notice whether some of them could be categorised in two or more ways, depending on the context and the reader's interpretation of the sign.

Discussion

The first sign is used to refer to biological males and is contrasted with the female sign:

Whilst the female sign could arguably be said to be vaguely iconic of a person (though not necessarily female), it would be relatively difficult to argue for a resemblance between men and their sign, unless the arrow is supposed to be phallic, and even then it is hardly lifelike! Let us, therefore, assume that this is an arbitrary symbol, used by scientists as a kind of shorthand for *male*. The second sign is iconic of people in wheelchairs, though we could argue on analogy with the knife and fork example earlier that it is simply indexical of ramped access to buildings, since it clearly has applications for people wheeling babies and small children too. The third sign is iconic of the word *Parking* which is in turn a purely arbitrary symbol. The final sign is more obviously iconic, although simplified, since it depicts a lift with people inside. The arrows indicating movement up and down, however, are conventional and arbitrary symbols, although the direction they point in may be iconic, assuming that the notice is posted on a vertical surface.

It will become important during the course of this book to recognise relationships between signs that belong to systems in the various ways that have been introduced here. In the meantime, let us consider what we are doing when we try to analyse meaning in English.

1.4 Pinning the Butterfly?

There is an automatic assumption in any book about language that the study of human language is worthwhile and is not equivalent to killing a butterfly in order to see how beautiful it is or in order to own it. The analogy, however, is a useful one because it helps us to see that the study of language has evolved since the 1950s away from a dissecting and categorising science into a more field-based science which tries to observe the butterfly unobtrusively in its natural habitat.

The observer may no longer take home dead bits of language to display and label in dusty volumes, but there remains the well-known problem of the 'observer's paradox'. This states that simply by being present, the observer is changing the behaviour of what is being observed. In the case of language, for example, it is very difficult to observe people talking in their most casual style. The use of casual language depends on people feeling relaxed and unselfconscious. Even if the observer does not declare what she is doing, the atmosphere is likely to be subtly changed by the very fact of her observations.

The difficulties of collecting rigorous data from field studies are such that only the development of progressively smaller and more reliable tape-recorders has made it possible. For this reason among others, linguists in the early part of the twentieth century concerned themselves with describing what de Saussure called 'langue', the system of language from which all actual occurrences of language were drawn (he named this use of the system 'parole'). The distinction between the abstract language 'system' and the practical use of the system in everyday life has remained very important in language study. Even when Chomsky was changing the face of linguistics the distinction only changed slightly in emphasis. Chomsky depicted the system as a set of rules stored in the brain of a speaker which he named 'competence' and distinguished this from the practical use of the system or the (often imperfect) operation of those rules which he labelled 'performance'.

For example, the knowledge that verbs must agree with their subjects in terms of person and number would be part of a speaker's competence in English. However, he or she might know this 'rule' and yet in a stressful situation produce a sentence which includes *she decide*, instead of *she decides*. In Chomsky's model, this mistake would be a feature of performance and not properly part of linguistic study since the Chomskyan tradition aimed to describe the speaker's competence rather than performance. Similarly, a speaker will know at some level (although maybe not consciously) that the verb *be* must be followed by a complement. This does not prevent the speaker from saying *The bus was . . .* when something happens to interrupt him or her, such as a fit of coughing, a fire alarm or the telephone ringing.

In analysing meaning in the English language, we need to establish whether we are going to look for an idealised system of meaning separate from the messy reality of language use in real situations or whether context and performance will also feature in our description. The alternatives offered in the last sentence were, as the style of my own language shows, not equally sincere. It is now fashionable to decry the idealisation of language systems as false and irrelevant to the business of describing human communication. This may seem reasonable now, but rather like the pinning of butterflies by Victorian naturalists who 'didn't know any better', it is difficult to imagine how we would know so much about English and other languages if the dusty work had never been done. Nevertheless, we are now at a stage when features of language use as well as the abstract system can be studied.

The distinction between use and system that has loomed so large in linguistics and is taken for granted in the last paragraph is merely a simple model which in the past has made it easier to cope with the complexities of language by pretending that there is a clear boundary between our inefficient language use and the perfect system in our brains. It has been useful, but like any model it can be challenged. Although the realities of language use in real contexts are very difficult to describe, it is becoming clear that even performance 'errors' such as hesitations, false starts and inter-ruptions are patterned in particular ways, often in direct correlation with contextual features. Certainly there are patterns to the kinds of inventive uses we create every day. For example, some of the mass nouns that refer to liquids for drinking can also be used as countable nouns. So although 'coffee' is normally a mass noun, with no plural form, we can talk about *coffees* to mean *cups of coffee*. This usage is not established for all drinks, but might well be extended in certain situations. Imagine a very long order you are placing at the bar in a crowded pub. You might return to the large crowd at your table and say *how many wines was that?*. The mass noun *wine* will be understood as being used in a countable way here to mean *glasses of wine* by analogy with the more common *coffees*.

It is therefore equally possible to analyse the regular patterns of well-formed English sentences and to analyse the regular patterns of performance hesitations or creations by English speakers in different contexts. The process is the same; detailed observation and model-building. The latter is simply a bit more difficult.

What are we aiming to do in this book which claims to describe meaning in English? I hope the reader will become aware of the enormous complexity in the way that 'meaning' is structured through different features of language, interacting with context and with the shared knowledge of English speakers/writers. The description offered will use any model which seems to aid our understanding of meaning in English and will try to map out a range of features from the most systematic 'rules' to the most (apparently) messy data, including breakdowns in meaning and creative or changing meaning. In addition to understanding a little better how users of English make meanings, it is hoped that readers will be able to apply some or all of the models to their own data.

1.5 Is it All in the Words?

One of the popular images of linguistic meaning is that it is the words that carry meaning, whilst syntax and text structure are just fairly mechanical ways of arranging combinations of words.

We have already seen that all syntagmas of signs, whether they are combinations of linguistic units like words or non-linguistic units like aspects of holiday plans, tend to have restrictions operating between the different paradigmatic choices. Just as you cannot have a mountain-climbing holiday in Holland, so you cannot independently choose an intransitive verb and follow it by an Object:

The shopkeeper fainted a chair.

It is, of course, true that the choice of words in any text is a very important aspect of meaning. There is a significant difference in meaning resting on the choice of word as an Object in the following sentences, for example:

The dog ate the biscuit.   The dog ate the cat.

However, some simple sentence pairs can illustrate that word order and syntax are also very significant for meaning:

(a) *John kicked Tim.*   (b) *Tim kicked John.*
(a) *The lorry hit the bus.*   (b) *The lorry was hit by the bus.*

In the first pair of sentences, the word order is very important to distinguish between Subject and Object position. English relies on word order to signal to the reader/hearer that the noun phrase before the verb is the Subject and any noun phrase following a transitive verb will be the Object. Whilst the words alert us to the kind of event being described (hitting) and to the participants (John and Tim), their arrangement is significant to the meaning of the utterance as a whole.

The second pair of sentences is a typical example of an active–passive pair of sentences. Children learn the meaning of passive verb phrases quite late. Not having developed an awareness of the meaning of *be + past participle*, the child will assume that word order still dictates the relationship between the bus and the lorry in sentence (b). It will therefore be understood as saying that the lorry was responsible for the hitting just as in sentence (a).

If words only contribute some aspects of meaning, can they be said to 'have' meaning at all? Many words in English seem to change their meaning according to the context, and this has led to some claims that words only 'have' meaning when they are in a particular context. However, a single word said with no linguistic context and in no particular situation still has meaning to some extent. Take the word *body*, for example. On hearing this word, or seeing it written down in isolation, I imagine most English speakers would think of a human form, possibly unclothed and maybe dead! There is, then, a central, common meaning of the word that is most likely to be 'meant' by the word *body* in isolation. The fact that undertakers are more likely to envisage a dead body than the rest of us does not detract from the argument that the word has meaning. There will be subtle variations in the meaning of the word for each of us. I might be overweight and the word *body* will remind me of my diet. You might be a hairdresser and have a different central meaning of the word which refers to the thickness of people's hair. People interested in the buying and selling of cars may see *body* as primarily referring to the metal shell of the vehicle. This meaning is played upon with the 'corpse' meaning in the following joke advertisement:

1933 Rolls Royce hearse for sale. Original body.

These examples do not undermine the general point; words do 'have' meaning, though that meaning may be subtly different for different speakers and can, of course, change across time. The meaning (or meanings) of a word is (are) simply a consensus among speakers and cannot be set in concrete. Dictionaries can only ever be an approximate record of the current (or recent) meanings of the words of a language and they will inevitably be continually out of date. What a dictionary is trying to achieve is the description of the idealised system (langue) of word meaning as opposed to the performance or use of the system in all its messy reality. In the last section we partly denied the relevance of the system vs. use distinction because it gives a false impression of order versus chaos. The example of word meaning supports this viewpoint. It might be useful to describe the meanings of words *as though* they were static and systematic, but it must be recognised that this is simply a snapshot of an otherwise moving picture.

If utterance or text meaning is at least a combination of word meaning and syntactic/text structure meaning, context is also very important. In unambiguous texts, it is sometimes difficult to see the interaction of these different facets of meaning very clearly. By looking at ambiguous texts, for example in jokes, we can see the different strands of meaning interacting more clearly.

For example, the word *draw* on its own probably means something like 'use a pencil to make non-linguistic marks on paper' to most people. However, there are many other meanings of the word, two of which refer to the closing or opening of a pair of curtains. The linguistic context of the word would identify these meanings in a sentence like *Please will you draw the curtains?* However, the verb remains ambiguous between 'close' and 'open'. It is the situational context that will make the meaning clear. This sentence will obviously only be said in the presence of the curtains! The hearer will be able to work out very easily that if they are already closed, they should be opened, and vice versa. Jokes can, of course, play on the ambiguities of words like *draw*:

> *Why did the little girl take a pencil to bed?*
> *To draw the curtains.*

One famous series of related jokes plays on our understanding of the situational context of restaurants and also assumes some basic knowledge about hygiene and food. Among the possible answers to the complaint *Waiter, waiter, there's a fly in my soup!*, we find the following:

> *It's all right sir, it can swim.*
> *I am sorry, sir, I didn't know you wished to dine alone.*
> *Don't worry sir, the spider on the roll will catch it.*

It is partly the mixture of the appropriate and inappropriate that makes these answers funny. In each case the waiter is suitably polite (using *sir*) and often apologetic. However, the horror of the customer is misconstrued as anxiety about a fellow living creature in the first answer and as a wish to be left in peace in the second. The final answer understands the horror correctly but compounds the mistake by admitting that other food is also infested by creatures.

The kind of meaning and play on meaning illustrated by the

'waiter waiter' jokes is based on conversational habits and the cultural knowledge that we may have about typical situations like being in a restaurant. These aspects of meaning are at the other end of the scale from the decontextualised word meanings of the type described in dictionaries. Both extremes, and all types of meaning between the extremes, are aspects of what we mean by 'meaning in English'.

Activity: words and meaning
Write down the first meaning that comes to mind when you see the following words:

soak, tight, match, book, front, ruler, light, school, ferret, wicked

Describe in one sentence the context you imagined when you responded to the first part of this exercise.

What other meanings of these words do you know? Look up a good dictionary and see what you have missed. Are there any meanings that you know, which are not in the dictionary? Think about why they are not listed.

Discussion
If we take just two examples from the list above, we find that the most likely first meaning of *front* and *ferret* to come to mind are 'the side facing' and 'a small, vicious animal' respectively. It does not take long to think of other meanings, such as the place where opposing sides in a war meet and fight each other for *front*, and a verb meaning 'to seek for something fussily in a difficult place' for *ferret* which would usually be accompanied by *around* in the latter meaning.

Two of the words at least have meanings current amongst young people in the late 1990s, which are probably not in the dictionaries, and will only be listed in the future if they become well-established. These are: *tight* meaning 'unfair' or 'bad luck' and *wicked* meaning 'very good'. Youth culture in particular is responsible for many new and changing word meanings, particularly those that can be used as exclamations in this way.

1.6   The Scope of the Book

Chapter 2, Sounds and Meaning, asks whether the sounds of English can have meaning in themselves – or only when they take part in word meaning. Are animal noises in English really evocative of the noises they refer to? Why do words which begin with /sn-/ often mean something unpleasant? These questions are answered by taking examples from a number of different sources, including sound-symbolism and onomatopoeia. Such meanings are not usually consistent across the language and are often quite general meanings, such as 'beauty' or 'slipperiness'.

This chapter also looks at the ways in which people's voices 'mean something' to other speakers. For example, regional and social accents place people geographically and in terms of class and education. But there are also other clues which help people categorise new acquaintances – these include the overall pitch and volume of the voice (which can, for example, help identify gender) and the voice quality.

Chapter 2 also tries to establish whether there are meanings attached to the more temporary and context-bound aspects of such features as volume, pitch and speed. For example, word and sentence stress can be used for emphasis, whilst volume and pitch demonstrate the speaker's emotions from anger to surprise.

The rhythmical and musical potential of English is most effect-ively exploited in poetry and song lyrics. The literary meanings of rhythm and musicality are explored in Jeffries (1993), but here more everyday uses of these features of English are discussed, including alliteration, rhyme, rhythm in slogans, advertising and speeches

Chapter 3, Words and Meaning, asks readers to consider whether there are, in fact, words which have no meaning – only a gram-matical function. In apparent contradiction to the discussions in Chapter 2 of the meaning of sounds, this section also introduces the reader to the notion that there are units known as 'morphemes' which are smaller than the word and are the smallest consistent carrier of meanings.

Having looked at the structure of words, Chapter 3 considers the meanings of words by dividing them into components of meaning. The advantages of being able to compare meanings by this method are illustrated. The relationship between words with overlapping meanings is also introduced and illustrated.

Part of a word's meaning is carried in the information speakers have about its relationships with other words. Partial synonymy, oppositeness and inclusiveness are three of the main relationships explained. Whilst words can be said to have central aspects of meaning in the dictionary sense of the word, they may also be known to appear primarily in certain contexts, or be used by certain groups of people. These aspects of meaning are usually known as connotations and include, for example, the scale from formality to casual use. The effect on meaning of, for example, choosing to use a particular style is also discussed.

Finally Chapter 3 asks what kinds of multiple meaning are there and how do these operate in texts?

Chapter 4, Structure and Meaning, explores the many different kinds and strengths of restriction on the possible combinations of words in English. Some words are strongly attracted to each other in, for example, idioms and set phrases, while some words have only general restrictions on their co-occurrences. This chapter will also question whether abstract categories such as noun or verb or basic clause elements such as Subject and Object can be said to 'have' meaning. Information structure – where you put the information in a sentence – is the next feature of structural meaning to be explored.

In order to understand how the word meanings introduced in Chapter 3 interact with the structural meanings, Chapter 4 includes a discussion of how we understand ambiguous words from their context as well as the creation of new, text-based, one-off relationships between words. The meanings which are taken for granted by sentences are also investigated here.

Chapter 5, Textual Meaning, explores the textual phenomenon normally referred to as cohesion. The reader is introduced to the different semantic effects of putting the sentences of a text into different orders. The question of 'where' meaning resides is also addressed by this chapter. It asks whether the creator of a text has the last word on a text's meaning – or whether the audience's interpretation is just as valid. The concept of 'negotiating' meaning is introduced.

Chapter 5 continues by questioning the assumptions made by a text. For example, texts may assume that the recipient has certain shared knowledge or it may try to persuade or coerce by making assumptions about the attitudes of the recipient. This chapter also considers ways in which English texts might be structured so that the narrative makes most impact on the reader or hearer.

Finally the reader is invited to consider how the interaction between people who are simply 'having a chat' might contribute to the meaning of the conversation, in addition to the word, sentence and text meanings already introduced. The meanings of devices such as interruptions and turn-keeping are discussed, as well as the more text-related aspects of body-language. The co-operative principles underlying conversation are introduced.

Chapter 6, Contextual Meaning, looks at fashion in clothes and language. Since cultural meaning can be 'read' in the way people present themselves physically as well as their language, a discussion of body language is introduced. Having established the importance of cultural and social meaning, the influence of social context on the meaning of any text is illustrated. The participants, their relationship, the place, the time and what has happened previously are all potentially meaningful parts of any interaction.

The remainder of Chapter 6 investigates whose meaning is being communicated – that of the originator of the text (writer or speaker) or does the receiver have some input into the construction of meaning? The question of powerful language arises and we consider whether texts can impose their own ideologies on the receiver.

Chapter 7, Meaning and Reality, attempts to summarise and survey some of the issues surrounding debates about the relationship between meaning and reality. It introduces the Whorfian hypothesis of linguistic deter- minism, which has had a huge impact on linguistic thinkers, considers the special place of literary meaning and returns to the 'chicken and egg' question of who really has the power to create meanings.

2

Sounds and Meaning

2.1 Beauty in the Ear of the Hearer?

One of the first questions that we might want to ask about meaning in English is 'What is the smallest part of the language to carry meaning?' It is unlikely to be anything as large as a clause or sentence, it might be the word, or even part of a word. In fact linguists often use the idea of 'the smallest unit of meaning' as the definition of a 'morpheme', the term used for both independent words like *cat*, *ball*, *jump* and for meaningful affixes that can be added like '-s' (meaning plural as in *cats*) or '-ing' (meaning continuing as in *jumping*).

The meaning of English morphemes will be investigated in Chapter 3. This chapter, however, will challenge the notion that there is no element in English smaller than the morpheme that can carry meaning. On the contrary, English appears to be threaded through with rich veins of sound-symbolism and onomatopoeia and these sound–meaning connections form the subject matter of this section.

Let us consider, for a moment, the different ways in which words can be stored, whether in the brain or in books. The most obvious way of organising a long list of words is alphabetically, because it is easy to look up the words you need as long as you know the alphabet. In fact, the alphabet, though useful and consistent, is really an arbitrary way of ordering words, as any reader of dictionaries will know. You find words like *finch* next to *find* and *motive* next to *motley* and they have no relationship except the accident of being closely linked alphabetically. On the other hand, a reference book like Roget's *Thesaurus* attempts to order words according to their relationships of meaning in groups like *discover, rediscover, invent, explore, strike, hit upon, find, locate, detect, expose, unearth, elicit, spot* and so on. Of course these books are only usable because there is an alphabetical list at the back where you can look up a word to find out which groups it occurs in.

There is some evidence that speakers store words in at least two different ways which are similar to the dictionary/thesaurus methods of storage. When you next have a word on the tip of your tongue, ask yourself what sound the word begins with, what it ends with and how many syllables it has. Having established something about its sound, you could then try to think of some words with similar meanings. In trying to think of the word *paradigm*, for example, you might remember that it begins with /p-/, that it ends in /-m/, that it has three syllables and that it means something like *list* or *options*.

When we are trying to think of a word, we usually know what it means. It is often exactly the meaning we require for our context and that is the reason we are trying to think of it. However, we sometimes come out with completely inappropriate words because they sound so similar to the word we are seeking. While I was writing the last paragraph, I tried to remember one of my mother's famous mistakes in word-retrieval. I knew it happened on the beach when we were watching a number of sailing boats which had those large billowing sails that are sometimes used on the front of a yacht to catch the lightest wind. She said *Look at those lovely pinnacles!* and we both started laughing because we knew the word was close in sound, but wrong. The word, of course, is *spinnakers*, so she had the right number of syllables, the right vowels and most of the consonants right too. If we write them in phonological transcription, we can see how similar they sound: /spɪnəkə/ vs. /pɪnəkəl/. My version, whilst trying to dredge up the story from my own memory was not so close. I thought to myself *It is something like 'bazooka'* which in phonological script is /bəzuːkə/! I had only retrieved the right number of syllables, the right *kind* of first consonant (i.e. a bilabial plosive, though voiced instead of unvoiced) and the right consonant, /k/, at the start of the final syllable.

If English speakers have words stored away in both semantic and phonological forms, is the phonological storage as arbitrary and meaningless as the alphabetical storage of the dictionary? In the case of English, possibly not. There are a very large number of small groups of English words which share a little of both their sound and their meaning. Whatever their origin, these sounds have become imbued with the meaning they seem to share, although the examples in this section will show that the sound–meaning connections of this kind, unlike many meaningful morphemes, are not consistent throughout the language.

The most obvious direct connection between sound and meaning is usually called 'onomatopoeia'. It is the only aspect of the English language that can be said to try and reflect the world directly. As we discovered in Chapter 1, most language is made up of symbols, which are arbitrary signs connected simply by convention to their referents. Onomatopoeic words make some claim to being less arbitrary than this by trying to sound like the sound they describe.

For example, the animal and bird noises in English include the following:

bird	*warble, trill, whistle, shrill*
bird (young or small)	*cheep, chirrup, tweet, twitter*
cat	*mew, miaouw, purr*
cow	*moo, low*
crow, rook, raven	*caw*
dog	*bark, yap, yelp, howl, bay, whine*
donkey, ass	*bray, hee-haw*
dove, pigeon	*coo*
duck	*quack*
frog	*croak*
hen	*cackle cluck*
horse	*neigh, whinny*
lamb, kid	*bleat*
geese	*honk*
insect, bee	*buzz, hum, drone*
owl	*hoot*
parrot	*squawk*
pig	*oink*
sheep, goat	*baa*

Some of these words are more clearly onomatopoeiac than others. For example, it is easy to see that the potentially long voiced sibilant /z/ at the end of *buzz* sounds like the buzzing of bees and flies. The words that children often learn very early are also quite effective in mimicking the sounds of cows (*moo*), sheep (*baa*) and cats (*miaouw*).

Other words are less close in sound to their meaning. The opening consonant cluster, /gr-/, of *growl* and *grunt*, for example, makes use of the back of the mouth, specifically the velum or soft palate, and is quite similar to the kinds of sound made in the throat by lions and pigs respectively. However, the rest of the word is not so clearly a straightforward reproduction of the sound being described. It is rather a kind of abstraction which symbolises the sound. The long diphthong /aʊ/ in *growl* gives the sound appropriate length, whilst the short vowel and plosive ending of *grunt* makes it suitably short, although it still does not sound exactly like a pig.

Just like the BBC pronunciation unit, which advises newsreaders on the nearest English sounds that will approximate to difficult foreign names, the English animal noises are an Anglicised approximation of the sounds of our most well-known animals.

English is also rich in onomatopoeia of other kinds. The sounds associated with inanimate objects, for example, are often described by words which mimic the sound to some extent. If we look at words with a single syllable to begin with, we can see that English syllables often consist of an initial consonant cluster, a vowel and a final consonant cluster. Any of these segments of the syllable may be onomatopoeic, and quite often the onomatopoeia extends over two or more of them.

Taking the initial consonant cluster first, we see that many of the words describing sounds with a sudden onset have single plosive consonants at the beginning. The plosive consonants are articulated by the speaker creating a complete closure in the mouth, allowing the air coming up from the lungs to build up pressure. The consonant is sounded when the pressure forces its way through the closure, causing an explosive rush of air. These plosives can be articulated using the lips (/p/, /b/), the tongue and ridge behind the teeth or 'alveolum' (/t/, /d/), or the back of the tongue and the soft palate or 'velum' (/k/, /g/).

The sound of the initial plosive in words like *ping, bang* and *tick* are therefore at least partially evocative of the sounds they describe. Similar effects can be achieved by using plosive sounds at the end of a syllable to indicate that the sound being referred to is not only sharp at its onset but also stops quickly and cleanly. Words like *clunk* and *clank*, often used to describe the rather dull metallic sound of heavy metal doors or chains, end in a voiceless plosive /k/. This has the effect of signalling that the sound stops abruptly rather than resonating as a more musical metal gate might *clang*. This word ends in a voiced velar nasal and has a much more drawn-out finish because nasal sounds last as long as the air continues to vibrate around the nasal cavity.

Apart from the plosives, the other major consonant groups in English can be used onomatopoeically. The nasal sounds, /m/, /n/ and /ŋ/ are a bit like plosive sounds, but because they involve air entering the nasal cavity and escaping through the nostrils, there cannot be the same build-up of pressure as in the non-nasal plosives. The result is that the sound of the nasals is largely made not by the eventual (ex)plosion of the air leaving through the mouth, but by the air which resonates around the nasal cavity. This resonant sound can continue for as long as the speaker has breath. Try 'singing' a nasal consonant for as long as you can and for contrast try 'singing' a /d/ sound. The latter will be short and the nasal quite long. Words using nasals for onomatopoeic effect include *hum*, which can be used about human beings and machines (like fridges) as well as bees. Many of the words describing the sounds of different bells end in the velar nasal, /ŋ/ — *bong*, *ding*, *dong*, *ping*, etc.

The fricatives are another group of sounds that are potentially quite long. They are sounded by air escaping through an incomplete closure in the mouth, such as between the top teeth and the bottom lip in the sounds /f/ and /v/. The difference between these two sounds is that the /v/ is also voiced; the vocal cords are vibrating at the same time as air is escaping between the teeth and lip. Fricative sounds are useful to signify the continuous sounds indicated by words like *scratch* and *scrunch* in which both the initial /s/ and the final /tʃ/ are voiceless fricative sounds. Common onomatopoeic uses of fricative sounds include groups of words which use /ʃ/ to signify the sound of water: *splash*, *splosh*, or to indicate a rush or air: *whoosh*, *swish*.

The vowels are also significant in English onomatopoeia. Their length can be significant as in the words *rasp*, *squeal* and *grate* which have long vowels /ɑː/ and /iː/ or diphthongs /eɪ/ respectively, to give an idea of the length of the sound being described. Other words like *snap*, *bang* and *click* have short vowels /æ/ and /ɪ/ to emphasise the short duration of their sounds.

As well as length, the English vowels are distinguished according to whether they are articulated with the mouth open, closed or halfway between. There is a tendency for relatively high pitched sounds to be indicated with words containing a very closed vowel like /iː/, /ɪ/ and /uː/ as in, *scream, chink* and *pule* respectively. Low pitched sounds, on the other hand, are most likely to be represented by open vowels, such as /æ/, /ɑː/ and /ʌ/ as in the words *babble, rasp* and *crunch* respectively.

As well as the individual sounds and combinations of sounds, many onomatopoeic words in English make use of syllable structure to evoke a particular sound. Repetitive sounds are often signified by a word which has two syllables, symbolic of the repeated sound. The words *grumble* and *splutter*, for example, denote noises that continue in bursts for a considerable length of time. They could be compared with similar words such as *groan* and *splash* which represent single sounds and have only one syllable.

There are many more words in English that are onomatopoeic to some extent. It is important to remember that this apparently intrinsic connection between sound and meaning is similar to the kind of visual sign often called iconic because they look rather like their referent. If you take the common example of the pictures used on men's and women's toilets in public places, many of the 'people' look unlike any real person we have ever seen. However, they have enough of the features of human beings for us to understand them. As well as looking 'a bit like' a person, they are part of our society's convention for signalling gender on toilet doors and our experience makes us 'see' them as directly representing men and women respectively. Onomatopoeic words, then, sound rather like their referents and those of us attuned to English-type speech sounds have conventional knowledge that makes us hear them as more accurate representations than they really are.

Because onomatopoeia is actually quite an abstract form of representation, it seems appropriate to describe sound-symbolism as being very similar to onomatopoeia. The only significant difference between the two seems to be that onomatopoeia refers to sounds and sound-symbolism refers to other categories of meaning. We will see shortly that many words in English are both onomatopoeic and sound-symbolic and it is not always clear where the division between these systems lies.

First let us consider the kinds of meaning that can be indicated in English sound-symbolism. Many groups of words describing contact, often some kind of hitting, seem to share part of their sound as well as part of their meaning. A fairly violent hit might be connected with the initial consonant cluster /sm-/ as in *smash* or *smack* or with /b-/ as in *bash, beat* or *boot*. Smooth but rather inaccurate attempts to make contact seem to be symbolised by /sw-/ as in *swipe* and *swat*. Other kinds of contact do not involve hitting. For example, there is a kind of desperation to hold on indicated by all of the following group of words which begin with /kl-/: *clench, clasp, clutch, cling, clinch, cleave to*. Another group uses two-syllable structure to indicate repetitive movement, but also has the consistent ending /dəl/ which may indicate the emotional side of the shared meaning in this group of words. The group includes *cradle, dandle, cuddle* and *fondle* and they all seem to be used most often with children as Objects, though their use may be extended to other intimates like lovers or pets.

The area of meaning that might be generally termed 'movement' is also rich in sound-symbolism in English. There are certain uncontrolled or careless movements, for example, that are connected with the initial consonant cluster /fl-/: *fling, flop, flap*. It should be noted that these connections seem to operate at a very deep level for English speakers. Whilst the meaning of a morpheme like *-ation* will not be hotly disputed as being something like 'the process of . . .' as in *nationalisation* and *privatisation*, there is no consequent feeling among English speakers that the sounds which make it up, i.e. /eɪʃən/, symbolise that meaning in any direct way.

Other groups of movement words also share sound-meaning similarities. There is a strong impulse behind the words *throw* and *thrust*, for example, which seems to be 'contained' in the initial /θr-/. The speed and changing direction of *scuttle, scurry* and *scamper*, on the other hand, seem to lie in their shared initial /sk-/ and two-syllable structure respectively. Combinations of vowel plus final consonant clusters may also be sound-symbolic as in the words *scurry, flurry* and *hurry*, which share a feature of meaning related to speed as well as their ending /ʌri/. Note that the last two sentences have effectively claimed that the word *scurry* is sound-symbolic in three different ways, two of which relate to speed of movement and the other to changing direction. This is not unusual for English words, many of which share a number of sound-symbolic features with a number of different groups of words. Various networks of sound-symbolism will be explored later in this section, but here we will briefly consider a number of general features of sound-symbolism in English.

If there is some physical basis for onomatopoeia, then there are also some sound-symbolic words that have direct connections between their sound and their meaning. For example, if a long vowel or a continuant consonant can symbolise a long sound (e.g. *buzzzzz* . . .), then they should also be able to symbolise long movements as illustrated by the diphthong of *winding* (/aɪ/) and the long vowel of *weave* (/iː/). We might also argue that the initial /sn-/ of *sneer, sneaky* and *snide* are 'nasty' sounds because they make you screw up your nose or that *grumble, grouch* and *grouse* contain the very 'growl' that their meaning implies in their initial /gr-/. However, there is a danger of seeing far-fetched rational explanations for the connections because they are so deep-seated in the language and speakers often feel that a particular sound sequence has certain meaning.

Another feature of sound-symbolism in English is that it mainly occurs as a feature of groups of words, rather than individual words. This would support the argument of the last paragraph which warned against making too many assumptions about non-arbitrary connections between sound and meaning. If words share a bit of their meaning and some of their sounds, there will probably develop a feeling that the shared meaning 'resides' in the shared sound. What is harder to explain is the occasional word which seems to have sound-symbolic properties, but does not appear to belong to a group sharing those properties. The examples that come to mind are words like *nag, career** (as in 'career down a hill'), *cudgel* and *carp*. Maybe all nasal sounds have the potential to sound nasty and *nag* is therefore an honorary member of the *sneer* group? Possibly the diphthong /ɪə/ in *career*, which moves from a high front vowel to a central vowel, sounds out of control and this connects with the

---

*This is one of a number of fascinating words in English that seem to have two opposing meanings. Chapter 1 mentioned the two meanings of *draw*, which seem to be contradictory as they are synonymous with *open* and *close* respectively. Here we have a movement meaning of *career* which has the additional feature of meaning of being out of control and implies a downhill trajectory. This contradicts the usual, metaphorically 'upward', meaning related to a progressive and successful working life, which is normally seen as being completely under one's control! Another example of opposing meanings of a single word is 'cleave', which can mean 'cling to' on the one hand, but also has a fairly outdated meaning to indicate a splitting process.

meaning in the speaker's mind. It is also possible that in thinking so carefully about sound-symbolism for the purposes of writing this section I am beginning to see it where the reader will not find it!

There are two other striking facts about the sound-symbolism to be found in English. First, the systems of words which share their sound–meaning pairs are quite small. There are probably many hundreds, if not thousands of words in English which begin with /h-/, for example, but only a small number of them share the meaning element which dignifies their initial /h-/ as sound-symbolic. The verbs *harry*, *hound*, *harass*, *hassle*, *hector* and *harangue* share an element of meaning that indicates the verbal equivalent of sheep-worrying. This meaning is not indicated by the /h-/ in *huge*, *hungry* or *horse*. Neither do we find the meaning connecting *clench*, *crouch* and *bunch*, which could be paraphrased as 'pushed tightly together', in words like *finch* or *lunch*.

The networks of sound-symbolism (including onomatopoeia) in English are very complex, but in order to illustrate them we will focus on individual words and look at the different groups they belong to. A number of the onomatopoeic words also have sound-symbolic relationships. For example, in some accents of English (including RP) *groan* shares with *moan* a diphthong and final nasal consonant, /əʊn/, which directly echo the sound that people make when groaning or moaning. But *groan* also has a sound-symbolic relationship with *grumble*, *grouch* and *grouse*, as we have already seen. The 'complaining' part of its meaning, then seems to be carried by the initial consonant cluster, /gr-/.

This kind of sound-symbolic relationship with two different sets of words is common in words that denote a sound, but which also strongly imply that the sound is made by a movement. These words have two possibilities for relationships, with other similar sounds, and with other similar movements. The word *bong*, for example, belongs most obviously with other resonant sounds ending in /-ɪŋ/ such as *ding*, *clang* and *dong*. However, it also shares the opening /b-/ of hitting words like *bash*, *biff* and *bang*.

A different kind of overlap is seen in the word *glare*, which at first sight belongs with other words of 'looking at' such as *glower*, *glance* and *glimpse*. The initial /gl-/ seems to symbolise this meaning. But *glare* also shares both sound and meaning with words which are apparently very wide ranging in their central meaning. These include another looking word, *stare*, as well as *flare* and *blare*. The interesting aspect of this example is that the meaning shared by these words is a rather subtle feature corresponding to something like 'suddenly, strongly and for a long time'. Thus when a fire *flares*, it suddenly starts to burn strongly and for a time at least, fairly steadily (compare *flicker*), and when music *blares* from you neighbour's house in the middle of the night, you would probably not disagree with the description 'strongly (which in auditory terms means loud) and for a long time'.

The final example of sound-symbolism in English is the group of words we use to describe laughing. It is a useful example to show the kinds of interlocking onomatopoeic relationships that can occur. Many of the words have a two-syllable structure which we have already seen can be used to imply repetition. Here it specifically carries the echo of laughter, that is usually made up of repeated pulses of sound: *Ha ha!*. Two-syllable words include the following:

cackle, snigger, titter, giggle, chuckle, chortle, gurgle, guffaw

The dictionary often describes laughter as being made up of 'a series of explosions in the throat'. It is no surprise, therefore, to find that there are a great many velar plosive sounds (voiced /g/ and voiceless /k/) in the laughing verbs, since plosives are explosions and the velum, or soft palate, is very nearly in the throat. The laughing words using velar plosives include:

cackle /kækl/, snigger /snɪgə/, giggle /gɪgl/,
chuckle /tʃʌkl/, gurgle /gɜːgl/

There is a final syllabic /l/ in many of the laughing words. This sound in many accents of English is also a velar sound, with the back rather than the blade of the tongue making contact with the soft palate. Being softer than the plosives, because the air escapes gradually from the lowered sides of the tongue, the effect is of a softer sound following the plosive, implying a more gentle laughing sound:

cackle, giggle, chuckle, chortle, gurgle

The vowels in these words are also symbolic. The higher-pitched laughter is depicted by closed front vowels, usually /ɪ/:

snigger, titter, giggle

The lower-pitched laughter, however, has either open back vowels (/ʌ/ or /ɔː/) or long central vowels (/ɜː/):

chuckle, chortle, gurgle, guffaw

Finally, there are two words which do not seem to share many of these features, but which remain onomatopoeic because their whole sound seems to echo the sound they describe:

hoot, roar

Notice that these sounds describe the relatively unusual single laugh by having only a single syllable.

The final point to make about sound-symbolism in English is that this section has described only the systematic (langue-like) and decontextualised kind of symbolism. In literary works and also in other real-life contexts such as advertising, reporting and even in some private conversations, there can also be a text-based sound-symbolism or onomatopoeia at work. The creative use of sound is discussed in section 2.4.

Activity: conventional onomatopoeia and sound-symbolism

For each of the following groups of words, consider whether they are onomatopoeic or sound symbolic. Which part of the word carries this meaning? Describe in a sentence how the meaning is symbolised by the sounds you have picked out. If possible, compare your answers with a friend's. Are the differences between your answers due to inaccuracies, level of detail or different hearer/reader-responses?

creep, crawl, crouch, cringe
slap, snap, tap,
flutter, flap, flicker

Discussion

The first group share their opening consonant cluster, /kr/, and seem to share a feature of meaning which might be summarised as 'reducing the space taken up by the body, specifically by rounding the upper body and lowering the head'. Of course, there are many other features in the meanings of these words. Nevertheless, their similarity of form and this shared strand of meaning combine to produce another small area of sound-symbolism in English. The second group is one of many forms of onomatopoeia created by a short sharp single syllable, with a short vowel and ending in a plosive consonant, in this case /æp/. The sound imitated by this group is also short and sharp and unlike resonant sounds, which are often represented onomatopoeically by nasal sounds, it lacks any musical note or pitch and is rather a dull sound. The final group share their initial consonant cluster, /fl/, and also share a strand of their meaning that indicates small repetitive movements over the same space. In the case of *flutter* and *flap*, this often involves movement of some flexible material, such as the fabric of a flag or clothes. In the case of *flicker*, it refers to light (often flames) apparently moving backwards and forwards in the same way. *Flutter* and *flicker* share with other two-syllable words such as *giggle* and *chortle* the symbolism of repetition based on the double syllables.

2.2 'Her Voice Betrayed Her'

Of course, it is not only women whose voices betray their feelings, but it is a cliché of certain kinds of romantic novels that we recognise:

> With a blithe goodnight *in a shaky voice* she stumbled towards the bungalow. At the door she heard Webb's *voice, mocking as ever,* behind her. 'Night, Russ!'
>
> (Roumelia Lane, *Himalayan Moonlight*
> [Mills and Boon, 1977] p. 71)

Before looking at the kinds of meaning carried by our voices, we need to distinguish between two types of feature of human language, usually called 'segmental' and 'non-segmental' features. The segmental features, as their name suggests, can be distinguished from each other relatively easily in the flow of language. Although we tend to run our words together in casual speech, we still have a clear notion of where the word boundaries are. For example, we can divide a sentence pronounced /weərɑːðəsɪzəz/ into a number of words thus: *Where are the scissors?*. We can also to some extent distinguish between the individual sounds which make up the words. The word /sɪzəz/, for example, starts with a fricative consonant, followed by a closed front vowel /ɪ/ and so on.

By contrast, the non-segmental features of language cannot always be clearly distinguished from each other and usually extend over a variable number of the segmental features of language just discussed. One example of a non-segmental feature of language is pitch. We will see shortly that it is not a simple feature in terms of its meaning. But in physical terms, we notice that the pitch of any utterance may be high or low or anywhere between the speaker's highest and lowest pitches. An utterance is most often said on a variable pitch which may gradually ascend or descend from beginning to end, may 'step' up or down in pitch from word to word or phrase to phrase, or may go up and down in pitch in even or uneven periods. It might be useful for the reader who has not previously encountered the distinction between segmental and non-segmental features to choose a simple utterance and try out aloud some of the pitch options given above. They will not all make meaningful sense. The utterance might be, for example, *Give me a spoon for my sugar*, and variations in pitch might make it sound like a request for action, an order or a request for a spoon as opposed to some other implement.

All of the features of language discussed in this section could be seen as non-segmental in that they affect the segmental features in a variable way. They also range from features that are self-consciously meaningful, in that the speaker has some element of choice in their selection, to features that are only implicitly meaningful in that the recipient will draw conclusions that are either subconscious or completely unintended by the speaker/writer. The other common factor in the features discussed in this section is that they are relatively permanent aspects of any speaker's language.

One of the relatively permanent features of a person's speech is their dialect. I will use the term 'dialect' to cover the range of regional features that may occur in someone's speech, whether it is standard or non-standard. These features will include phonological, lexical and grammatical features and will therefore subsume the most obvious way in which English speakers' language varies: accent. Whilst non-standard dialects may be, and sometimes are, written down, they are most often encountered in the spoken language and will therefore form part of the aural impression we have of speakers, whether because of the words they use, the way they pronounce them or the way they are combined grammatically.

Geographical dialects occur towards the latter end of the range described above, where any meaning derived is unintended. There are occasions, of course, where people deliberately adopt a regional accent or dialect (either their own or someone else's) for some purpose. Most commonly, however, if people change their accent or dialect at all, it is a subconscious action.

There are many native dialects of English in all five continents as well as the dialects to be found in England itself. In most situations where English is used as a daily language, there exist side by side a standard variety of the language with high prestige and one or more regional varieties with lower prestige. It is often the case that the standard language is taught in the schools, with the result that regional varieties are seen as uneducated or lower class. A very common situation in Britain is for educated speakers to speak standard English, but with a more or less strong regional accent (i.e. pronunciation only).

Whilst there is an element of choice in the variety of English that you speak, it is often a subconscious choice. There is also a great deal of luck involved. If you are born into a family whose natural dialect is Standard British English, Standard Indian English or one of the other standards, you are immediately and almost automatically seen as being educated and middle to upper class. On the other hand, if you are a speaker of Geordie, Scouse, Scots or Jamaican English, you might retain your dialect in such a strong form that your hearers will mistake you for someone uneducated and lower class, when in fact you are neither. Many speakers of English, of course, speak two or more dialects and quite naturally change their variety according to the situation and the people they are addressing.

We might consider here the difficult question of whether varieties of English as described above can be said to 'mean' anything. In the same way that we can either dress very self-consciously to give a particular image or throw some clothes on because we are in a hurry, we can consciously adopt an accent or dialect for particular reasons, or simply speak in the way that comes most naturally to us. I would suggest that we must assume that both kinds of choice, and all the shades of consciousness in between, are aspects of meaning, however subconscious. For one thing, it is impossible to know when we have reached the cut off point between conscious and subconscious meaning. We should also consider the role of the hearer who will draw conclusions about the speaker's dialect whether or not the speaker has made a deliberate choice.

It is becoming increasingly common for linguists to reject the established view that meaning is a simple kind of 'message' initiated by the speaker/writer, transmitted by the language, and received rather passively by the hearer/reader. We will return to this theme in later chapters, but anticipate here the idea of the recipient as being active in the negotiation of meaning.

If the recipient is partly responsible for the meaning that arises from any utterance/written text, then meaning can emanate on a number of levels without the speaker/writer's conscious involvement. The conclusions we draw from the fact that a new acquaintance has a Welsh accent or speaks an African variety of English will partly reflect our own social background, including our prejudices.

Whilst it is clear that there are some choices available to the speaker in the varieties of English available to them, it is not so clear that there are choices in the general quality of a speaker's voice, including the pitch and volume range they have. However, if we accept that some meaning is received by the hearer, irrespective of the speaker's intentions, then we can see that there are certain 'facts' communicated by the general features of pitch and volume that could be seen as meaningful in many English-speaking societies.

Most accessible are the gendered meanings that tend to be drawn from features of pitch. We have an expectation that men will speak on average with low pitch and women with higher pitch. This is analogous to the 'strong men'/ 'weak women' assumptions on which much of our society is built. However, we are perhaps less surprised by the small and evidently weak men and tall, strong women we meet than by the deep-voiced women and squeaky men. For some reason the pitch stereotype, which like all stereotypes is based in some truth, seems less easy to challenge than the strength one. So deep voices 'mean' masculine, if not male, and higher average pitch 'means' feminine or more probably female.

A closely related permanent feature of voice is that of volume. We will investigate temporary aspects of volume in the next section, but here we are concerned with average overall volume of a person's voice. The most obvious meaning of a generally loud voice is 'authority' or 'confidence'. Because the history of many English-speaking societies is very largely male-dominated, we may also extend the meanings of loud to include 'male'. The converse is true of generally soft voices. Shakespeare draws on this stereotype in *King Lear* when Lear is lamenting the loss of his favourite daughter, Cordelia, and cannot believe she is dead:

> What is't thou sayest? – Her voice was ever soft,
> Gentle, and low, an excellent thing in woman.
> (*King Lear*, Act V, Scene 3)

Whilst we may now reject the value judgement that women *should* be quieter than men, it remains true that we react strongly to women who sound loud or men that speak softly. How often are the interpretations of tabloid newspapers based on this prejudice when they describe women who speak out in public, as aggressive or masculine? Examples include the first woman Prime Minister of Great Britain, Margaret Thatcher, who was first persuaded to take on and then villified for having male characteristics in her speaking voice, including more volume. Prior to the development of technology for amplifying sounds, political success could depend on the speaker's ability to address large gatherings of people and be heard. This emphasises the link between loud voices and public speech, which has long been considered the province of men, rather than women.

A soft voice, then, is seen as meaning 'demureness' and 'passivity' or 'lack of confidence' and by extension 'female'. You might reflect, next time you meet a loud person, what meanings you are drawing from the volume of their voice. It may be that readers in English-speaking places other than Britain will argue that their society treats overall volume as meaning something different. American visitors to Britain, for example, often seem unbearably confident to English people. This may be partly based on the confidence children are given by the American system of education. Or it might be as simple as the fact that they all speak on average slightly louder than English people. Perhaps there is just more space in the United States and probably British people seem rather too shy and retiring to Americans. I find that I feel people are cross with me when I first arrive in Spain because they generally seem to speak more loudly than English people. Volume communicates something about the speaker to the hearer, depending on the backgrounds of both participants.

There are also other features of the voice over which speakers have no obvious control. Some of these have been rejected by linguists as being non-linguistic, even though they do communicate something. At the most basic level, for example, breathing communicates that someone is alive, snoring that they are asleep (and possibly that they have a cold or adenoidal problems), sneezing communicates hay fever or a cold, and yawning tiredness. Some of these features of voice might be controllable, though they are usually all interpreted as being involuntary. Coughing, for example, can be 'put on' to gain sympathy and yawning can be used deliberately to try and make people leave you to your well-earned rest. It is of relatively little interest to us to spend much time on these physiologically determined features of the voice, but we should remember that a single yawn could conceivably have the same meaning as a full English sentence such as *I am tired*.

One final feature of the voice that some linguists have noted is called 'timbre'. This is roughly equivalent to what might be recognisable as 'resonance'. How resonant your voice is might be a feature that hearers will notice, but it is difficult to tie it down to a specific meaning. High resonance tends to occur with loud volume, and will be described by words like *boom* and *call*. Low resonance, by contrast is often connected with virtual whispering and is sometimes mentioned in potentially romantic situations:

> Dreamily she gazed into the coals, sipping her drink, totally relaxed. When Michael spoke, it was almost as if it was part of the dream. 'The firelight's shining in your hair,' he said softly.
> (Sandra Field, *Out of Wedlock* [Mills and Boon, 1985] p. 140)

Activity: responding to voices
Find a situation in which you can listen to someone speak without being involved in the interaction. This could be achieved by listening to a radio presenter or by eavesdropping on a conversation

between people near you on a bus or in a cafe. Try not to listen particularly to the content of the conversation, but listen to the voice or voices of the people speaking. Then ask yourself some of these questions about the voice(s) you are listening to:

- Is the speaker using a regional accent or dialect that you recognise? Do you have any aesthetic reaction to this variety of English?
- Is the speaker talking relatively loudly or softly, considering their gender, the situation, the proximity of other speakers etc. What does the loudness/softness signal to you? What kind of person might you expect to react differently from you to the same speaker?
- Is the general pitch of the speaker's voice high or low? Does this pitch fit with the gender, age and regional background of the speaker? If not, what kind of impression do you get from the clash of information?

Discussion

Whilst there may be a general tendency to react to permanent features of voice in certain ways, it is noticeable that in individual instances, the situation and what you already know about the speaker(s) have a great influence on your interpretation of vocal features. The most influence a voice will have on us is perhaps when a stranger telephones us and we are unaware for a moment who they are and what their intention is. As soon as the conversation begins to develop, factors such as content begin to supplement our information about the gender, regional origin and age of the speaker. I recently played a tape to some students of a very upper class RP-speaking woman describing her elderly mother's intention to stay with a brother for the Christmas period. Whilst the content was stereotypically female, the voice is rather low-pitched and the students all guessed that she was a man. Some of them acknowledged the influence of the content by saying that they had thought how unusual it was for a man to go into such detail about domestic arrangements!

2.3 Shouting and Squealing

The previous section looked at ways in which our voices 'mean' something to people we talk to, whether or not that meaning is consciously intended by the speaker. The features discussed there are usually fairly permanent and are probably partly independent of which language you speak. There are other non-segmental aspects of speech, however, that are tied to the context and utterance concerned as well as being rather different for different languages. These include stress, temporary changes of volume (as compared with a permanently loud or soft voice) and intonation.

There are at least two levels of stress in English, usually known as word-stress and sentence stress. Word-stress is very difficult for foreign learners of English because it is not regular as it is in some languages. Spanish, for example, has word-stress on the penultimate syllable of all words ending in a vowel, however long it is. So the stress on the following words is:

pláya (beach), caramelíto (little sweet)

The only exception to this is the relatively small group of words that end in consonants, which have the last syllable stressed:

corazón (heart), Madríd (Madrid!)

English, by contrast has a very complicated system of word stress, often related to whether the word has a Greek, Latinate or Germanic origin. The relevant point to be made here, however, is that although it is more complicated, the English word-stress system is just as permanent as the Spanish one. The following words are almost without exception stressed in the following way, wherever they occur:

cómmunist, beréavement, desígn, Portuguése

The fact that word-stress is almost unalterable in English (apart from some differences between dialect forms) makes it virtually meaningless and therefore of no interest to us here. Much more interesting is the use made of sentence stress. The label 'sentence stress' is not very accurate, since the clause is often taken to be the most natural domain of this kind of stress. The following sentence, for example, has two clauses conjoined by *but* and naturally seems to demand two main stresses if it is read aloud:

Féw heard the general's farewell speech, but somehow it did not mátter. ('Haitian military ruler leaves to allow reinstatement of exiled president Aristide', *Guardian*, 11 October 1994)

The most neutral stress used in English clauses is on the final clause element. This often coincides with the newest and therefore most interesting information in the clause. For example, the following sentence (for convenience only one clause long) would most neutrally be stressed on the word *principles*:

We haven't borrowed our prínciples. (Tory Party conference: 'Major waves flag to rally the troops', quoting John Major, *Guardian*, 11 October 1994)

Any stress that is put in a non-final place in the clause is seen as 'contrastive': it implies that the stressed element is important and different from another specific option. As in many political speeches, the excerpt above sees John Major, the British Prime Minister in 1994, trying to criticise the Labour Party by implication. It would not have been at all surprising, therefore, if he used some kind of contrastive stress instead. He may, for example, have stressed the first word, *we*, indicating that there were obviously others (i.e. the Labour Party) who had in fact borrowed their principles. On the other hand, he might have stressed *haven't*, giving the listener cause to think that he has previously been accused of something which he is hotly denying.

Seeing a quotation written down means that we would assume that the stress was neutral unless there is evidence for contrastive stress. Returning to the previous example, of a sentence with two conjoined clauses, we find evidence for contrastive stress in the first clause:

Few heard the general's farewell speech

Here, the subject *few* is a contrastive choice, emphasising the *many* who stayed away from this event. It would therefore be the most likely word in this clause to take the stress if the sentences were to be read aloud.

It is clearly important to English speakers to be able to use sentence stress to emphasise a word or phrase, or to make contrastive implications. This is shown by the ways in which writers try to indicate stress using italics, bold lettering or capital letters in their attempts to emulate the stress in the voice. The following excerpt from *Notes of a Native Son* by James Baldwin, show him using italics to emphasise what the repeated structure already gives emphasis to:

> That was all we said. It was awful to remember that that was all we had *ever* said.
>
> (Baldwin, *Notes of a Native Son* [Pluto Press, 1985] p. 108)

In this case, the fact that the words *that was all we said* are repeated exactly makes the added words *ever* and *had* stand out from their context. The italics add the orthographic equivalent of contrastive sentence stress.

If sentence stress is the way in which English speakers alert their hearers to the important parts of their utterances, then the pitch movements of the voice tell us why they are important. Stress itself is a complicated physical process involving more than a simple increase in loudness,* but it is relatively easy to hear and we are concerned not with production but with meaning. When a speaker has chosen (albeit subconsciously) to stress a particular word, they also decide which way the pitch will move and over what stretch of speech.

At one extreme, the speaker may decide to stress every word they say. This normally only happens in circumstances where the speaker is trying hard to make themselves understood or when they are having trouble getting each word out. For example, if you are dictating a message on the telephone and it is being written down by your hearer you may stress each word and leave long gaps between the words in order to make sure that the message is correct. This often happens when people phone in to ask for information or for a job application and need to leave their address. The stressing of

---

*Briefly, stress is usually assumed to correlate with increased loudness, though from the producer's point of view this could be defined as increased effort or force. Some argue that it is the pitch prominence that alerts us to stressed words. Thus we notice stressed words because they stand out from their surroundings, either through their force or their different pitch. For more detailed discussion of the properties of stress see Crystal (1969).

each word happens most typically when children are just learning to read and each word is a challenge to them. Nearly all readers go through a phase when they stress and separate each word, giving each one a full intonation pattern:

> The – turnip – seeds – grow. – One – turnip – grows – and – grows – and – grows.
>
> (from *The Enormous Turnip* [Ladybird Books, 1980])

The sign of a fluent and mature reader is when the number of sentence stresses becomes close to the normal number for an adult which is roughly one for every clause:

> As time went *by* Belinda lost her creased-up *wrinkles* and began to look altogether more *attractive*, though never *beautiful*.
>
> (Jeremy Strong, *The Karate Princess* [Puffin, 1989])

Activity: stress
Look at the following sentences and decide where you think a neutral sentence stress would occur:

> *She went for a fortnight.*
> *There were three eggs in the box.*
> *Harold arrived at four o'clock.*

Ask a friend to read them aloud and listen to see whether they have used the stress that you predicted. Try stressing different words to produce contrastive stress. What kind of context do you have to imagine to make them make sense?

Discussion
A neutral version of these sentences would produce stresses on the words *fortnight*, *box* and *clock* respectively. Some examples of contrastively stressed versions are the following:

> *She* went for a fortnight. (*He* stayed at home)
> There were *three* eggs in the box. (Not two as you claimed)
> Harold *arrived* at four o'clock. (Though he should have been leaving by then)

There are a number of other possibilities obtained by choosing different words to stress. Notice that although words with word stress usually carry the sentence stress, there are occasionally contrastive needs that can cause a normally unstressed word to become stressed:

Harold arrived *at* four o'clock. (Not before or after)

Assuming that most utterances do not have every word stressed, what is the status of the words that are left unstressed? Linguists have claimed that utterances are divided into sections, called 'tone-units', each containing a word carrying sentence-stress, but usually also containing other syllables. The stressed word, known as the nucleus, does not have to carry the whole of any intonation, but the pitch change is spread out over the remainder of the tone-unit, known as the 'tail'. Often there will also be a few syllables before the nucleus begins, known as a head:

Head	Nucleus	Tail
I am	tired	of the country

A fairly neutral reading of this sentence would probably have a low pitch on the Head words, *I am*, and step up to a higher pitch on *tired* which would then fall gradually through the tail. As shown in Table 2.1, there are five possible pitch patterns in English which are used in this way, beginning on a Nucleus and extending to the end of the tone-unit.*

There is some evidence that the 'meanings' of the four moving-pitch tones can be divided into two groups according to whether they end in a rise or a fall. The falls have a more finished and definite sound to them, whilst the rises are inconclusive or unfinished. Level tones, however, are more non-committal, often being used when a speaker is 'quoting' words or is in some sense not wanting to give the words any further meaning. If you try to imagine a friend telling you a story about who was at the party last

---

*I am presenting relatively clear examples here, although it is not always easy to tell when tone-units begin and end, where nuclei occur and which pitch pattern is being used. For more information on and practice in the details of analysis, see Kuiper and Allan (1996). The concern here is with patterns of meaning in English and how they are presented partly through intonation.

Table 2.1

Name of tone-type	Transcription	Approximate pitch patterning
Falling tones	ˋ	
Rising tones	ˊ	
Fall-rises	ˇ	
Rise-falls	ˆ	
Level tones	ˉ	

night, you will probably imagine the following list being said with a series of rises and a fall at the end:

Jáne, Wéndy, Róger, Péter, Míriam, Sùe

On the other hand, a teacher reading out the names on a register might well use a series of level tones which would have the effect of making the names stand apart from each other.

The two main types of pitch change have a range of meanings, from the grammatical to the emotional, but the difference between them can also be summed up in a few words. Brazil and Coulthard (1975) use the labels 'referring' for rises and fall–rises and 'proclaiming' for falls and rise–falls. The intention is to group together those tones that refer to some kind of common ground between speaker and hearer (rises) and those that seem to be introducing an element of new information (falls). Thus the first two sentences below seem to belong together, as do the second pair:

Whát did you say? *Whǎt did you say?*
The milk's in the frìdge. *The milk's in the frîdge.*

In both of the first pair of sentences, the pitch movement occurs across the whole clause, with the second (fall–rise) falling on *did* and sounding more incredulous or cross (depending on context) than the first (rise) more innocent question. In the second pair of sentences, the simple fall in the first example indicates a statement with no hidden agenda. The second version (rise–fall) indicates that there is something significant about the siting of the milk which could probably only be discovered from the immediate linguistic and social context of this sentence.

As we have seen above, however, tone-units do not operate in isolation, but follow each other in sequence. Some researchers, like David Brazil, have suggested that the sequences of tone-units are patterned in various ways with some level of meaning being attached to the sequence itself. The simplest example of a tone-unit sequence is the list. As indicated above, the most normal (and therefore neutral) intonation for a list is a series of tone-units with rising tones with a final tone-unit on a falling tone:

Get me some bútter, súgar, éggs and a pàper

Other typical sequences include a fall–rise followed by a fall, echoing the lexical and grammatical meaning of the words, which give some kind of background to the main new information:

When I've washed the dĭshes, I'll clean the flòor

This is the most neutral intonation for this sequence of clauses; the speaker is setting the scene in the first clause and giving new information in the second. We might guess that the question immediately before this sentence was something like *What are you going to do later?* However, intonation is independent of grammatical or lexical structure and can be used with the same words to create the opposite sequence of given and new information:

When I've washed the dìshes I'll clean the flŏor

The effect is to make the washing of the dishes the new information and the floor-cleaning something already referred to in the conversation. The prompt question in this case is something like: *When are you going to clean the floor?*

There are, of course, more extensive and in some cases more specialised examples of tone-unit sequences. One that is particularly interesting to listen to is the commentary of a horse race. The pattern of tones in commentaries is like a very long series of level tones or rising tones, always pitched higher than the tone before, so that the overall effect is of a gradual building up of pitch from the beginning until the first horse passes the winning post. After the winners are home, the pattern reverses with lower and lower pitches occurring until the final tone, which is, of course, a falling one and is often very deep in the speaker's voice. The pattern is reinforced by the rhythms and by the speed of the delivery which tends to start at a medium pace, speeds up considerably during the height of the battle for first place and then slows down almost to a drawl as it becomes clear which horse will win. There is not much for the commentator to say after the race is over, but like the horses themselves, it is as though he or she needs to ease off slowly rather than stopping short.

The racing commentary example introduces the other temporary non-segmental features of speech: rhythm, pitch, speed and volume. Rhythm will be discussed in the next section as part of a consideration of musical aspects of speech. Although pitch, speed and volume are also often musical, they are dealt with here because their meaningful use can be seen to relate very closely to both stress and intonation. Nevertheless, there are aspects of all three which are independent of the stress and intonation systems in English.

Pitch, speed and volume tend to be similar in some ways to the features discussed in the previous section which were distinguished as being more-or-less permanent features of the speaker's voice. So a speaker who has a generally loud voice may within her/his natural range still speak loudly or softly. And a speaker who has a generally high-pitched voice can still speak in a relatively low part of their range. Specific pitch changes which are tied to the text have been discussed as intonational features. Here, however, we are dealing with the intervening level of temporary, but not intonational, pitch speed and volume. So, for example, it is meaningful to the hearer if a speaker is using an unusually high general pitch level – for her. And a speaker who has a normal rate of delivery may suddenly speak much faster, with consequences for the hearer's interpretation.

Fast speeds and high pitches tend to be interpreted as indicating the speaker's nervousness, either through excitement or some more negative emotion, such as fear or anger. Abnormal volumes tend to have similar meanings to those postulated for the permanent features of the voice; loudness means assertiveness or anger (or attempts to be heard), softness means self-effacing emotions like shyness or reluctance to be heard.

Activity: intonation
Practise producing the following intonation patterns. Remember that the pitch movement (fall, rise–fall, etc.) takes place over the whole of the tail of the tone-unit. The head is simply the syllable where the movement begins:

> *I want a banána, / three ápples, / a pássion fruit / and a bunch of gràpes.*
> *Whĕn she finishes the novel / she's going to write a biògraphy.*
> *Whèn she finishes the novel / she's going to write a biõgraphy.*

Practise the two versions of this sentence, using neutral and contrastive stress respectively. When you have the differences clear in your mind, try the same variation on the following sentences:

> *After the match in Sheffield, we went to the night-club.*
> *Before he noticed the body, he saw that the wardrobe had been opened.*

Discussion
Do not worry if you find this exercise difficult, it is not easy to hear the difference between rising and falling tones to begin with and you need to take into account how high the pitch is to begin with. Try exaggerating the patterns until you are used to it. There are some types of spoken language that are more likely to yield clear patterns than others. Try listening to horse racing and other sports commentaries and notice how the speaker's tone units alter around the exciting moments (e.g. ends of races and goals). It is also interesting to listen for patterns in the intonation of political speakers, particularly at grand moments of oratory, such as party conferences or in the run-up to elections.

2.4 Rhythm and Music

Musical use of sound in English is usually associated with poetry or song lyrics. It is true that one of the defining features of much poetry in English is an awareness of sound, even in free verse which has no formal rhythmical structure. However, it seems unlikely that our appreciation of rhythm and other musical features of English is confined to poetry and lyrics. More probably we respond to the heightened use of these features in poetry because we already have a great deal of experience of similar features in our everyday lives.

Although it will be useful here to describe the rhythmical structures of English and other sound effects, we will try to concentrate on their meaning rather than their form. The question underlying this section, therefore, is: 'What is the effect (intentional or otherwise) of a speaker choosing to use a particular sound effect?'

Languages are sometimes said to fall into one of two categories distinguished by their ways of regulating the timing of syllables in connected speech. No categorisation is ever perfect and this distinction does not fit exactly with the facts, but it is quite a useful model for the ways in which rhythm in language operates. Under this categorisation, English is said to be a 'stress-timed' language, whereas other languages like Spanish or Greek are said to be 'syllable-timed'. In other words, there is an impression of even lengths of time between each main sentence-stress in English and other 'stress-timed' languages whereas in 'syllable-timed' languages each syllable has roughly the same amount of time in which to be articulated. The 'pulse' of these languages is therefore much more even in tempo and often sounds staccato to those of us with an English-trained ear. Thus the stresses in Spanish sound something like the following:

/ / / / / / / / /
Mi madre está en la casa.

In English, by contrast, the stressed syllables may have any number of unstressed syllables between them and in order for the stressed syllables to occur at regular intervals, the unstressed ones may be speeded up considerably:

-   / - - -   /   /   / - - - - -   / - / -
My mother is in the old cow shed cleaning out after the evening milking.

Try saying this sentence really quickly and notice how it is the unstressed syllables that are squeezed as a result. One of the problems that arose with this model came when linguists started to measure in milliseconds the length of syllables or the time between stresses. The model started not to seem so accurate when tested scientifically. However, if we restore it to its status as an aid to understanding, it does seem to explain some of the features of English that contribute to its rhythmicality.

English words from the major lexical words classes (noun, verb, adjective, adverb) usually carry word-stress, either on their single syllable or on one syllable of a polysyllabic word. The grammatical word-classes (e.g. prepositions, conjunctions) usually only carry very light stress unless it is a contrastive sentence stress deliberately emphasising the word concerned:

I told you to go *up* the ladder. (i.e. not down it)

The rhythm of English is therefore made up of unstressed syllables (i.e. grammatical words and unstressed syllables of polysyllabic words) and stressed syllables (monosyllabic lexical words and main stresses in polysyllabic words). If the time between stressed syllables is perceptually even, then whatever the number of unstressed syllables in between, they will be 'squeezed' to fit in the gap. The resulting effect may sound rather rushed when there are more than a couple of unstressed syllables to fit in:

- - / - - - - - / -
In the sanctuary of the cathedral

Here there are at least five unstressed syllables between *sán-* and *thé-* of *cathedral*, or six if you make a meal out of the end of *sanctuary*. If you say this sentence with exaggerated stresses and quite fast, you can hear the unstressed syllables being compressed, leading to the elision of at least one of the vowels in *sanctuary*, giving /sæŋktjʊriː/ instead of /sæŋktjʊəriː/.

Clearly the most regular rhythms in English are made up from regular patterns of stressed and unstressed syllables. The most famous of these patterns is 'iambic', which means that the rhythm has pairs of unstressed and stressed syllables. These matters are most important for poetic metre, which is not considered in detail in this book. Here we will consider whether there is any meaning attached to the choice of a rhythm in everyday language.

Perhaps the most obvious choice of rhythm a speaker makes is whether or not there should be any regular rhythmical pattern in what they say. In casual speech it is probably quite unusual for regular rhythms to occur, except by accident. In speeches, advertising and slogans, on the other hand, it may be very consciously chosen as a way of making the hearer remember the message. The context of the utterance, as always, partly predisposes the hearer to certain kinds of meaning. Listening to political rhetoric, for example, we expect to hear simple and memorable slogans, often made more weighty and formal by the pulse of stressed and unstressed syllables. For example, in September 1996, at the last British Labour party conference before the 1997 election, the leader of the opposition, Tony Blair, echoed a well-known football song ('Football's Coming Home') when he repeated a number of times and with heavy emphasis:

/ - / - /
Labour's coming home.

It was convenient for Mr Blair that in a phrase of five syllables, only two of them (the second syllables of 'Labour' and 'coming' respectively) were unstressed, leaving him the opportunity to use the vocal equivalent of thumping a fist on the table to drum his point home.

In other contexts, for example in advertising, the choice of regular patterning often underlines the light-hearted nature of the utterance. Regular metrical rhythms often give the message that the approach of an advertisement is either childlike or amusing:

My mate, Marmite. My mate, Marmite.
(repeated rhythmically by soldiers during a route-march)

This advertisement uses a play on the product name, *Marmite*, as well as the rhythmic framework, to produce a strong, macho image of a product (vegetable spread) that is often associated with babies.

Most examples of use of rhythm in more everyday contexts are fleeting impressions often quickly succeeded by other stress patterns. One example of the kind of rhythm used in this way is the emphatic phrase containing a number of stressed syllables in succession with no (or very few) intervening unstressed ones:

```
 -  /  - -  /  - /  /  /
```
I'm going to have a long hot bath!

Other ways of being emphatic also seem to involve regular rhythms, but they may have unstressed syllables between the stresses:

```
 -  /  - -  /    -  /  - -  /
```
We're going to fight, we're going to win!

Activity: stress
Look at the following sentences and try to decide where the stresses will occur in a neutral version (i.e. containing no contrastive sentence stress that would stress a grammatical word such as an article or a preposition):

> *Why don't you come to the party?*
> *Take a long hard look at yourself.*
> *I want a Barbie doll on Christmas Day!*

Are the rhythms regular? Do they seem to contribute in any way to the meaning of the utterance?

Discussion
The first sentence has a regular, dactylic metre (i.e. a stress followed by two unstressed syllables), though it is doubtful whether speaker or hearer will be respond to this beat consciously. It does seem to be the case that requests and persuasive utterances often resort to some kind of regular metre, so to this extent the regularity might signal persuasion. The second example has one of the emphatic clusters of three stresses in a row. The effect is to emphasise the stressed words and it is also iconic in that the word *long* involves a nasal sound and *hard* involves a long vowel in most accents of English and therefore they symbolise the meaning of the phrase in their physical shape. The third sentence is a more extreme form of rhythmicality equalling persuasion – or in this case demanding. The child knows automatically that a foot-stamping episode accompanied by a rhythmic utterance will be more effective, because it will be remembered, than less metrical whinges.

The musicality of English is not only carried by rhythm, but also by combinations of sound which can vary from the most musical, which could be said to have no definable meaning, to the iconic, where the sound has a close and even non-arbitrary meaning. The latter situation has already been discussed in connection with individual English words which have onomatopoeic or sound-symbolic meanings. The previous discussion was based on the 'language as system' model, which sees English as an identifiable object, separate from its realisation. Here we are more interested in the textual build-up of sounds in such a way that meanings are enhanced.

What can happen is that the originator of a text will draw on the recipient's knowledge of conventional sound-symbolism and exploit it by causing a build-up of particular sounds in the text. For example, although I have already suggested that not all words ending in /ntʃ/ share the 'tightly together' meaning of *bunch*, *clench* and *clinch*, it would be possible to suggest this symbolism by a build-up of words containing this sound:

Over lunch she clenched her teeth thinking she would never forget the stench of that day . . .

Another example to is the use of a large number of fricative sounds in a passage about windy weather:

I lay in an agony of imagination as the wind
Limped up the stairs and puffed on the landings,
Snuffled through floorboards from the foundations,
(Peter Redgrove, 'Old House', in
Alvarez [Penguin, 1962] p. 214)

This kind of mimicry is most common in poetry, but that does not mean that we are otherwise insensitive to sound impressions. Many speakers will be able to describe texts by using rather inexact, but indicative adjectives such as 'bouncy', 'spiky', 'rounded', 'smooth', 'rough', etc. These are the rather general, but nevertheless real, meanings of texts which make unusually frequent use of different groups of consonants. Because of their manner of articulation for example, a preponderance of plosive sounds in a text might well sound quite 'sharp' or 'spiky' and in conjunction with the word-meanings and syntax-generated meanings they might contribute to a general impression of 'anger' or 'accuracy' or 'excitement'.

An overwhelming number of nasal consonants in a text, on the other hand will contribute to meanings that have more to do with 'stability' or 'connectedness' whilst fricatives in abundance can breathe 'suspicion' or 'secrecy' into a text. Vowels also have an effect on the meaning of a text if they seem to reinforce the words and structures. For example, long vowels and diphthongs slow a text down, even if it is a written text, whilst short vowels give an impression of speed which could be interpreted as 'vitality' or 'excitement'.

All the kinds of meaning discussed in this book, including those based on sounds, are only ever a part of the whole picture. It is necessary, if we are to learn anything about the way that language works, to divide the material into manageable layers and chunks. But the division is only a useful model and should always be supplemented by the knowledge that all the different aspects of linguistic meaning operate together in real situations.

3

Words and Meaning

3.1 Empty Words

Chapter 3 approaches meaning from the level of the word. This, in many ways is the most 'comfortable' level of meaning for non-specialists, since we tend to talk casually about meaning as though it were all carried by words. I have already suggested (section 1.5) that words do not 'have' meaning in quite the way that is implied by the existence of printed dictionaries. These publications are merely a snapshot, as it were, of the current state of usage of words. Nevertheless, we can treat words and parts of words as though they 'have meaning' for the purposes of documenting and analysing the relationships between words and their contribution to textual meaning. It is simply important to keep in mind the fact that we are only documenting a consensus at a particular time and in a specific speech community and even then individual speakers of that time and place might disagree with some of our conclusions. To begin with, we will consider whether there are words which, even in this modified sense, do not seem to carry meaning.

In everyday conversation, when we use the phrase *empty words*, we normally mean that the person we are referring to is insincere, that they are *mouthing platitudes* or *paying lip-service*. In other words, we are not claiming that the words themselves have no meaning but we are claiming that this meaning is not intended by the speaker concerned. Are there, however, any words in English that really are empty in the sense of not having any meaning? Are there words that are the equivalent of mortar between bricks; not the substance of the wall, but important to make the wall hang together properly?

One of the problems of discussing meaning is that we are inevitably using language to talk about itself, and that is a rather circular occupation. If foreign learners ask the meaning of a word like *beseech* and are told it means *implore*, they will be none the wiser if they have never heard of *implore* either. If they then ask the meaning of *implore*, it would be extremely unhelpful to tell them that it means *beseech*!

This example is only a more extreme version of what happens in any discussion, using a language, of the meaning of that language. Circularity is endemic. However, there *are* meanings that are relatively easy to define, because they almost manage to break out of the circle. The most concrete of words, like *table, chair, lake, people,* can be quite neatly defined by referring to their physical properties. They have legs, they are used for sitting on, they contain water and so on. If necessary the circle can be broken completely by using either examples of the referents of these words, or pictures of them. So a table can be pointed to and the hearer told that it is *table* in English. A speaker can show a photo of Lake Geneva and say this is a *lake*.

Words referring to activities are a little harder to define, though there are usually also physical properties that can be described. *Cutting, singing* and *breathing* could be described as involving the use of a sharp instrument, the vibrating of the vocal cords and the drawing of air into the lungs respectively. Alternatively an example of these activities can be shown, either live or on videotape.

Once the meanings being described are more abstract than this, the description of meaning becomes much more complicated, especially when human emotions are involved. Try defining words like *sorrow* or *retribution* without looking at the dictionary. It is not easy, especially when you ask yourself whether you have correctly distinguished them from very similar words like *sadness* or *revenge*.

Whilst there are clearly differences in the difficulty with which word meanings can be described, we can still ask the question posed above: are there any words that are empty of meaning? The verb *be*, for example, is often no more than a filler for the obligatory verb slot in English sentences such as *She is a teacher* or *He is very tall*. Some languages do not have an equivalent verb, since it does no more than act as a kind of linguistic 'equals sign'. Words which can fill the subject position in certain structures, but which add nothing to the meaning could also be defined as empty. These include *there* and *it* in sentences like *There isn't any tea left* and *It is raining again*.

Apart from these virtually empty words, the most obvious

candidates for this category are those words that operate in sets known as 'closed-systems'. These sets of words are usually quite small in number and are historically stable in that they change much more slowly over time than the open classes of words. An example of a closed-system in English is the pronoun system. The subject pronouns in English are the following:

I, we, you, she, he, it, (one), they

It is many years since this system changed. There used to be a familiar second-person pronoun, *thou*, rather like the *tu* of French or Spanish. Except for archaic usage in some church liturgies and in certain regional dialects of English, this pronoun has virtually died out in the twentieth century. It is just possible that the pressure from feminists for English to have a sex-indeterminate singular pronoun will result in a new pronoun emerging in the next few decades. However, these changes are very small compared to the constant invention of new nouns and verbs to match the changing society we live in and to name some of its consumer products and new pastimes. The computer revolution alone has spawned many such new words in the open classes of word. Thus we have *download*, *laptop* and *user-friendly* occurring in the verb, noun and adjective classes respectively, but no new pronoun yet and certainly no new article to go with *the* and *a*.

In addition to being fairly small classes and relatively stable, closed-systems of words are mutually defining. The idea of a 'system' as a way of modelling relationships between signs was introduced in section 1.3. The basic design of a system requires all its parts to be in a network of relationships such that you cannot interfere with one part without affecting all the other parts. This means that if the set of words changes, the meanings of other words in the set have to change too. Either some words reduce their area of meaning to accommodate a new word or they have to expand their meaning to cover the gap left by a word that dies out. In the case of English pronouns, the loss of *thou* meant that the other second-person pronoun, *you*, had to change from meaning 'second-person respectful' to covering all second-person usage.

Clearly the pronouns in English do have some meaning, although it is rather general in its scope. This is for a very good reason. The pronouns are supposed to be able to replace any noun that accords with their own meaning. So the word *he* can only replace male individuals whilst *we* must refer to the speaker and at least one other person. The pronouns, therefore, reflect only the differences in meaning that are important to the society in which the language is spoken. Thus, in the singular, at least, English makes a fundamental distinction between human reference (*I*, *she*, *he*, *you*, *we*) and inanimate or non-human reference (*it*). Notice, however, that the problem of when something can be defined as human is behind the common use of *it* when referring to babies before birth and for a short time after their birth.

Another factor also comes into play here. We meet someone we know with their new baby. We cannot remember whether it is a boy or a girl and the blankets and winter bonnets prevent us from working it out. The use of *it* might carry us through this moment, although sensitivity to the mother/father's feelings might make us hesitate to categorise their new offspring with the animals. I often find myself using a quaint or twee euphemism when in this situation, something like 'the little one'. The double bind is that we do not want to be seen to relegate the baby to the 'less-than-human', but we do not want to admit that we are ignorant of the very important defining characteristic of gender. If society ever manages to change fundamentally so as to see gender as a relatively unimportant feature of human beings, we may become more relaxed about this kind of encounter.

Personal pronouns, then, have meaning in so far as they are distinguished by features such as 'human' vs. 'non-human' or 'first person', 'second person' and 'third person' or 'female' vs. 'male'. What about the other closed-systems of words?

The prepositions are such a large group of words, they are probably close to being an open class like nouns and verbs. And they have meanings which are summed up in *A Grammar of Contemporary English* (Quirk *et al.*, 1972) in the following way:

In the most general terms, a preposition expresses a relation between two entities, one being that represented by the prepositional complement. (Quirk *et al.*, 1972, p. 306)

As well as having similarities of meaning, the prepositions range very widely within this:

So varied are prepositional meanings that no more than a presentation of the most notable semantic similarities and contrasts can be attempted here. (Quirk *et al.*, 1972, p. 306)

Possibly the closest to empty words in English is the system of articles. There are only two: *the* and *a(n)*. According to Quirk *et al.* (1972) 'the articles have no lexical meaning but solely contribute definite or indefinite status to the nouns they determine'. It is important to recognise that *A Grammar of Contemporary English* is written in a tradition that has divided the grammatical from the semantic so consistently that it perceives this split as being real and absolute. The definition of lexical meaning, if it were given, would probably involve some recognition that lexical meaning can stand on its own, whereas grammatical meaning only functions in contexts. Thus, the word *cat* has meaning to an English speaker, even out of context, whereas *the* does not. Whilst this model of meaning has some uses, it ignores the great overlap between these two kinds of meaning. Perhaps, as so often in linguistic matters, the distinction being drawn as absolute is really a gradual shading from one extreme to the other.

The prepositions, for example, which we passed over rather quickly above, are on the one hand clearly context-bound and on the other hand, have definable meanings of their own. Thus *above*, even out of context, means 'higher than', but clearly requires the context to complete the meaning and say what it is that is higher than what! The demonstrative pronouns are another closed-system that both has context-free meaning, and requires context for that meaning to be fully realised. For example, Quirk *et al.* (1972, p. 217) define the meaning distinction between *this, these* and *that, those* in this way: 'The general meaning of the two sets can be stated as "near" and "distant" reference.'

In other words, *this* and *these* refer to things that are either physically or psychologically near to the speaker, whereas *that* and *those* refer to things that are distant from the speaker either physically or emotionally. For example, I might speak of *this book in my hand* and *that book on the shelf* or *this problem I'm having* or *that problem you were having*. Notice that the usage is meaningful in its own right. If I change the last example, I can identify myself more closely with 'your' problem: *this problem you were having*.

To return to the articles in English, we find that they are no more than the most extreme example of meaning being largely dependent on context. This does not imply that they are therefore empty of meaning in any significant way. The definite article can refer outside the text to something or somebody in the immediate situational context:

Look at the willow tree in the moonlight!

This sentence would, unless found in a romantic novel, be said in a night setting near to a willow tree. The article refers to this tree. It can also, however, refer to anything or anyone that has been previously mentioned in the text. So, for example, the first introduction of a character into a story is normally indefinite:

An old grey donkey called Eeyore . . . (adapted from Milne, 1926)

And later references will be definite:

The old grey donkey, Eeyore, . . . (Milne, 1926)

This usage is seen as making connections within the text, known as cohesive ties (see section 5.1). Whilst it is difficult to define the 'meaning' of the definite article used in this way, it nevertheless seems certain that there *is* a meaning along the lines of 'as referred to earlier in this text . . .'.

Many of the so-called empty or 'grammatical' words show a type of meaning known as 'deixis' (noun) or 'deictic' (adjective). This kind of meaning is variable in that the word has only very general meaning when the word is out of context, but is fixed more exactly when the positioning or identity of participants is established by the surrounding text. For example, it is difficult to teach a child what the word *I* means, since it appears to change meaning, depending on who is speaking. It means 'Mummy' when she says it and 'me' when I say it. For a while during the development of children, then, the surrounding adults and older children instinctively use the third-person pronoun, or the name of the person concerned. So a mother will say *Mummy's going to put on Susan's coat now*, when she is talking directly to Susan, because the names do not shift their reference in the same way as the first- and second-person pronouns.

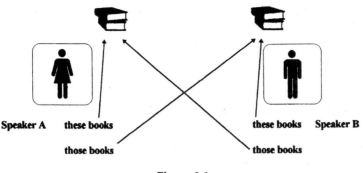

Figure 3.1

As I mentioned earlier, the demonstrative pronouns, *this*, *these*, *that* and *those*, also have shifting reference, depending on the location of the item(s) concerned in relation to the speaker. Things that are near the speaker are identified by *this* and *these*, whereas things at a physical or psychological distance are identified by *that* and *those*. If two speakers are each standing near a pile of books and one of them (speaker A) says *Give me those books*, it clearly makes *those books* refer to the pile furthest away from speaker A. The identical phrase, said by speaker B will refer to the other pile of books, the ones near speaker A (see Figure 3.1).

Activity: closed systems

Make up the article system of a new language. You can use sounds, written language or symbols to identify the different articles, but instead of having just two, as in English, your language will have articles meaning the following:

- Definite reference (like *the*) but only singular and mass items (e.g. *the* cat, *the coffee*).
- Definite reference (like *the*) but only plural items (e.g. *the* cats).
- Indefinite reference (like *an*) but only singular and mass items (e.g. *a* cat, # coffee).
- Indefinite reference (like *an*) but only plural items (e.g. *some* cats).

Notice that in English, there is no indefinite article used with mass nouns like *coffee* or *air*. Also, we do not consider *some* to be an article, although it roughly translates the indefinite plural article, it is normal in English to use indefinite plural count nouns without an article: *cats*.

Now add a new pair of definite/indefinite articles, which are used to introduce mass nouns:

- Definite reference (like *the*) but only mass items (e.g. *the air*).
- Indefinite reference (like *an*) but only mass items (e.g. *some* air).

What has happened to the meaning of your other articles? Have they all been equally affected?

Discussion

Here is an article system from an invented language, called TALK, compared with the English system:

TALK	singular/mass	plural
definite	spa	spalk
indefinite	pa	palk

ENGLISH	singular/mass	plural
definite	the	the
indefinite	a	

What happens if we add two more articles, to cater for the mass nouns separately? The following table shows how the effect is to narrow the meaning of *spa* and *pa* so that they only refer to singular items:

	singular	mass	plural
definite	spa	spag	spalk
indefinite	pa	pag	palk

Activity: deixis

You will remember that 'deixis' refers to the ability of some words and expressions to change their precise reference, depending on who is speaking. Thus the pronouns *you* and *I* refer to different people when the speaker changes. Four out of the following six utterances contain a deictic element. Which are they? What is the deictic element? How does this element shift its reference depending on the speaker?

(a) *The cake is on your kitchen table.*
(b) *He gave her a blue coat.*
(c) *Those flowers need chucking out.*
(d) *Here is my glove – I thought I'd lost it!*
(e) *Miriam thought it was a lovely dress.*
(f) *My parents are coming to dinner.*

Discussion
The two sentences not containing deictic elements are (b) and (e). Although third-person pronouns (*he, she, it* and *they*) have shifting reference, the shift does not depend who the speaker is. The other utterances contain the following deictic elements:

(a) The cake is on *your* kitchen table.
(c) *Those* flowers need chucking out.
(d) *Here* is *my* glove – *I* thought *I'd* lost it!
(f) *My* parents are *coming* to dinner.

The first- and second-person pronouns (*I, me, my, you(r)*) depend for their reference on who the speaker is and who the addressee is. The demonstrative pronoun, *those*, indicates flowers that are at a distance from the speaker, whereas the adverb *here* indicates proximity. The verb *coming* (as opposed to *going*) indicates movement toward the speaker's position. Notice that in other languages, the verbs of movement are not always deictic in this way. Thus in Spanish, if you were not at home when you said utterance (f), you would use the verb *go* to indicate movement toward the house, rather than toward yourself.

3.2 The Smallest Units of Meaning

In an earlier section (2.1) I claimed that certain individual sounds and combinations of sounds carry meaning in limited areas of English. However, most linguists would argue that the smallest consistent units of meaning were not sounds but morphemes.

Most independent words of the kinds to be found in the dictionary would be seen as free morphemes. These are often known as lexemes and as they are listed in dictionaries they are in a 'root' form, with no affixes. Thus *dance* will have its own entry, but not *dancing* or *danced* and *tortoise* will be listed, but not *tortoises*.

It would be very uneconomical to have every past tense of a verb and every plural of a noun listed in the dictionary alongside the present tense verbs and singular nouns. Because there is a great deal of regularity in the physical form of these additional meanings, they can be listed separately, usually in the grammar books rather than in dictionaries.* They are usually known as 'bound' morphemes: morphemes which cannot occur alone, but are always attached to a free morpheme.

English has two major groups of bound morphemes: inflectional morphemes and derivational morphemes. The inflectional morphemes are always added at the end of the free morpheme and are often called suffixes for this reason. This group of suffixes is very consistent in its form–meaning relationship. For example, there are very few countable nouns in English which do not use the regular form of the plural morpheme. The normal realisation of this morpheme is as /z/ after voiceless consonants, /z/ after voiced consonants and vowels and /ɪz/ after sibilants (i.e. after /s/, /z/, /ʃ/ and /ʒ/) and affricates (/tʃ/ and /dʒ/). Thus we have:

cat	/kæt/	cats	/kæts/
dog	/dɒg/	dogs	/dɒgz/
horse	/hɔːs/	horses	/hɔːsɪz/

and only a few exceptions, that foreign learners often commit to memory in lists:

sheep	/ʃiːp/	sheep	/ʃiːp/
woman	/wʊmən/	women	/wɪmɪn/

Because of this small number of commonly occurring exceptions, there is a tendency among morphologists (i.e. scholars studying the structure of words) to propose that the morpheme is an abstract idea, with a fixed meaning but with a number of different physical

---

*For a comprehensive and detailed account of word-formation in English, see Appendix 1 of Quirk *et al.* (1972) pp. 973ff.

realisations. The plural morpheme would therefore be given the symbol {Pl} and be said to have three common realisations, /s/, /z/ and /ɪz/ and a number of less common ones such as ∅ (i.e. no affix) as in *sheep* or /æ/ to /e/ as in *man* replacing *men*.

You will notice that what is happening here is an attempt to make the model fit the data a little better than if we claimed the morpheme had physical as well as semantic consistency. The human habit of categorising the world around always leaves a small debris of material which cannot be categorised. The most successful description of the data (or model) will be that one with the smallest pile of exceptions left at the end.

Since the inflectional morphemes in English are very few in number, we can list them exhaustively:

- Nouns – plural (*cats*) and possessive (*cat's*)
- Verbs – third-person singular present tense (*dances*), past tense (*danced*), continuous (*singing*), perfective (*spoken*)
- Adjectives – comparative (*safer*), superlative (*safest*)
- Adverbs – comparative (*more strongly*), superlative (*most strongly*)

They are very general in their meaning and, though very useful, they are not very interesting because of their consistent nature. The derivational morphemes are much more numerous, more restricted in their range of application and more specific in their meaning.

A small proportion of derivational morphemes are prefixes, occurring before rather than after the free morpheme. Some of these prefixes have a negative meaning and can be attached to a number of different word classes:

'un-' *unkind* (Aj), *unbutton* (V), *unsuccessfully* (Av)
'in-' *indelicate* (Aj), *invert* (V), *involuntarily* (Av)

Notice that the word class does not change when a prefix is added. Thus, the adjective *kind* remains an adjective, even when it is negated by adding *un-*. Unlike this relatively small class of prefixes, the large majority of derivational affixes are suffixes and by their addition cause a change of word class. So, for example, by the addition of a morpheme meaning *to make* – the adjective *private* becomes a verb: *privatise*. By the addition of a morpheme meaning *the process of –* or *the product of –* this verb in turn can become a noun: *privatisation.* The resulting word means *the process of making private* and other words demonstrate that these two morphemes are consistent in their meaning when attached to different free morphemes:

> *standardise, tenderise* (to make . . .)
> *frustration, condensation* (process or product)

What makes the derivations of English particularly interesting for the linguist and frustrating for the second or foreign language learner is that they are far less widespread than the inflections. Not all English adjectives can have the *-ise* suffix added, not all verbs can be made into nouns by the addition of *-ation.* Here are some examples which might not exist, though they are perfectly understandable (particularly when spoken):

> *contentise* (to make content), *fluentise* (to make fluent)
> *derust* (to get rid of rust from), *judgementation* (the process of
> judging)

Other examples of the kinds of meaning carried by derivational suffixes in English include the changing of gradable adjectives to manner adverbs by the addition of *-ly*:

> *stupidly, hurriedly, madly, beautifully, happily, sadly*

The meaning of such a morpheme would be something like *in a* ____ *manner.* Notice that the kinds of meanings here, though more specific than the 'plural' or 'past' of inflectional morphemes, is still rather general and assumes that there is a meaning coded in the free morpheme to fill the 'gap'. The meanings carried by bound morphemes, therefore, are contextually refined at the level of the word.

The derivational morphemes in English range from those that are petrified in their usage and those that continue to be productive in the language. The first extreme can be illustrated by words beginning in the morpheme meaning *to make* ____ realised as *be-*:

becalm, besmirch, belabour (?)

By contrast the suffix '-ish', which is added to adjectives and means *fairly* ___ , is very productive:

biggish, smallish, darkish, roundish, cleverish, sane-ish

Towards the end of this list it becomes clear that we are entering the area of English that is spoken but not often written. Notice that you would probably not blink if you heard the last two words, though they look very strange written down. This is the kind of mechanism that allows changes to take place and how new words are often coined. But it is true that many 'one-off' inventions are remade over and over again. Speakers feel able to use such productive suffixes quite freely with adjectives whether or not they have heard it used in that way before.

Another suffix of this kind is '-able' meaning 'capable of being Ved' (where V stands for the verb from which it is derived and 'ed' represents the past participle form):

understandable, moveable, saleable, singable, copeable with

Thus we have words meaning 'able to be understood/moved/ sold', etc. I have heard the last example many times, though each time it feels as though the speaker is inventing it anew. There is no evidence that this phrase in this form is going to catch on, but it does not sound 'wrong', simply rather ungainly or inelegant.

We will return later to the question of creativity in English. Here we will simply note that bound morphemes seem to carry meaning of a fairly general kind and always with the need for a free morpheme to 'fill the gap' in their meaning. So *-ion* is one of the suffixes that indicates 'the process of Ving' and *-er* means 'one who Vs'.

digestion (the process of digesting)
baker, craver, doer (one who bakes, craves, does)

A slightly different, but very important process of derivation in English is known as 'zero derivation' because it does not involve adding affixes to the base word. With zero derivation, the word simply changes to another word-class, without changing its form. One set of words that exhibit this behaviour are the nouns describing tools in English. Thus we have *hammer, nail* and *saw*, not only as nouns, but also as verbs describing the action typically associated with these nouns:

Give me the hammer (n).   *I want to hammer* (v) *this floorboard down.*
Where's the nail (n) *I dropped?*   *I need it to nail* (v) *the box together.*
I'll get the saw (n).   *Which bit of wood shall I saw* (v)?

Although no affixes are added to produce the new derived form, once a word has changed class, it will take the usual inflections for that new word class. So the nouns shown above, once they have been made into verbs, can have the usual verbal endings where appropriate:

She's hammering the nail into the chair.
I nailed the table to the floor.
Have you sawn that wood yet?

One final major grouping of complex word forms should be introduced here: the compound words. These words consist of more than one free morpheme and are interesting from the point of view of their meaning because they signify 'more than the sum of their parts'. The form of compounds is simple: two or more words (free morphemes), are usually written as one, although sometimes a hyphen is added between the morphemes:

blackbird, tablecloth, dog-collar, ice-cream, handbag

The meaning of these words is both derived from, and more than, the meaning of the two parts added together. The word *blackbird* does not apply to any bird that happens to be black, but to a specific garden bird to be found in Northern Europe. Other birds of the same colour have to be satisfied with a phrasal description: *black bird*. Similarly, a *handbag* is not just any bag that is carried by hand, but indicates a socially and culturally determined item used by women to carry some of a wide range of items including money, diaries, pens and make-up (another compound).

The more anti-European sections of the British press often rail against the intrusion of European legislation on British labelling and naming. One of the contentious issues has been the claim that other Europeans would like to ban the use of the word *ice-cream* to describe the product which in many of the cheaper versions contains no cream at all. The definition of compound words as having a meaning separate from and in some ways different to the sum of its parts might solve such debates! It could, after all, be argued that *ice-cream* is an *icy* product with a *creamy* consistency.

Activity: inflection, derivation and compounding

Which of the following list of words were formed by the three main processes of word-formation in English, inflection, derivation and compounding?

> *completely, reversal, socialist, trying, house-hunt, contemptible, arrangement, harmless, danced, meanness, buses, pollution, lawnmower, discovery, subnormal, harder, baby-sit, deafen, sunny, popcorn*

You will notice that some of these words have more than one affix and it is, of course, possible to add inflections to any word in addition to any derivational affixes it may have. So, for example, the verb baby-sit may be used in any of the usual forms that English verbs take:

> *I am baby-sitting tonight.*
> *We baby-sat for her last week.*

The words form the following groups:

inflection	derivation	compounding
trying	completely	house-hunt
danced	reversal	lawnmower
buses	socialist	baby-sit
harder	contemptible	popcorn
completely	arrangement	
	harmless	
	meanness	
	pollution	

discovery
subnormal
deafen
sunny

Taking the derived words, work out where the affixes are and try to
define their meanings (remember they will usually have a 'slot' for
the free morpheme to fill). Then work out in what way the meanings
of the compound words differ from the meaning of their constituent
parts.

My rough attempts at answering these questions follow:

bound morpheme	definition
-ly	in a ___ manner
-al	the process of __ing
-ist	a person who has ___ attitudes or beliefs
-ible	the property of attracting __
-ment	the process or product of __ing
-less	without ___
-ness	a quality of being ___
-tion	the result of __ing
dis-	reversing the action of __ing
-y	the process of __ing
sub-	below ___
-en	to make ___
-y	the property of ___

The compounds signify the following in addition to the joint
meaning of their parts:

compound	joint meaning of parts	additional meaning
house-hunt	hunting for a house	in order to buy it
lawnmower	for mowing the lawn	a machine
baby-sit	sitting, babies	looking after
popcorn	popped corn	often with added flavours

Choose a sample of the affixes from the derivational list and try
making up new words using them. How productive do they seem to
be? How convincing are the resulting words? Are they the kind of

derivations that are likely to be repeatedly remade in spoken English, or are they potential new permanent words of the language, destined for the pages of the dictionary?

3.3 Analysing Word Meaning

Having established that many English words are made up of free and bound morphemes in a variety of combinations, how do we proceed to describe and analyse the meanings of English words, whether they are simple (a free morpheme) complex (free and bound morphemes) or compound (free morphemes in combination)?

One model of word meaning that has been proposed is known as 'componential analysis'. This approach to word meaning relies on an assumption that the meaning of a word can be analysed in terms of a set of semantic features, many of which will form part of the description of other words in the same language. There is a similarity here with the kinds of meaning we saw in the last section, but here there is no physical form, like the bound morpheme, to carry the meaning.

The first examples to illustrate this approach are taken from Lyons (1977) and illustrate the origins of componential analysis which arose independently in two places and disciplines. Linguists first used the notion of 'sense components' (I will call them 'semantic features') in Eastern Europe and did so as a result of extending their structuralist (Saussurean) view of language from including only phonology and grammar to include semantics as well.

Briefly, the structuralist view that developed out of de Saussure's ideas was that language consisted of a number of systems at the various linguistic 'levels' and these systems had internal patterns which could be described without recourse to factors outside language – such as the 'real' world. From this perspective semantics was viewed as the study of the similarities and differences in meaning between different words. Inevitably, these similarities and differences were seen as 'components' which were likely to be standard throughout the language concerned. For example, *man* was analysed as consisting of the components: **male + adult + human** some of which would be shared by *woman, child, boy*, etc. Similarly *chair* was analysed as having the components: **for sitting upon + with legs + with a back + for one person** which would partly overlap with the meanings of *stool, bench, pouffe,* etc.

The other group of scholars who came up with componential analysis at about the same time were working in America. This time it was the idea of anthropologists, working with previously little-studied tribes which usually appeared to embody different kinship priorities in their languages. For example, some languages may not only have the equivalent of English *aunt* [**female + sibling of parent**] and *uncle* [**male + sibling of parent**], but may further distinguish between what we would paraphrase as 'aunt on my mother's side' and 'aunt on my father's side'.

It should be noted here that with circumlocutions and long-winded expressions, languages can usually express equivalent meanings, but any single language chooses culturally important differences to emphasise by building them into its vocabulary. An example from within the variety of Englishes is the range of meal titles that exist throughout the English-speaking world. Whilst there is some difference between the regions of England itself as well as between the classes of British English society, there are some meal names that are very specific to other ex-colonial areas of the world. Thus a working-class Northerner in England may eat *dinner* at midday and *tea* at 5 o'clock, whilst a middle-class southerner may eat *lunch* and *supper* at roughly the same times (probably 1 p.m. and 6 or 7 p.m.). There are still areas of India previously colonised by the British where the afternoon high-tea is called *tiffin* and the Americans have contributed the very useful blend of *lunch* and *breakfast* – *brunch,* which is a large mid-morning meal that obviates the need for two meals.

There have been some fairly strong claims made for componential analysis. For example, some people claim that the semantic features which make up word meaning are universal (i.e. there is a stock of standard features of meaning on which all languages draw). Given the very wide range of human cultures in the world this seems unlikely to work at the most detailed levels. Others have tried to make their features all have a binary form: two opposing sides to a single feature that can be represented as 'plus' and 'minus' for that feature.

For example, many have represented the sex features of human words in terms of + or − **male**. Apart from the obvious sexist prejudice in this particular example which defines females by a lack of maleness, binary features in general are too restricting for the data. Many words are found to overlap in meaning, but differ in a way that cannot be represented by plus and minus features. We will see some examples later in this section.

One of the main problems with the way in which componential analysis has been discussed in the literature is that only a very few examples have been discussed. One detailed study (OUP, 1983) into the effectiveness of componential analysis for wide-ranging description of the meanings of English words resulted in the following general conclusions:

1. Only at the most general level can semantic features be universal.
2. Componential analysis is a very useful way of describing the meanings of many lexical words in English, though it has huge theoretical problems.
3. There are many kinds of semantic features: single, binary, multi-term.

Some examples of componential analysis in English will illustrate these points. If we look at the general area of **movement verbs** in English, we might conclude that they share the basic components:

- **change location** (changing from one place to another)
- **animate** (for now setting aside inanimate movement)
- **using legs** (narrowing down the field for now to leg-based movement)
- ± **(plus or minus) continuous contact** (the importance of this feature will become clear shortly)

These main features of meaning may deal with the important differences between *walk* and *run*, because they share the first three features and are distinguished by the fourth. Although most speakers, when asked about the difference, would say that walking is slower than running, it does not take many moments of reflection (and possibly experimentation) to realise that what is significant about their difference is that when walking we always have one foot

on the ground, but running involves short moments when both feet
leave the ground at the same time.*

But what about other verbs which are more specific in their
meaning? For example, the following group share a **human actor**
and the feature **each step the same length**: *stride, pace, march* and
goosestep. They also need features of a more specific kind to
distinguish them from each other:

stride	**long steps**
pace	**repeatedly covering same ground**
march	**placing feet down firmly**
goosestep	**placing feet down firmly + legs straight**

If a model of word meaning is to be useful, it needs to be able to
operate at this level of detail in a language like English which is so
rich in near-synonyms. Clearly the more restricted kind of ± feature
is not adequate to the task.

The following group share the feature **movement judged as
abnormal**: *shuffle, shamble, waddle, hobble, limp*. They can be divided
into two groups by the following features:

dragging both feet – *shuffle, shamble*
with difficulty or uneven steps – *waddle, hobble, limp*

But this group needs further individual features to distinguish the
individual words from each other:

waddle	**body moves from side to side**
hobble	**constricted movement of legs**
limp	**one leg injured/deformed/restricted**

Clearly it would make no sense to force all features into a binary
pattern, since that would result in defining, for example, *waddle* as
not having one leg injured, *not* having a constricted movement of the
legs, etc. This would seem to be taking the structuralist notion of

---

*I am indebted to Nida (1975, p. 90) for this observation about the difference between
'folk' definitions of words and definitions which more accurately capture the way we
use the words in fact.

words being mutually defining to absurd and not very useful extremes.

If componential analysis is a useful model for analysing word meanings, we are almost bound to accept another structuralist theory of relationships between words known as Semantic Field Theory. The analysis of word meanings into components is only useful if these components are shared and the examples given above illustrate the fact that most often they are shared by words with very largely overlapping meanings. In English the most widespread relationship between lexemes is partially shared meaning and there are many areas of the vocabulary where a number of words seem to divide up the semantic space between them.

The theory of semantic fields was first suggested by the German linguist Trier (1934), who suggested that all areas of meaning were neatly and economically divided up like a mosaic and that each sub-area of meaning was assigned to a different word. The advantage of this theory over earlier models of meaning was that it recognised clearly that human meaning is on a continuum and is arbitrarily divided by specific languages.

Early discussion of lexical fields almost always quotes the example of the colour spectrum which is known to be a continuum, making clear to English speakers that our words (*blue – purple – red – orange – yellow – green*) represent arbitrary divisions. It is also a useful example because different languages use a different number of words to divide up the colours.

English	Welsh
	gwyrdd
green	
blue	glas
grey	
brown	llwydd

This example (from Hjelmslev [1953] and quoted in Palmer [1976]) shows that there is indeed very little connection between the 'real' world and lexical items. The colours that we tend to treat as 'given' are not even adjacent on the spectrum – grey and brown in particular are mixtures of other colours.

The strongest versions of field theory claim that the entire lexicon consists of a neat, interrelating structure of word senses. There would be no overlaps between word meanings, no areas of meaning that are not lexicalised, and words would belong in one field and only one field.

However, it is generally agreed that 'lexical fields', the linguistic realisation of the semantic fields as envisaged by Trier, are not nearly as clearly separated or as perfectly organised as early structuralists thought. This does not automatically make the notion of lexical fields less valid. Lyons (1977, pp. 267–8) argues that while 'what is lacking so far . . . is a more explicit formulation of the criteria which define a lexical field', there is as yet no 'alternative theory of the structure of the vocabulary', which has been 'tested against an equal amount of empirical evidence'.

What is a lexical field? Miller (1961) writes that a semantic domain* is 'any set of words implied by an incomplete definition'. In other words, words which can be grouped together in a field share the most central part of their definitions and differ in the peripheral parts of their meaning. Such definitions avoid a taxing question: which conceptual areas are most fundamental when you are making the first divisions into large fields of meaning? For example, do you group *swim* with *run* on the grounds that **move** is part of its definition? Do you also group *come, go, arrive, depart, enter, exit, advance, retreat* together since they are all **directionally oriented**? Or do you group *swim* with *sail, water-ski* and other **water** words or with more precise near-synonyms (subordinates), *crawl, breaststroke, butterfly*. And do you group *depart* with words indicating the same direction (i.e. away): *leave, go away*?

Clearly, once you get to this level of detail, there is no one correct way to organise a lexical field and as with other types of human categorisation, it depends what you are hoping to show through such organisation. The analyst, in deciding to group *smell* with *inhale, sniff, breathe in*, is focusing on that part of the 'incomplete definition' which relates to taking air into the lungs. Another analyst might decide to group together all the 'sense perception' lexemes, giving a different insight into the relationship between these verbs.

---

*Note that Miller is using the term 'semantic domain' to refer to the linguistic system, not just the area of meaning that might be covered by the linguistic units. This is equivalent to our use of the term 'lexical field' here.

Note, for example, the different range of meaning between *smell* and *taste*:

She smelt the food	*The food smelt delicious*
She tasted the food	*The food tasted delicious*

The verb *taste* differs from *smell* in that the conceptual subject of the verb remains the person referred to by *she*, i.e. it is still her doing the tasting, whereas the food can 'give off scent' in an almost active way when it is the grammatical subject of the verb *smell*. This phenomenon will only be clearly seen as one of the distinguishing features of these items if the words are grouped together.

As it developed, lexical field theory became increasingly linked with componential analysis, described at the beginning of this section. If you are going to establish how a set of words divides up an area of meaning, you are almost certainly going to be working out the relevant semantic features that distinguish the words. For example, in the area of 'language and communication' verbs there is a group of words denoting **quiet speaking** which include the following: *mutter, mumble, murmur, whisper*. These words can be distinguished from each other in the following way:

mutter	**voiced/indistinct words/low pitch**
mumble	**voiced/indistinct words/blurred articulation**
murmur	**voiced/distinct words**
whisper	**voiceless**

They also share general features of meaning, including **language and communication, specific medium, speech, quiet**. This kind of analysis of word meaning combines the two theories of lexical fields and componential analysis.

While early structuralists made very strong claims for lexical field theory, Nida (1975, p. 164) takes a more realistic standpoint in arguing that there are many different dimensions to language and that no one theoretical model can capture *all* the different aspects of meaning: 'there are too many claims that a particular model can and must explain everything about languages'. Field theory, then, may show some of the meaning relations between words; it cannot show them all.

One problem is that lexical fields are traditionally only two-dimensional and cannot capture all the relationships that exist between lexemes. They are, in effect, giving priority to the relationship of near-synonymy and subordinating all other relationships such as oppositeness and multiple meaning. It is as though we were using a two-dimensional model of a patchwork quilt when we needed a three-dimensional model closer to the spatial relationships of the stars in their constellations. There are also many parallel relationships of meaning that will not automatically be displayed by a lexical field grouping. For example, the lexemes *see* and *hear* are likely to be placed in separate and unconnected fields with their phrasal counterparts *look at* and *listen to*. The distance between the fields may fail to show up the parallel distinction between these pairs of sentences:

> *He saw the policeman.*   *He looked at the policeman.*
> *He heard the radio.*   *He listened to the radio.*

It is likely that this objection – to the two-dimensionality of lexical fields – could be overcome as a result of recent developments in technology. It would be quite possible, now, to store words and their semantic features in a computer-readable database which could sort and sample the data on a number of different dimensions, allowing different groupings of word-senses to be placed together for different reasons.

Although lexical fields sound very attractive in theory, in practice there are other problems with Trier's strong version of the theory. By comparing different languages we sometimes find not only different patterns for breaking down the semantic space, but we also find that some languages have gaps where other languages have words. It may have happened to you, if you speak another language fairly well, that you find English lacks a word for something expressed very aptly in the other language. Cultural contact often results in one of the languages 'borrowing' the other's expression where the gap exists, e.g. *le weekend, je ne sais quoi.*

Lexical fields are, however, useful in describing the different levels of lexical structure. For example, if we take an area of meaning roughly covering 'language and communication', we find the following English words:

glare, grimace, wink, frown, smile, shrug, beckon, bow, nod

These seem like one field describing the full range of body language until you realise that each one is merely the first word in a more specific field of its own:

glare, *glower, look daggers, give black look*
grimace, *scowl, lower, pull face at, pout*
wink, *bat eyelids at, flutter eyelashes*
frown, *raise one's eyebrows, knit one's brows*
smile, *grin, beam, smirk, leer*
wave, *salute, bow, genuflect, nod, curtsey*
nod, *shake one's head*

Once you get down to the more specific fields, the words are closer to being near-synonyms. They are then more and more difficult to distinguish by semantic features and are sometimes simply distinguished by their grammar (*raise/rise*) or by their connotation (*loo/bog*) or by their collocation (see Chapter 4).

Activity: semantic features and lexical fields
The following groups of words seem to belong in two separate lexical fields. What features of meaning would you use to characterise each group as a whole (i.e. the incomplete definition that they share)? Also consider how you would define the more detailed differences between the members of each group, using semantic features.

crease, crumple, crush, wrinkle, crinkle, pucker
hum, drone, buzz, whine

Discussion
The first group seem to involve some **change of state** whereby there is a relative **change of position** of some of the parts of the item being crushed, crumpled, etc. The item concerned is normally perceived as largely **two-dimensional** (e.g. something made of fabric like a handkerchief) and the result is that this flattish item becomes folded in a number of places and is seen as spoiled by this. Thereafter, we need to distinguish between the different words in the field. We might, for example, characterise *wrinkle* and *pucker* as having

parallel folds, whilst *crush* and *crumple* have intersecting and cross-cutting folds. We might also make some distinctions according to the kinds of material which tend to be described in this way. Thus paper as well as fabric typically *creases* and is *crushed*, whereas fabric and skin may be described as *wrinkled* or *puckered*. Notice that these groups concern word-senses, and there will be other, closely related senses of the words here, which do not seem to have exactly the same set of semantic features. This is the case, for example, with *crush* in the above group. There is one sense which *is* a member of this group and other senses (*I felt crushed./The car was crushed by the lorry*) which belong elsewhere.

The second group seem to share features describing them as a **long noise** which is **smooth in pitch** and **even in volume**. They are distinguished by the fact that *whine* is particularly high-pitched whilst the others are typically **mid-to-low pitched**. We may also consider that *drone* and *whine* have unpleasant connotations, whilst *hum* and *buzz* seem to emphasise the accompanying vibrations. These semantic features are partly a matter of consensus amongst English speakers, and partly differ from speaker to speaker. Do not be surprised, then, if your answers are different from mine.

Activity: semantic features and lexical fields
The following text is taken from the autobiography of Ellen Kuzwayo, an activist in the struggle against apartheid in South Africa. This passage occurs just after she has heard that her son, also involved in political activity, has been arrested. If you look closely at the text, you will notice that its vocabulary is made up of a number of interwoven lexical fields. Try identifying them.

It was during one such moment, when my mind was blank, that I heard a knock on the door. I don't remember saying, come in; all I know is that I turned, stopped and stared. As if in a dream, my son, my dear son Bakone, walked in accompanied by a young white man whom I soon got to know was a plain-clothes policeman. Within the space of a few hours, he appeared taller and thinner, his lips dry, as if he had not eaten for days on end. I was lost for a moment about what to do or say; then suddenly we were in each other's arms. I led him to the office couch where we both sat down. I took him and placed him on my lap, tall as he

was, with his legs dangling on the floor. The instinct of motherhood took complete control of me. I kissed him.

(Kuzwayo, 1985, p. 187)

Discussion

There are many things one would like to say about this passage, not
least to try and analyse how it communicates so strongly with the
reader the emotion that takes hold of her. However, we should stick
to our task here and look at how the text is constructed from a
number of lexical fields. The tension of this passage partly exists in
the two contrasting sets of words, one of which emphasises inaction
and the lack of control felt by the narrator, and the other which
shows her taking decisive action and trying to exert what little
control she could over the situation:

blank	*turned*
stared	*stopped*
dream	*to do or say*
lost	*led*
instinct	*sat down*
took control	*kissed*

Interestingly, these two sets of words are not separated in the
sequence of the passage, but are intertwined to show the see-saw of
emotion and inaction–action that characterised her response. In the
end, the control that is taken over her will is not that of the state, but
that of the instinct of motherhood. At this point, the two lists
converge, since it is the controlling force, motherhood, that enables
her to act – to kiss her son. Another field of words that is prominent
in this passage is that relating to parts of the body and characteristics
of the body:

mind, taller, thinner, lips, arms, lap, legs

This set of words emphasises the physical, rather than the mental or
psychological effects of what has and will happen. The effect, in a
book that is full of historical and political detail, is to fill this passage
with an immediacy and overwhelming emotion that contrasts
strongly with the surrounding text.

3.4 Meaningful Relationships

The previous section claimed that it was useful to look at word
meaning as being made up of components, or 'features', because
many groups of words in English shared part of their meaning. It
was also proposed that words had close relationships with each
other, and could be organised into lexical/semantic fields to
illustrate their overlapping meaning.

Defining word meaning is inevitably circular, since we are using
language to define language. However, the attempt to analyse
meaning into components aims towards making the circle very
wide, but with some referential 'pointing' to the real world as well.
The fact that we cannot avoid comparing words when we are
discussing their meanings also indicates that the relationships
existing between words constitutes part of the speaker's knowledge
about them, and is therefore part of their meaning.

These relationships between words are known as 'sense relations'.
They can be illustrated by reference to the notion of 'system' that
was introduced earlier (section 1.3). If the vocabulary of a language
like English is made up of systems of words, like the pronoun
system but much larger, then a word's meaning is partly determined
by what it does not mean, i.e. the area of meaning that is covered by
other related words. The addition or subtraction of a word from this
kind of mutually defining system will inevitably change, however
subtly, the meaning of the remaining words.

The easiest illustration of this phenomenon is to compare the
same area of meaning from two different languages. For example,
the names of parts of the day and night are not equivalent in English
and Spanish:

Spanish	*mañana*	*tarde*		*noche*
Standard English	*morning*	*afternoon*	*evening*	*night*

Whilst *mañana* and *morning* are almost equivalent, the word *tarde*
covers most of what we mean by *afternoon* in English as well as a
good part of the evening. The later evening, when Spaniards tend to
still be out and about, is covered by *noche*, although it also means
night in the English sense of the time when we are in bed.

The term 'sense relations', then, is used to convey the idea that
word-senses have not only denotation (the referential part of their

meaning), but also a complex set of relations with other words. We have already seen the relationships between word-senses in the same field. Another simple example of sense relations is opposition:

slow/fast
happy/sad
break/mend
raise/lower
woman/man
buy/sell

In terms of sense relations, these words each have, as part of their meaning, the opposites shown here. We will return to opposition shortly, but first let us consider the other different kinds of sense relation.

Synonymy is a word we all use casually. What does it mean? That two words have the same meaning. What does 'the same' mean? If we expect it to refer to identity in all aspects, it is not a very useful relation to talk about, because there are so few exact synonyms, even in English. What, for example, are the synonyms of the word *sad*? The following might qualify:

unhappy, melancholy, heavy-hearted, mournful, doleful

English has had such a rich input in its history that it has a comparatively large vocabulary compared with other languages. There is, therefore, every chance of finding synonyms from Germanic, Greek and Latinate origins. However, these potential synonyms usually end up having a number of subtle differences of meaning and/or usage which make them less than exact synonyms. Most speakers of English would agree that the list of potential synonyms for *sad* have differences of meaning and are therefore only partial synonyms. It does not follow that the differences are easy to describe.

Let us focus on the structure of the English vocabulary and its hierarchical nature. If we look back at some of the examples from earlier sections, we often find that there is a single word which seems to sum up the overlapping words in a lexical field. The group *shuffle, shamble, limp, hobble, waddle, stroll, saunter, amble, swagger, stalk, strut, mince,* for example, all share the meaning of the word *walk.* Other related words such as *jump* and *run* also have a number of more specific words associated with them:

jump	run
vault	jog
leapfrog	sprint
hurdle	trot
leap	scurry
spring	scamper
bound	scuttle

These examples imply that there is a certain amount of 'hierarchy' in the structure of vocabulary. You will remember the specialised meaning of this term (section 1.1) which is nothing to do with levels of importance as it appears to be in human hierarchies like government. If there are hierarchies in lexical structure, it indicates that there are more and more specific and general levels of vocabulary. So a specific word like *rose* could be replaced by a more general word like *flower*, *cow* by *animal* and *spring* by *season*. The more general term, known as the 'superordinate', has a meaning which forms the core meaning of the more specific word, called a 'hyponym'. In terms of semantic features, the more general word will have fewer features than the more specific word which will have additional features, marking out its particular specialised meaning. There is a relation of implication between superordinates and their hyponyms: if something is a rose, it must also be a flower; if you are a mother, you are also a parent. Some hierarchies have more than two levels of generality. This means that words on intermediate levels are at the same time hyponyms of the more general terms and superordinates of the specific terms on lower levels. For example:

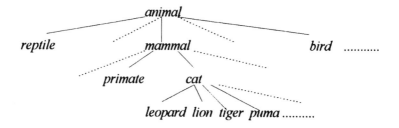

The words in the middle layers of this partial hierarchy each relate to those on either side in a relationship of inclusiveness. The meaning 'animal' is in all of them; the meaning 'mammal' is in all except *animal* and so on. The relation of implication works throughout these levels, even when one level is missed out. So a cat is a kind of mammal and is also a kind of animal. A leopard is a kind of cat, a kind of mammal and a kind of animal. Notice also that the kind of hierarchy you devise will be partly dependent on its purpose. Thus a scientist interested in the categorisation of living things will no doubt include levels such as the division into vertebrate and invertebrate animals and others I do not even know about, all of which I have conveniently ignored here.

Although there are a few areas where hierarchies map out quite well the apparent relationships between words, in fact the English vocabulary is not hierarchical all the way through. There are some hierarchical relationships to be found among the verbs. For example, walking is a kind of moving and hobbling is a kind of walking:

However, there is not one single top-level word over all other words. Rather, there seem to be a number of general words in English which are the top superordinates over sections of the vocabulary. A fairly comprehensive list might be:

person, place, thing, stuff
act, move, become, get, be, make

However, readers might like to try thinking of words which do not fit under one of these very general superordinates.

In conversations, we repeatedly choose the appropriate level of vocabulary to suit the occasion. For example, if we received one of those competition forms with hidden messages that need to be scratched off, we would probably say *Give me a coin to see if I've got the winning combination* rather than *Give me a twenty pence piece . . .* Similarly, we ask a child to *run round the corner for a pint of milk,* not *scamper*. When guests enter our homes, we do not say *pull up a corner unit*, we say *pull up a chair*. And we avoid using inappropriate levels of vocabulary, where the result is that our choices are too close in their meaning: *What would you like to eat? Some food!*

Let us now return to oppositeness as the last sense relation to be discussed in this section. The word 'antonymy' is often used as the opposite of synonymy, but we should be aware that there are various types of opposition in lexical structure and what is known as antonymy is only one of them.

First, let us consider what oppositeness is not. Although we may be tempted to draw this conclusion, it is not the opposite of 'sameness of meaning'. Although we have noted that there are very few exact synonyms in English (and probably even fewer in other languages), we do know what the 'ideal' synonyms would be like. For a start they would share the following features:

- Denotation (i.e. all of their semantic features)
- Sense relations (i.e. the same superordinates, hyponyms, opposites, near-synonyms)
- Grammatical behaviour (e.g. verbs would both be transitive, nouns both count/mass)
- Connotation (see section 3.5)
- Collocation (see section 4.1)
- Polysemy (see section 3.6)

We might expect the opposite of synonymy to mean that all of these features are not shared, but exactly opposed. To put it simply, 'real' opposites would have nothing in common at all. This would not be a very close or useful relationship as a few examples can show. If we try to choose words which are as different as possible from words such as *cat, sing, palpitation, ringworm, gelatine,* we find ourselves thinking of words like *porcupine* for *sing* or *meditate* for *gelatine*. The answers are disparate – we do not agree on this kind of opposition – it is not culturally important and is therefore not enshrined in our vocabulary.

What, then is opposition as found in vocabularies? Opposition is essentially a special kind of partial synonymy. Two words are partial synonyms when they share many of their components of meaning. For example, *pour* and *spill* share features like **movement of liquid**

+ **change location** + **from solid container**, but they differ in one important cultural respect: *pour* is an intentional action whereas *spill* is unintentional.

With opposites, then, the feature which differentiates them is either of some cultural importance or is fundamental to human life and is therefore highlighted by the words themselves having the special status of being 'opposites'. Notice the large number of books available for teaching toddlers about opposites. The culturally important contrasts need to be introduced; they do not just pick them up naturally. Another quite straightforward pair of opposites is *shorten/lengthen* which share features like **change of physical form** + **change of size** + **in one dimension**. They differ in that *shorten* involves making that single dimension smaller and *lengthen* involves making it larger.

Note that not all words which could have opposites do have them. In this area of size, for example, there is no opposite for *elongate* or *deepen*, although there is the standard pair *widen* and *narrow*. Opposition seems to operate most frequently at the level of meaning that comes between the rather vague superordinates listed above (e.g. *thing*, *stuff*) and the more specific hyponyms of the lower levels. There may be a pair of opposites like *pull* and *push* which are conventional opposites, but a very similar pair like *tug* and *shove*, with a more specific meaning (i.e. the strength of the movement) may lack the emphasis on opposition.

As we noted earlier, there are a number of different kinds of opposition. 'Gradable antonymy' involves words that mark out the two extremes of a range of meaning, where there are degrees between the two extremes, but they are not normally lexicalised. Thus in the area of adjectives we have opposites such as *hot/cold*, *large/small*, *sad/happy*, *light/heavy*. Between these extremes, there are clearly different amounts of heat, size and weight, but English lexicalises and opposes the ends of the gradation for convenience. Note that in some important areas of the vocabulary, there are in fact lexical items for the gradations along these scales, but their opposition is not normally invested with the same importance as the ends of the scale. The scale of temperature, for example, has its extremes opposed as *hot* and *cold*, but the intermediate 'pair' *cool/warm* and the solo item *tepid* do not seem to take part in any conventional opposition.

A second type of opposition, which involves no gradation, is known as 'complementarity'. In this case, the words concerned denote referents which are mutually exclusive so that *a* entails *not b* and vice versa. Examples of complementaries include *man/woman*, *alive/dead* and *in/out*. In each case, both of the words cannot apply at the same time. Thus a person cannot be both a *man* and a *woman* (at the same time); things which have the potential for life cannot be both *alive* and *dead* at the same time; and if you are describing the position or situation of something or someone, they cannot be both totally *in* and completely *out* of the room at the same time. Notice that we exploit the relationship of complementarity in a number of idiomatic phrases:

> *this is a dead-and-alive town*
> *she is more man than woman*
> *you're half-in, half-out*

These phrases do no damage to the basic mutual exclusivity of the pairs of words. Rather their meaning depends on the understanding that in the normal run of things, both words cannot be applied together to the same thing.

The third type of opposition that can be identified is 'converseness'. Words that are converses take a different perspective on the activity or relationship that they describe. Thus the relationship between spouses is embodied in the words *husband* and *wife* and if one person is known to be a wife, there must be a husband lurking in the background. Notice the difference here with *woman* and *man*, where to say that someone is a woman says nothing about the existence of a man. There are also pairs of verbs that regard the same activity from different perspectives. These are often connected with transactions and include pairs such as *buy/ sell* and *lend/borrow*. In a commercial transaction, then, the words *buy* and *sell* are both equally relevant, but one emphasises the action taken by the seller, and one the action by the buyer. Similarly with the words *lend* and *borrow* which both apply to non-commercial loans. If one person is lending something, there must be another person borrowing, and vice versa. Notice that this pair is one that seems to be undergoing change for certain English speakers who use only one of the verbs for both 'ends' of the transaction. Once we understand the converse relationship, it is not so surprising to find people using them in this way:

Can I lend your ruler for a minute?
Could you borrow me your umbrella at lunchtime?

Whilst these are not currently the Standard English forms, the presence of the possessive pronoun *your* makes very clear in which direction the lent/borrowed item is travelling. There is, strictly speaking, no need for both of these verbs in English.

The final type of opposite that will be introduced here is called 'directional opposition'. The pairs of opposites that we might identify as directional opposites are those which describe the reversal of a process or direction. Examples include pairs of verbs such as *break/mend, button/unbutton* as well as directional prepositions such as *towards/away from* and *up/down*.

Although we have been discussing opposition, and other sense relations as though they mainly operate between words, irrespective of context, it is important to remember that all of these relationships between words reflect constructs of society and can therefore be changed in context:

Labour say he's black
We say he's British

This Conservative party slogan from the 1979 election shows how parallel syntax sets up the expectation of opposition. Both of the sentences have the structure SVO (Subject – Verb – Object) and in both cases the Object is a subordinate clause with the structure SVC (Subject – Verb – Complement). This parallelism leads the reader to make comparisons between the pairs of items in each of these positions. The two grammatical subjects, *Labour* and *we* (i.e. Conservative), are culturally opposed in Britain. The two verbs, *say*, and the subjects and verbs of the subordinate clauses, *he's*, are identical. So far, then, the reader has been offered opposition followed by similarity. The expectation as we approach the end of the second sentence is that there will be another opposition in the complement. The final element of any clause is usually its focal position, where the new information is situated, so the parallelism of the early part of the two sentences leads us to expect a conventional opposition in complement position. This is how we are led toward interpreting *black* and *British* as opposites, specifically complementary opposites, which are mutually exclusive. The reader is therefore encouraged to conclude, with the Conservatives, that for Labour to label people *black* is in some sense denying their *Britishness*.

Activity: sense relations
What other words do you think the following have connections with? These connections may be any kind of sense relation, such as synonymy or partial-synonymy, any kind of opposite, relations of hierarchy (hyponymy):

loud, anorak, take

What kind of oppositions do you think the following words enter into in English?

uncle, wet, always

Look at the following sentences and find a sense relation that has been 'created' in that context (i.e. would not be seen as existing out of this context):

Were we the independent thinkers we thought ourselves to be, or were we the dupes of a cynical government?

There were the road campaigners; outrageous people, the dregs of society.

The noise was a high-pitched whistle, one of the eeriest sounds I've ever heard.

Discussion
The adjective *loud* is a gradable antonym with the opposite *quiet* or possibly *soft*. It has a number of partial synonyms, some of which include *noisy*, *high volume* and *ear-splitting*. Some of these partial synonyms seem to be hyponyms of *loud*, since they encompass its meaning as well as being more specialised. The noun *anorak* belongs in a lexical field with words like *jacket*, *blazer* and *kagoul*. They are all

hyponyms of the more general superordinate *coat*. The verb *take* has a converse opposite *give*, although one could also explain their opposition in terms of directional opposition: 'I gave it to her and then took it back.' The partial synonyms *receive* and *get* seem to emphasise the same (taker's) end of the process and also operate at a fairly similar level of generality. In the same lexical field as *take* there are also more specific hyponyms such as *steal*, and *grab*.

The opposite of *uncle* would normally be seen as *aunt*, although this is a 'catch' in a way, since the words both emphasise a relationship, but that relationship is not the dimension on which the opposition works. If someone is an uncle, there must be a nephew or niece and vice versa. But these relationships are culturally less important than those between male and female in our society. Therefore the opposition is a complementary, not a converse, with *uncle* and *aunt* simply being mutually exclusive versions of 'people who are siblings (or spouses of siblings) of one's mother or father'. This is identical to the relationship between *man* and *woman*, and not like *wife/husband* since there can be an aunt without an uncle and an uncle without an aunt.

The adjective *wet* has a gradable opposite *dry*, and there are clearly stages between the two, though not many are lexicalised: *damp*. Some degrees of wetness are difficult to place; they may exist outside the range, depending on whether *wet* and *dry* are perceived as absolute extremes or simply as typical positions on a gradient. Examples such as *soaking* and *bone dry* seem to indicate that the traditional opposites are simply convenient opposites whose exact meaning probably depends on the item concerned and the context in which the humidity is being discussed.

The adverb *always* is interesting because the continuous nature of its meaning is apparently brought into focus by the opposite *now*, which refers only to a single point in time. By contrast the aspect of its meaning that seems to encompass 'all time' is brought out by the opposite *never*, which refers to 'no time'. These two are different kinds of opposition: *always/never* are gradable opposites, although we often read them as being complementaries. Thus there are, in fact, things that occur for part of the time, and we even lexicalise this concept in English with the word *sometimes*. Even the apparently more absolute end of the scale, *never*, can be shown to have some flexibility: *hardly ever*, *almost never*. The other opposition, *always/now*, is only apparently an opposition, since the two are neither mutually exclusive, nor two perspectives on the same phenomenon and they are not ends of a gradient or directionally opposed. Nevertheless, we sometimes treat them as though they were converses, as the first line of this Philip Larkin poem shows:

> Is it for now or for always,
> The world hangs on a stalk?
> (Larkin, 1945, XXVIII)

Here, Larkin is addressing the old question of whether his love will last. The choice between it being either very short-lived (i.e. *now*) or lasting for ever (*always*) is clearly over-simplified, since there are in fact many other options, including love lasting for some time, but not for ever.

The 'created' sense-relations in the three sentences above, are complementary opposites (*thinkers* vs. *dupes*), synonyms (*campaigners = outrageous people = dregs*) and hyponym/superordinate (*high-pitched whistle* is a kind of *eerie sound*). Notice that as soon as these words and phrases are taken out of context, the sense-relations dissolve. Nevertheless, causing such relationships to be produced in texts is a very powerful persuasive tool for the text-producer.

3.5 You Know a Word by its Reputation

Earlier we saw that the distinction between language system ('langue') and language use ('parole') was a model which sees an abstracted 'language-system' as underlying everyday usage whereas, in fact, it is a simplification of the accumulation of all prior usage and experience of the language in the community. However, it was also pointed out that the notion of the abstract language system was a convenient model for the description of language and would be used where appropriate.

So far we have considered linguistic elements as though they had meaning independently of their situational context. To this extent we have been looking at the language system, rather than usage. However, the meaning of a word is not separated from its use, but is dependent on the accumulated experience of the speaker in the use of that word. There is at any one time, and in any linguistic community, a consensus about the meaning of a word. There will also be changes in the pipeline at any one time and differences of opinion about shades of meaning. However, there will be enough overlap or consensus to allow the community to operate and for people to understand each other.

One aspect of word meaning that we will deal with as though it were part of the abstract language system is known as 'connotation'. We will describe words as though they 'had' connotations, although it will become clear that connotation is in fact largely dependent on the context of usage of any word. Rather like sense relations (the knowledge about how words are related to each other) connotation is not part of what we traditionally understand as 'meaning'. However, it becomes clear when we compare words with identical denotation that it is necessary to distinguish them in some other way.

In order to give a simple example, we could take all the words in English that refer to the 'toilet' or 'lavatory'. Because excretion is a taboo subject for many human societies (including all English-speaking ones), we tend to associate the words describing *the littlest room* with the deed itself and they thereby become tainted with taboo. In such a strong area of taboo, this process happens over and over, resulting in a very long list of words all referring to exactly the same place.

One of the noticeable aspects of the English words for *loo* is that the more casual the situation, and the more intimate the participants, the more explicit or amusing become the references to the *shit-house* or *bog*. On the other hand, polite company requires more and more euphemistic names for the *bathroom* or *w.c.* and some of the references to women's *conveniences* are positively misleading about what happens inside the *powder room* or *ladies' retiring room*! Clearly many of the synonyms that arise in these sensitive areas will be euphemistic, Nevertheless, they have in addition the connotation of being either formal or informal, according to the social context in which they are likely to be used.

Connotation is a word we use lightly and often in everyday language to refer to obvious, but indirectly expressed emotion. We might hear someone say, for example: 'I don't use the word *husband* – for me it has the wrong connotations.' But for us the term *connotation* has a more specialised meaning. The connotation of a word is related to the situational context and typical conditions of its use and there are many types of connotation found in English.

As we discovered above with reference to *toilets*, there are areas of the vocabulary where the choice of a word may depend very much on how formal the situation is. Some semantic areas have a range of terms:

Informal ...	Neutral ...	Formal
nick, knock off	steal	purloin
chinwag, chat	talk	converse
	tell, order	bid, charge enjoin

Others seem to lack the full range:

Informal ...	Neutral ...	Formal
?	?	bemoan, lament
do your nut	explode	?

It is interesting to speculate why English apparently only has formal words for the particular kind of complaint embodied in *bemoan* and *lament*, which sound rather old-fashioned as well. On the other hand, getting very angry suddenly seems to have both neutral (*explode*) and casual forms (*do one's nut*). These two sets almost seem to complement each other as though formal situations preclude sudden uncontrolled anger (and the words to describe it) whereas informal situations rarely result in polite *bemoaning*.

A small number of English words are associated primarily with certain groups of people, either because they are used *by* this group, or because they are used *to* them. Examples are almost exclusively connected with children. Language used by and to very young children often reflects the kind of sound patterns that children use, especially reduplication (repetition) of syllables, e.g. *bye-byes*, *wee-wee*, *quack-quack*. Slightly older children also have words that would seem either inappropriate or childish in adult-only company, e.g. *fib*, *own up*.

The attitude of the speaker sometimes forms part of the connotation of a word which may convey approval or disapproval, humour or distrust, but belongs in a lexical field alongside neutral words. For example, a speaker may choose to use the word *warble*, rather than *sing* if the quality of the singing was not appreciated. The neutral *smile* may be replaced by *beam* to show appreciation or *smirk/leer* if the smile is thought unpleasant. If *grouse* or *gripe* are used in place of the more neutral *complain*, it indicates that the speaker is doubtful whether the person complaining has good grounds for complaint.

For some words the situation in which they would be used may be well-defined. For example, a formal meeting would be the obvious setting for using words like *move* or *propose* as in phrases like 'I move the following motion . . .' or 'May I propose this amendment?' Some words have a primary religious use and their meaning is shot through with religious connotation as a result: *worship, glorify, laud, magnify, pronounce.* The last example here refers to the use of *pronounce* in the wedding ceremony: 'I now pronounce you man and wife.' There is another sense of this word which has different situational connotation, being used in or about courts of law: 'The judge then pronounced sentence.' Clearly there are also other senses of *pronounce* which do not have strong situational connotations: 'Can you pronounce this sound in Turkish?', 'Her limp seems very pronounced.'

We dealt at length with sound-symbolism and onomatopoeia in Chapter 2. It is worth noting here, however, that these features of the sound of a word do appear to be important aspects of the knowledge we have about the meaning of the word, especially when connected words are spread across a wide range of semantic fields: *snivel, snide, sneaky, snooty, sneer.*

If we accept that any description of the 'system' of vocabulary is inevitably a 'freeze-frame' snapshot of an ever-changing picture, then we will see that at any one time there are words that are either coming into fashion or going out of fashion. The 'era' of a word is also part of its connotation in so far as speakers are conscious of its age. For example, when a word is old-fashioned it can be striking, especially in a surprising context. There is one small area of meaning that seems to be completely occupied by old-fashioned words in English:

beg, beseech, implore, entreat, appeal, plead, intercede

Few of these words are used without a feeling of formality, often associated with a rather stiff, old-fashioned approach. I wonder whether the changing attitudes of the twentieth century have finally eclipsed the feudal tendency *to plead* with our superiors, since we are now so much more likely to *claim our rights* instead? A similar change in attitude might be reflected in the gradual loss of words which *acknowledge* or *admit* guilt or responsibility. To *grant* that other people may have a point or to *own* that you have done something wrong both sound rather dated.

On the other hand, the modernity of a word may also be relevant to its connotation, although it is much harder to document examples carefully because of the constant and rapid change in the vocabulary. One example that is always worth investigating is the various synonyms for 'good' and 'bad' that are in currency at any time amongst children and young adults. Read a few old children's books (e.g. the classic Enid Blyton adventures about the Famous Five) and you will find Julian saying 'You're a marvel' or 'I say – this is too bad!' More recent variations on *good* and *bad* have included:

> *triff, brill, ace, wicked, bad, cool* (all meaning *good*)
> *mean, tight* (meaning *bad*)

Some words enter the standard language from other dialects and even other languages. Whilst their origins remain in the folk memory of the speech community, they are part of the word's connotation. Whilst *yodel*, for example, simply refers to a particular kind of singing, it cannot be separated from the alpine areas of Switzerland and Austria where it originated. When *I guess* first became current in British English, its American 'flavour' was very noticeable, although historians can document its origins in English dialects which were later exported to the United States. The American flavour of *I guess* has faded over the years. There are some interesting examples of the 'wrong' connotation attaching to words from other languages. It seems likely that the rise of fast-food restaurants in many parts of the English-speaking world is associated with the United States. This results in the word 'pizza' carrying an American (or American-Italian) connotation rather than a clearly Italian one.

As well as the range of sense relations discussed in section 3.4, words are sometimes more closely associated with certain other meanings of the same word-form than with others. For example, the word *beam* has a metaphorical meaning associated with smiling which has a closer relationship to a *beam* of sunlight than to a *beam*, or *plank* of wood. A more abstract example is provided by the word *consider*, which has two closely related meanings:

> *consider* =   talk about different aspects of a topic: 'In my
> lecture I will consider . . .'
> *consider* =   think about different aspects of a topic: 'I have
> been considering leaving . . .'

These meanings seem to share a closer relationship to each other than either of them share with the third meaning:

> *consider* =   have an opinion about a topic: 'I consider that was a
> most unkind remark.'

Whilst it is useful to differentiate between different kinds of connotation, these categories are clearly not discrete; they will overlap to some extent. For example, it would be unsurprising to find that words that seem old-fashioned were also associated with old people, or to find that modern words tend to also be casual or informal rather than neutral or formal.

Activity: connotation
The following groups of words seem to largely share their denotation, but can be differentiated by their connotations. Which kinds of connotation do you think are in play here? (NB: some groups may be differentiated by more than one kind of connotation.)

> *clarify, elucidate, shed light on*
> *elaborate (on), waffle*
> *inform (on), expose, denounce, grass (on), shop*
> *wed, get spliced, get hitched, marry*
> *flagellate, whip*
> *mention, allude to, touch upon*

Discussion
Most of these words are distinguished from the other members of the group by the formality of their connotations. The most formal word in each group seems to be *elucidate, elaborate on, denounce, wed, flagellate* and *allude to*. The really informal end of the spectrum is represented by *shed light on, grass, get hitched*. Neutral words include

clarify (or is this relatively formal?), *inform on, marry, whip, mention.*
Other connotations include the fact that *wed* sounds dated, unless it
is used in a tabloid headline, in which case it is informal, and the
derogatory or light-hearted: *waffle, grass on, shop, get hitched.*

3.6 Multiple Meanings

This chapter concludes by discussing one of the most self-evident
aspects of word meaning in English; the fact that many English
words have more than one meaning. Earlier we met the following
rather childish joke:

> *Why did the little girl take a pencil to bed?*
> *Because she wanted to draw the curtains.*

At the risk of ruining the joke, I will point out that it depends on two
meanings of the word 'draw'. But how are these meanings of what
is apparently the 'same' word related to each other?

There are two kinds of multiple meaning known as 'homonymy'
and 'polysemy'. These mildly off-putting technical terms can be
translated as 'the same name' for homonymy (compare, for
example, *homogenous* means 'the same type') and 'many senses'
for polysemy (note *polygon* means 'many sided'). The words which
share these kinds of multiple meaning are known as 'homonyms'
and 'polysemous senses'.

Homonyms are two separate words which share the same sound
and spelling. They are, however, unrelated in meaning. The most
commonly quoted examples are words like *bank*/1* (institution
which deals in money) and *bank*/2 (river-side). Another, slightly
more obscure example is *found*/1 (establish) and *found*/2 (melt and
mould). They share neither their etymology (Latin fundare/fundere
and French fonder/fondre) nor their contemporary meaning. Note
that there are also pairs of words that share *either* their sound
('homophones' e.g. *sight* vs. *cite*) *or* their spelling ('homographs' e.g.
content /kˈɒntent/ vs. *content* /kənˈtent/.

The second, more widespread, type of multiple meaning is

---

*Note that the usual dictionary convention for differentiating between homonyms is
to use a numbering system.

polysemy. Many English words have a number of related meanings, which are, however, different enough to warrant being treated separately. For example, *foot*/a (bottom of leg) and *foot*/b (e.g. of a mountain) are polysemous. The second sense is created by metaphorical extension from the first, but is nevertheless identifiably different from it. Their relationships with other words are different in that *foot*/a is in a semantic field with *arm* and *leg* whereas *foot*/b belongs with *summit* and *foothills*.

Note that in the earlier sections of this chapter, I have implicitly been using polysemous senses to illustrate all of the other issues surrounding words and relationships between words. So, for example, in the last section, the group of words *tell, order, charge, bid, enjoin*, includes specific meanings of *order, charge* and *bid*, which might be paraphrased as 'communicate with someone whom you have power to command about what they should do'. These are clearly different from other meanings of these words such as the following:

order/b	to request goods in advance
charge/b	to require money in exchange for goods
bid/b	to offer an amount of money for goods with no fixed price

Different polysemous meanings of lexemes tend to belong to different lexical fields and have different ranges of sense relations (e.g. opposites, hyponyms) Thus *order*/b belongs with *request* and *charge*/b with *price*, whilst still further senses belong with *organise, put in sequence, classify* (*order*/c) and *accuse, name* (*charge*/c) respectively.

Note that these polysemous senses are quite clearly related to each other, but different enough to warrant separate dictionary definitions. Thus *charge*/b can be defined both in terms of its similarity to *charge*/a or *charge*/c and also in terms of its similarity to the other members of its lexical field:

charge/b	to order someone to pay (in terms of *charge*/a)
charge/b	to make someone responsible for the price (in terms of *charge*/a)
charge/b	to order or enjoin someone to do something (in terms of lexical field)

Further examples from the very large number of polysemous English words are:

broadcast/a	make public by word of mouth
broadcast/b	make public through media
broadcast/c	spread out over a wide area
exemplify/a	be an example of
exemplify/b	give examples of
pronounce/a	articulate
pronounce/b	declare
pronounce/c	give an opinion about

If you look in dictionaries for some of these words, you will find that different dictionaries come to different conclusions about the number and meaning of the senses of common words in English. If you regard the meaning of a word as being the sum of all its uses, then one extreme attitude to take would be that for each speaker, in each context, on each separate occasion, the word means something slightly different. To a certain extent this analysis is true, but it is not a useful model of description since it does not simplify the data at all (see Chapter 1 for a discussion of the purpose and limitations of descriptive models). At the other extreme, we might argue that all related uses of a single word-form mean the same. This is clearly an over-simplification and contradicts the intuition of English speakers. The more satisfactory analysis, exemplified by the polysemous idea, proposes that the individual uses of a word are in fact clustered into groups which share their meaning in most respects. The disadvantage of this is that different analysts, including the reader, will have slightly varying opinions about the clustering of meanings.

To finish with a metaphor alluded to in an earlier section, we might see each polysemous sense of a word as being a star, with a number of relationships to other stars nearby. Each group of senses, then, will form a constellation, like the Plough or Ursa Major, and are unified by this patterning of their connections. The constellations are a convenient human construct that makes sense of the mass of heavenly bodies in the sky. They could have been constructed with different combinations and this would have given rise to different patterns and names for the signs of the zodiac. With regard to words and their senses and sense relations, the same point can be made. We can organise them to reflect our own priorities at any one time. Note also that stars may be less solid than they seem from a distance and may really be made up of tiny pieces of dust and stone or swirling gases. Polysemous senses may similarly appear to disintegrate if we look too closely! They are nevertheless real for all that.

Activity: multiple meaning

Think of as many uses of the following words as you can:

ring, tip, cast, wave

Now decide which uses are so close to each other that they really count as one meaning. Having established the 'clusters' of meaning, decide whether any of the resulting senses are different enough from each other to be considered homonyms, rather than polysemous senses.

Discussion

There are probably two homonyms for *ring*, which seems to have a group of senses related to circular shape and another group related to sounds. If this is so, we can then divide these homonyms into a number of related senses as follows:

Sense	Meaning	Sense	Meaning
ring/1a	make the sound of bells/metal	*ring*/2a	to make a circular mark round something
ring/1b	phone up	*ring*/2b	to encircle
ring/1c	sound like	*ring*/2c	an item of jewellery worn on the finger

A glance at the dictionary will establish that this is not the whole story for the word-form *ring*, but it is enough to illustrate the issues raised by this section. Note that any one person's command of the language is likely to include a sub-set of the meanings of many common words in English. So there will, perhaps, be meanings of *ring*, for example, that readers have not encountered before.

The other words you have considered are represented in the tables below. I should stress that these are only partial pictures and the fact that our notion of 'language system' is imperfect means that we may well disagree on the finer points of any analysis. Your solution, in other words, is not wrong because it differs from mine!

Sense	Meaning	Sense	Meaning
cast/1a	make into a shape by pouring molten material into a mould	*cast*/2a	throw (with a dated connotation)
cast/1b	choose the actors for roles in a play or film	*cast*/2b	throw a fishing line into a river or sea
		cast/2c	throw (metaphorical), e.g. *cast aside*

Intuition plays a large part in our feelings about these words. Whilst analysis should be based on evidence, such as the fact that different homonyms will have different sets of sense relations, we often find ourselves reading connections into their relationship and wanting to recast them as polysemous senses. Students often disagree, for example, with my analysis of *cast* into two separate homonyms, because they can easily see how the senses of *cast*/1 could be defined in terms of *cast*/2:

cast/1a   throw into a mould to make into a shape
cast/1b   chuck actors at a script and see which slot they fall into

As you might see from my (biased) representation of their argument, I disagree! However, the point remains that as human beings we tend to look for connections and that the job of a lexical analyst is not made easier by this.

Sense	Meaning	Sense	Meaning
tip/1a	the end of something narrow or tapered	*tip*/2a	upturn
tip/1b	a small piece of advice	*tip*/2b	a place for throwing rubbish
tip/1c	a small amount of money left over from a bill and paid to the person serving	*tip*/2c	a mess (casual style)

The analysis of *wave* which follows illustrates that there is different practice in dictionaries and what we are doing here is not the same as the work of lexicographers. For example, there appear to be two major areas of meaning covered by *wave*: movement backwards and forwards and undulations made by ridges and troughs in a surface. However, the difference could be accounted for very simply by pointing to the difference between verbs, which describe actions, and nouns, which often describe states. The different senses of *wave*, therefore, will stress action (i.e. agitation) or resulting state (i.e. undulation), depending whether they are verbs or nouns. The difference, therefore, between what we are attempting here and what a dictionary usually does, is that we are concentrating solely on meaning, whereas a dictionary is obliged to give grammatical information as well.

Sense	Meaning
wave/1a	a rising and falling movement of the sea or other water
wave/1b	(metaphorical) of hair – looking like a wave
wave/1c	a large social or cultural movement or change
wave/1d	an overwhelming physical or emotional feeling
wave/1e	to move backwards and forwards
wave/1f	to move the hand backwards and forwards

4

Structure and Meaning

We tend to think of meaning as being 'held' by the units of language, such as words, whilst the arrangement of those units, their structure, is simply a convenient storage-system for tidy containment of those meaningful units. This chapter aims to undermine this model of language, whereby the form of language is not only seen as being independent of its content, but is seen as lacking any contribution to the meaning of utterances or sentences.

4.1 Words in Combinations

We have observed that part of the knowledge that speakers have about English words is their possible combination with other words. This could be described as their potential immediate linguistic context. Some of the possibilities, and restrictions, on combinations are quite grammatical in their nature and others are more clearly semantic. They all, however, have some impact on the meaning of the text.

If we begin at the least restricted end of the scale, we find a few words that have very few limitations on their co-occurrences. For example, the only restrictions I can think of on the verb *be* are the grammatical ones that apply to it because it is a verb. It can occur with any noun or noun phrase as its subject and any noun phrase, adjective phrase, adverbial or non-finite subordinate clause as its complement:

Jane Broomfield is at the hospital.	(adverbial prepositional phrase)
The yellow duster was very dirty indeed.	(adjective phrase)
My highest ambition is to visit the moon.	(non-finite subordinate clause)

Of course, there are some (probably semantic) restrictions that hold between the subjects and complements of the verb *be*, otherwise we would have sentences like the following:

Stuart Hold's cat is transparent.
The blue glass is in hospital.
My dearest wish is very dusty.

We will return to the topic of 'breaking the rules' shortly. First, let us consider what slightly stronger restrictions on co-occurrence would look like. The kind of restrictions which are not general enough to be called grammatical, but are not particularly arbitrary or quirky, are often called 'selectional restrictions'. This term originated in a theory of grammar known as 'transformational grammar', which regarded grammar and semantics as largely independent of each other. Transformational grammar (often shortened to TG) has heavily influenced the way in which subsequent models of grammar see language. But one of the inadequacies of early TG models (see, for example, Chomsky, 1965) is that it suggests we draw a definite boundary between semantics and grammar. We may wish to question this suggestion later.

Selectional restrictions tend to be defined as restrictions on verbs, or sometimes on adjectives, because they are most economically described in this way. They usually restrict a word, or group of words, to occurring with another semantically defined group of words. For example, there are verbs that occur only with animate subjects. These include movement verbs like *walk* and *skip** as well as more abstract words like *feel* and *think*. Some verbs are restricted even more narrowly to human subjects: *talk*, *assume*, etc. These restrictions seem to rest on universal categories that are very wide. There are also, however, restrictions that depend on much smaller categories of items and events. Only liquid or liquid-like substances can *pour* or *gush*. The words *nibble* and *eat* require edible objects. We can only *count* countable objects. Only objects giving off light can *shine* or *glow*.

Once we get to the very narrow restrictions like those at the end

---

*It should be remembered that most words quoted here are intended to be read as being a single polysemous sense of the word form printed. Thus skip here means to move in a particular way (double-jumping on one foot at a time) rather than to miss out items from a sequence as in 'She skipped the games lesson that day'.

of the previous paragraph, we are close to the next type of restriction, which is usually called 'collocation'. Indeed it is not clear where the dividing line is between 'selectional restrictions', which are usually based on semantic categories and are therefore semantically motivated, and 'restricted collocations', which can be completely arbitrary.

From selectional restrictions like the requirement that *rusty* is used about things made of iron to collocational restrictions that give us *tomato sauce* and *tomato juice* but not *tomato jam*, is a small step. It seems that as the restrictions get narrower, some remain based in the 'real world', whether physical or cultural, and others are completely arbitrary, though they may possibly be explained historically.

For example, it is clearly impossible for anything that is not made out of iron to go rusty and this explains the restriction on the word *rusty*. It is a more cultural fact that although tomatoes are technically fruit, we treat them as a savoury food and do not, therefore make jam out of them. The word is thus prohibited from this collocation.

Examples of apparently arbitrary collocations include the following sets of existing collocations and prohibited combinations (the latter being marked with an asterisk):

dinner set, tea set, *breakfast set, *lunch set
stark naked, *stark nude
stark staring mad, stark raving mad, *stark raving crazy

It may have become apparent that in discussing restrictions on co-occurrence of words, the more semantic and less grammatical the restriction, the easier it is to break the rule acceptably. It seems that at the grammatical end of the scale, the speaker is less ready to try and understand an utterance that breaks the rule, simply seeing it as 'wrong'. Breaking restrictions of the more narrow or arbitrary kind can be seen as creative and sometimes metaphorical.

The following examples break various different kinds of restrictions. You might like to question where the cut-off line is between acceptable creativity and ungrammaticality:

I *ate* three *floppy disks* for my lunch.
Three sticky answers fell on the floor.
The chair gave a *piercing murmur*

Let us revisit the term collocation, because it is a very useful notion in discussing the language of any text, including literary texts. It refers to the co-occurrence of words in syntagmatic arrangements, e.g. *fish and* _____ , *foot the* _____ . Sometimes, as with these examples (above), there is an almost invariable pattern, though note that *fish and chips* may be a specifically British collocation and *foot the bill* is more British-sounding than the American English *pick up the tab*. Other words have a semantically defined range of collocation, which is the type of restriction referred to above as selectional restrictions. The restrictions on combinations using the word *tomato* are easy to explain by reference to cultural norms – we see the tomato as a savoury food and yoghourt, ice-cream and custard as sweet. Except in the most exotic environments (Chinese food or cocktail parties, for example) they do not mix. At its widest, then, the notion of collocation is equivalent to the idea of 'selectional restrictions' introduced above. Some words are free to occur with a very wide range of words – often definable by some of the most basic, and possibly even universal, semantic features:

walk (Subject: any animate – or pseudo-animate – being)
break (Object: any inanimate object, made of rigid material)

One of the interesting ways of exploiting the knowledge of native speakers about selectional restrictions is to break them. In her poem, 'Mean Time', Carol Ann Duffy's narrator talks of walking through 'the wrong part of town', mourning a lost love. The weather echoes her emotions:

And, of course, unmendable rain
(Duffy, 1994, p.126)

Duffy uses the adjective, *unmendable* with a substance, *rain*, which is not normally thought of as capable of breaking, let alone mending. The adjective, then, has a selectional restriction to solid and usually rigid objects, rather than liquids, as in this case. What is the meaning of such a violation of selectional restrictions? It seems to me that the effect is to suggest that the rain, like her heart, cannot be 'put right', since it is necessarily perceived as *broken* by this description.

Often a broken selectional restriction will create a metaphor by pulling together two things that are not normally seen in each other's terms. In 'The Old Pantry', Peter Scupham describes the scene of stillness in a traditional pantry. One of the items he describes is a pitcher of milk:

> Anchored at the pitcher's rim, a ladle
> (Morrison and Motion, 1982, p. 154)

Scupham uses the metaphor of a boat anchored in a harbour to describe the ladle, and he achieves this simply by applying the adjective, *anchored*, derived from a past-participle, to the ladle although this adjective would normally be used to describe boat-like entities. Many unextended metaphors are created in this way.

Probably the most interesting, and certainly most mentioned type of collocation is the restricted type, particularly when it is not socially or physically explained and appears to be arbitrary.

> *roar/hoot* with laughter (but not *guffaw, snigger*)
> *clench teeth, fist, fingers, buttocks* (but not *knees, eyes)*
> *tea, dinner service* (but not *breakfast* or *lunch*)

Writers sometimes exploit our knowledge of restricted collocations to create unusual effects. In one of his 'Martian' poems,* 'An Inquiry into Two Inches of Ivory', Craig Raine, leads the reader to see the inside of a house as a large landscape, by playing on the set phrase *the great outdoors*:

> We live in *the great indoors*:
> (Morrison and Motion, 1982, p. 170)

This opening line of the poem leads us to expect an adventure of the proportions of those we are used to seeing in films of *the great outdoors*, even though it will clearly have a domestic setting.

Another very effective example of the exploitation of restricted collocations comes from from a short play called *Footfalls* by Samuel Beckett:

*The 'Martian' poems, written by Craig Raine among others, aimed to describe ordinary things and people from the point of view of someone outside the experience, such as a Martian. The effect is to 'make strange' the ordinary in an effort to see it more clearly.

Slip out at nightfall and into the little church by the south door, always locked at that hour, and walk, up and down, up and down, his poor arm (Pause) Some nights she would halt, as one frozen by some shudder of the mind, and stand stark still till she could move again.

Here Beckett exploits what we know about the usual, restricted collocations of *stark* and *stock*, which are *stark naked, stark raving mad* on the one hand, and *stock still* on the other. In combining the two sets of collocations, he evokes them all and makes us wonder whether the person he describes is not only very still, but also naked and/or mad.

Activity: selectional restrictions and collocations
What do you think are the selectional restrictions on the following words?

comb (verb), *dance* (verb), *shine* (verb), *wholemeal* (adjective)

How do these restrictions change when you consider other, non-literal or metaphorical uses of the same words?

Fill in the gaps in the phrases below, with the word or words you would most expect to occur there. Do they seem to be selectional restrictions, based on semantic categories, or restricted collocations?

There was a deathly _____ (noun)
He was stunningly _____ (adjective)
There was a major _____ (noun)
She is _____ (noun) perfect

Discussion
The normal selectional restrictions on literal senses of the words given would be something like the following:

Subject restrictions	Verb	Object restrictions
human (or animate being)	*comb*	*hair, head, beard, wig, fabric?*
human (or animal)	*dance*	names of dances
light sources	*shine*	(no Object)

adjective   **noun**
wholemeal   *flour, bread, pastry, cakes,* etc.

Notice that in these cases, you could define semantically the kinds of things that would co-occur with the word concerned, although I have sometimes given examples for clarity. Thus the verb *comb* has as Object things which grow (or in the case of wigs and fur fabrics, *seem* to grow) relatively long hair, and *wholemeal* is used to describe food products containing flour as a main ingredient. Notice, too, that these restrictions have quite a powerful influence on the interpretation of utterances which apparently contravene them. Thus any Object that follows the verb *dance*, will be interpreted as a new kind of dance that has been invented:

> *They danced the milkshake and the Pluto.*

If we consider the second question, these words can also occur in non-literal senses, but they may still be subject to selectional restrictions:

Subject restrictions	Verb	Object restrictions
human (or animate being)	*comb*	area of land, e.g. *neighbourhood, beach, district*
inanimate with independent movement	*dance*	adverbial of place
human or human actions	*shine*	(no Object)

Some sentences illustrating these uses follow:

> *They combed the neighbourhood looking for the lost child.*
> *The washing-machine danced across the kitchen floor.*
> *Your good deeds shine as an example to us all!*

The only one of these words that appears not to have any serious restrictions when it is used non-literally is *wholemeal*, where its use simply indicates (with derogatory connotation) the environmentalist or hippy style of living:

wholemeal sandals, wholemeal house, wholemeal children, . . .

This use is not well-established and this may be one reason for the lack of restrictions, since it sounds 'newly created' each time it is used.

Filling the gaps in the four sentences given may well have resulted in lists similar to these:

Given frame	gap to be filled
There was a deathly	hush, silence, stillness, . . .
He was stunningly	handsome, beautiful, attractive, ?pretty, ?old
There was a major	problem, hold-up, difficulty, cock up
She is _____ perfect	word, note, ?step (in dancing)

These collocational ranges are almost like selectional restrictions in that they generally include words with similar meanings. However, there is something arbitrary about allowing:

a deathly hush, stunningly handsome, major cock-up and *word perfect*

but treating as unlikely collocations, the semantically similar:

a deathly quiet, stunningly gorgeous, major mistake and *number perfect.*

Now that you have encountered those examples that I am claiming are unlikely collocations, you may well be saying to yourself that they sound perfectly natural and just as acceptable as the earlier list. However, this phenomenon is no more than the result of the 'consensus' view of 'langue' that I have been proposing throughout this book. That is, there is a great deal of flexibility in the language and much of it depends on new structures and meanings being created on analogy with old ones. Therefore, it would not be in the least surprising if a collocation that is statistically uncommon, but semantically similar to a common one, felt quite natural. We would not, for example, have difficulty interpreting phrases such as *stark crazy, stark nude,* or even *stock naked,* although they are arranged in decreasing order of likely occurrence.

4.2 'Naming' and 'Doing' Words

In this section we will ask whether the word-class a word belongs to adds anything to its meaning. Does it matter whether *hammer* is a noun or a verb, for example? Clearly many words can belong to different word-classes, although often with a tangible change in their sense:

*Will you **book** the hall for a party?*
*He picked a **book** from the library shelf.*

It is easier to assess whether the word-class itself contributes to the meaning of a word when both senses are as close as possible in their denotation. In other words, you would probably use almost exactly the same semantic features to describe their meaning:

King Henry's reign was long and tyrannical.
Will Prince Charles ever reign in Britain?

We could ask ourselves whether the two occurrences of reign here have any difference of emphasis. You would expect the difference to be subtle, since we have deliberately chosen an example where the major meaning components are the same. The first occurrence seems to describe a 'unit' or 'item' which has a length of time attached to it. Although King Henry's *reign* is not a concrete object that we can hold and look at, it does seem to have some kind of separate existence that the noun is 'naming'. This would work just as well if we made it a hypothetical, rather than a historical item:

Prince Charles's reign is bound to be short.

On the other hand, the verb in *Will Prince Charles ever reign in Britain?* seems to describe an action or an activity which by contrast with the noun has no 'edges' and focuses more on the relationship between the monarch and the 'reigning' and less on the length of time. Again, this subtle shade of meaning seems to be related to the

word-class and not the different context, as we can see by putting
the verb with old King Henry:

Did King Henry reign well?

Linguists have tried for a long time to establish a more scientific
basis for the word-classes than saying that nouns are 'naming'
words and verbs are 'doing' words. Part of the reasoning is that
these descriptions are not adequate because there are very inactive
verbs like *sleep* or even *be* and very active nouns like *dancing* or
demolition. However, pairs of closely related nouns and verbs
illustrate that there remains a vestige of 'doing' in almost any verb
and of 'naming' in almost any noun:

The fall broke my leg.
That's a nasty break – how did you do it?

Assuming that the second sentence also refers to a broken leg, we
have almost identical denotation (semantic features) in *broke* (verb)
and *break* (noun). However, there is a notion of 'action' in the first,
even though the subject is an abstract noun *fall*, which is not as
active as a verb would be. By choosing to phrase it in that way, the
speaker is emphasising the event when the breaking took place and
by choosing *fall* as the subject, rather than *I*, the responsibility or
blame is given to accident or fate. If the sentence had been '*I* broke
my leg when *I* fell', the emphasis would remain on the action, but
would have focused on it all being *my* mistake. By contrast, the
second sentence chooses to focus on the outcome rather than the
event by 'naming' it with the noun *break*. This is appropriate to the
likely context of such an utterance. We can imagine the doctor
looking at the X-ray of the broken leg and speaking to the patient.
The enquiry following the utterance is probably just polite
consideration rather than a refocusing on the event. After all, the
doctor's job is to deal with the result – the *break* itself.

It is not just nouns and verbs that seem to contribute to their
meaning by belonging to a word class. Adjectives are traditionally
known as the 'describing' words and this primary school definition
serves quite well to define the meaning contribution of the
word-class 'adjective'. Again, it is easiest to see the 'meaning' of the

word-class where words can belong to two or more classes. To extend the last example a little, we could use *broken* as an adjectival form:

My leg is broken.
My broken leg

Although these two contexts, before and after the noun, also change the meaning slightly, we are concerned here with how *broken* differs in meaning from the noun and verb used earlier. The adjective focuses on the break as a feature of the leg, rather than an event (verb) or an entity (noun). The same difference of emphasis can be seen with the following trio:

We have wasted a lot of food.
Look at all that waste!
The waste food was thrown away.

Here the verb emphasises activity and, in this case, the guilty party (*we*). The noun causes us to imagine the pile of waste as an item to be dealt with. The adjective has less impact, however, being portrayed as no more than a characteristic of the food, which human beings have to deal with, rather than cause. These examples indicate the extent to which even quite innocent-sounding texts can put over a particular angle on a subject, without necessarily stating this viewpoint directly.

The last main lexical word-class to deal with is the adverb class. Primary school grammar never came up with a handy definition for this class, partly because it really is a rag-bag of words forming sub-classes like 'manner adverbs' and 'time adverbs'. The adverb class does not seem to add consistently the same meaning to words, except in so far as they all contribute something to the 'setting' of the action or event described in the utterance. The adverbs in the following sentences, for example, by describing the way in which the action takes place, or the time and place it happened, all give us a fuller picture than if we had been left with the nouns, verbs and adjectives alone:

Suddenly the children were sent reeling by a sharp blow.
During the morning Jason played happily in the sand.

Suddenly and *by a sharp blow* show the means and manner in which the children were knocked down in the first sentence and *During the morning, happily* and *in the sand* respectively show when, how and where Jason played in the second.

What we find in looking at the adverb class is that there begins to be a much less clear dividing line between form and function. Up to now we have assumed that words could 'belong' to one or more word-classes, but sometimes they could be 'used as if' they belonged to another class, rather than being a fully-fledged member of that class. A relatively clear example of this phenomenon is the use of adjectives as the head of noun phrases:

We need to help the poor in this country.
This organisation exists to support the lonely.

This 'conversion' of adjectives into nouns is not usually seen as evidence of the adjective also belonging to the noun class, because there is a feeling that the noun *people* is lurking in the background and is missed out only because it is so predictable. The effect, however, is the same as if these words were nouns; they *name* a group of people who share the attribute described.

To return to adverbs, we notice that the relevant grouping of items here seems to be individual words like *happily* and *once* with phrases which behave in an adverbial way like *in the sand* and *by a sharp blow*. We can compare adjectives and adverbs with similar meanings, like *sudden* and *suddenly*, in the same way as we compared nouns and verbs:

The door banged shut suddenly.
The sudden banging of the door . . .

Here the adverb contributes something to the background and the manner in which the event happened. The adjective, on the other hand, allocates a feature to the noun *banging*. Once we start to look at phrases behaving adverbially, we can compare them with the other ways in which identical phrases may behave. The most convenient comparison is between prepositional phrases behaving adjectivally and behaving adverbially:

The cat in the basket is asleep.
The cat always sleeps in the basket.

Prepositional phrases such as *in the basket* can either occur as postmodifiers after nouns as in the first example, or as adverbial elements as in the second. The difference in meaning is the same as it was for *sudden* and *suddenly*. The adjectival use seems to assign a feature to the noun and make it part of the cat's identity, that it is in the basket. It implicitly contrasts this cat with others that are not in the basket. The adverbial use, however, gives a circumstance as the background to the rest of the utterance: any sleeping done by the cat occurs in the basket.

Our final examples show that the choice of wording of a text may involve some decisions about which word-classes to use. Some of these decisions have significant effect on the meaning, all the more powerful for being subtle. For example, a popular and vote-winning law might be claimed by the people who were responsible for it, with the noun phrase Subject showing clearly who did it:

The government passed this law.

A more unpopular law, which perhaps imposes more taxes or constrains civil liberties, might be presented with the government placed into an adverbial position:

This law was passed by the government.

Of course, the decision also involves a change of verb from active to passive. Most textual decisions are interdependent with other decisions in this way. However, it is no accident that awkward connections such as responsibility for unpopular legislation are often passed over with the 'guilty' party made to seem peripheral in an adverbial phrase.

Activity: word-class meanings
Consider the following groups of sentences and work out for each one, which word class the words in italics belongs to, and what it means as a result of this word-class

He issued *a strong denial* of his part in the affair.
He *strongly denied* his part in the affair.

They used to make *bears dance*.
They had *dancing bears*.
The *bears* did a *dance*.

The following pairs of words could have a different effect on the meaning of a sentence as a result of their word-class. Make up sentences to illustrate this difference. Note that to show the effect of word-class alone, the semantics of the words should be the same, irrespective of their word-class.

noun	verb
brush	*brush*
talk	*talk*
observe	*observation*

Discussion

The first pair of sentences uses the word *strong* (adj) to show what kind of denial was issued and the adverb *strongly* to show how the denial was delivered. You might like to consider which of these sentences convinces you more of the innocence of the man concerned. You might, for example, argue that the adverb seems to show a mannerism that could be construed as hot-headed or even 'protesting too much'. The strength of his case is not affected, only the manner in which he presents himself. The adjective, by contrast, seems to emphasise the earnest nature of his denial and may seem to favour his innocence.

The dancing bear examples illustrate verb, adjective and noun word-classes respectively. The effect of the first sentence is to keep the bears and their actions (dancing) separate from each other, so that the notion that it is not right or natural to make bears dance is quite easy to assimilate. The second sentence seems to assume that the bears were, in some sense, intrinsically, the kind of bears that dance. This is quite neutral with regard to the rights or wrongs of the situation, although it could be argued that there is an assumption being made that these bears dance as a matter of course. The third sentence apparently gives the bears their own will by making them the subject of the sentence. By using the noun *dance*, this sentence shows that the dancing was an event, which had a beginning and end and did not define the bear's whole life.

The words in the table above could have been put into sentences like the following:

noun	verb
He gave his muddy shoes a brush.	*He brushed his muddy shoes.*
I'm giving a talk on Georgian poetry.	*I talked on Georgian poetry*
That's enough talk – go to sleep!	*Stop talking and go to sleep!*
They made an observation of	*The astronomers observed*
Halley's comet	*Halley's comet*

If you included an actual brush in your sentences (e.g. a clothes brush), it would have been difficult to find a verb with identical semantics. I chose the abstract noun referring to the act of brushing, which indicates that the brushing had boundaries. In contrast with the verb, the brushing might seem to be rather shorter and possibly inadequate to deal with the mud. The verb emphasises the activity and there is a much stronger implication that the shoes will end up clean!

I gave two different senses of *talk* in both noun and verb forms. Notice that the poetry talk as a noun appears to be an undifferentiated unitary event where the content of what is said is secondary to the fact that it happened. The verb, on the other hand, almost invites you to ask for more details.

The two 'nagging' sentences, presumably telling children to be quiet, are harder to paraphrase, though one might suggest that the noun version would have more effect, since it gives a notional boundary to the talking by treating it as an entity, whereas the verb tacitly accepts that there is a continuing stream of talking happening. Partly as a result of this, the first version sounds more cross.

A very similar distinction occurs in the final example, where the noun *observation* seems to refer to a particular event, possibly one of a series of observations during the visible stage of Halley's comet. The verb, by contrast, is ambiguous between a particular occasion, with an open-ended timing, or a general activity undertaken by astronomers during the period. The noun version appears much more purposeful, almost implying that they were looking for particular scientific fact, rather than gazing up into the night sky.

4.3 Subject – Verb – Object

In the previous section we were asking whether the classes of word and phrase that grammarians identify in structural analysis of English have any meaning in themselves. These word classes are related to, but not identical to, the elements of structure known as clause elements or functions. There are five basic clause elements in English: Subject, Verb, Object, Complement and Adverbial.

I have already indicated that the class of adverbs is closely related to the adverbial function in that they share a very general meaning relating to the setting of the text. The kinds of form that tend to have an adverbial function in English are prepositional phrases (e.g. *on the table*), adverbs (e.g. *sometimes*) and some noun phrases (e.g. *one day* or *last week*). The meeting point between form and function is most obvious here, because all of these forms, when used in an adverbial position in a sentence, take on the 'meaning' of the word class of adverbs.

For example, the prepositional phrase *in the park* can be used like an adjective straight after a noun:

The swings in the park are broken

Here, it takes on the meaning of the adjective class and is interpreted as a descriptive characteristic of the swings. The same prepositional phrase, however, can be used adverbially to indicate the setting of the whole sentence:

We are going to play football in the park

Similarly, the noun phrase *next summer* can be used as a grammatical subject and have the usual naming effect of nouns:

Next summer will be wonderful

Like the monarch's reign in the last section, this use of the phrase has the effect of delimiting the summer and giving it almost a concrete quality. However, used in an adverbial function, the same phrase has the 'meaning' of the adverb class and seems to be setting the temporal context of the whole utterance:

Adverbial	Subject	Verb	Adverbial	Adverbial
Next summer	I	am going	to Spain	for my holidays

The most straightforward form–function relationship is between the class of verbs and the verbal function in English structure. There is a one-to-one correspondence between form and function, since verbs always function as the pivotal verbal element of the clause which thereby takes on the same 'meaning' as the word-class; action (e.g. *jump*), change (e.g. *break*) or definition (*seem*). The meaning of the word-class 'verb' was discussed in section 4.2 and need not be repeated here for the clause element also called 'verb'.

Another meaningful clause element that should be mentioned here is the complement. There are two kinds of complement in English, those that complement the subject and those that complement the object. Subject complements often follow the verb *be*, or one of the other copular verbs like *appear*, *seem* or *become*. They can be either adjective phrases or noun phrases:

Sheila is *a teacher*. (noun phrase complement)
Sheila is *very tall*. (adjective phrase complement)

There seems to be a more consistent meaning attached to this clause function than to subjects and objects. It has the role of 'attributing' the characteristic carried by the noun phrase or the adjective phrase to the subject. In these examples, then, Sheila is given the properties of being a teacher and being very tall.

Object complements work in a similar way, but follow one of a small set of verbs that take both an object and a complement, including *think, consider, make* and *call*:

They thought him a fool.
His brother made him angry.
The baker calls this loaf a batch.

Again the meaning of the complement is 'attribution', but to the object, not the subject. The *him* in the first example is attributed the characteristic of being a fool, the second one is characterised as *angry* and the *loaf* is given the name *a batch*. It does not seem to alter the meaning of the function whether the complement is an adjective (*angry*) or a noun (*a fool*). The choice of *a fool* (noun phrase) rather than *foolish* (adjective) *is* significant, since it implies a more permanent characteristic, but this meaning difference seems to be located at the word-class level, rather than in the complement function.

Two of the easiest clause elements to identify structurally are Subject and Object. They each are most typically made up of nouns or noun phrases, but may be subordinate clauses instead. The most stereotypical meaning of these functions is that the subject is the 'agent' of the action (verb) and the object is the 'patient', or the 'affected' of the action:

The child (S) *ate* (V) *the apple* (O)

Here, the child is clearly both active and instigating the action, the eating is the action and the apple is obviously affected quite dramatically by the action. However, these simplified meanings of the clause functions are not as consistent as those identified earlier for noun and verb word-classes. Many subjects, for example, are not obviously the agent of the action:

The map lay spread out on the floor.
The cupboard seemed empty.

Equally objects seem to 'receive' the action of the verb in a wide variety of ways, not all implied by meanings like 'patient' or 'sufferer':

Charlotte Brown wrote this book.
I have read the book.
The baby has torn her book.
David sang three songs.
The old man had an idea.

The book of the first three sentences respectively is created (*wrote*), *read* and then physically destroyed (*torn*). Each occurrence seems to have a subtly different relationship with the verb, making the meaning of the object function rather wide-ranging and unsatisfactory in any simple definition. The *three songs* and *an idea* of the last two examples are even less clearly related to the proposed meaning for objects. Because they have abstract referents, these words can not easily be seen as 'patients' of the action.

As a reaction against the kinds of grammars that were being written in the structuralist tradition, some linguists (notably Fillmore, 1968) proposed that English should be regarded as having cases in much the same way that Latin or German do. Although English clearly has very few inflectional endings of the sort that perplex English learners of German, it could be argued that there are a number of different ways that phrases in English sentences relate to the verb and these give rise to the kinds of meanings that in some languages are carried by case endings. For example, the subject of a clause may be an agent:

The doctor opened her bag.

But it may be an instrument:

The wall grazed my knee.

Or it may be more like a patient:

The whole cake was eaten by Uncle Peter.

Similarly, the object might be a patient:

Uncle Peter always ate the cake.

But it could be a product:

They made a giant snowball.

Or even an instrument:

Mr Carpenter used an old screwdriver to open the paint.

The meaning of these noun phrases appears to be largely determined by the choice of verb. There are, for example, some verbs that 'create' their objects and are therefore followed by 'products'. These include *make, paint, compose, write*:

> *Bach wrote music for the harpsichord.*
> *Grandma made us some dinner.*

Other verbs 'change the state' of their objects which could therefore be seen as patients. These verbs include those that change size (*enlarge, shrink*), or structure (*break, crack*) or other physical attributes (*paint, cover*) and also verbs that move objects such as *put* or *lower*:

> *Kathryn lengthened the rope.*
> *Mary broke the window.*
> *I'm going to paint the door brown.*
> *Please place your application form in the box provided.*

Whether or not we accept the proposal that case grammar is a useful model of English, it does seem to be clear that the five basic clause elements of English do not each have a simple meaning that can be added to the word meanings in a straightforward way to equal the sentence or utterance meaning.

Activity: clause elements and meaning

Practise recognising the different italicised clause elements in the following sentences. Where you decide they are subjects or objects, add a case label* (e.g. agent, patient, instrument), to indicate their meaning.

> *Our old house* is falling down.
> Sarah will be *delighted* when she sees you.

---

*Although there has been a considerable amount of work on the appropriateness of using case labels for English, no single system of cases and labels has emerged. For the sake of understanding the potential contribution of case analysis, readers should use the following labels as a working example: *Agent* – person, animal or thing which performs the action of the verb. *Patient* – person, animal or thing which is affected by the action of the verb. *Instrument* – usually inanimate object which is used by an agent to perform the action of the verb. *Product* – person, animal or thing created by the action of the verb. *Attribute* – a quality or characteristic attributed by the verb to one of the other participants.

Don't switch on *the lights* until I tell you.
Sadly, they never saw him *in his costume*.
The key opened this door easily.

Discussion
Notice how the stereotypical 'meaning' of subjects is that they 'do' something (i.e. they are agents or actors in the situation), but the two subjects in these examples could also be classed as patient and instrument respectively. The two meanings partly co-exist, since to choose to put *the key* into subject position, whilst recognising that it cannot act on its own, nevertheless lends the key some apparent abilities or independence that it would not have had in another position: 'I opened this door with the key.'

extract	clause element	case label?
Our old house	subject	patient
delighted	complement	attribute
the lights	object	patient
Sadly	adverbial	
in his costume	adverbial	adverbial
The key	subject	instrument

4.4 Information and Sentences

The last two sections have shown that structural meanings are composed of the class membership of an individual word or phrase and its positioning or function in a clause. This section will look at the structure of English clauses from the point of view of how information is given and how it may be emphasised on the one hand, or glossed over on the other.

English clauses have two features that are very important for the structuring of information. First we should note that the verbal element is pivotal and is normally expected to occur quite early, though not at the beginning of a clause. Secondly the information which is already shared by both speaker and hearer usually occurs near the beginning of the clause, often in the subject, whilst the new information and focus of the English clause is usually at the end, on the last clause element. These two principles work together because shared or 'given' information normally takes up few words and is therefore responsible for making the early elements of the clause quite short. This enables the speaker to arrive at the verbal element quite quickly and allows the hearer to focus on the meaning of any new information.

If we imagine that we are listening to a conversation between two friends, we might hear the following sentence in the middle of a series of utterances on the same topic:

She'll probably give it to him on Wednesday.

As outside observers, we are unable to understand who *she* is, what *it* refers to and who *him* is. The only information that we can grasp, because it is new, is that the giving is going to happen on Wednesday. In the absence of any particular markers of emphasis, the final clause element is the one carrying focus and is often also the one containing most new information.

It is important to remember that invented 'textbook' examples quoted with no context can often sound as though they are full of new information:

The little girl wanted a new bike.

This sentence seems at first sight to be completely explicit and contain all new information. However, the definite article *the* shows that there is some assumption that we know which little girl is referred to, and unless the sentence is uttered with some kind of contrastive intonation,* the verb is not likely to be the main focus. This leaves us with *a new bike* as the new information in object position. Since information structure is clearly closely related to text structure, sentences like this should usually be considered in their textual context.

If the picture was entirely rigid, we could assume that information structure as described above contributes very little to meaning, apart from the general usefulness of hearers knowing when to listen out for new information. In fact the picture is not as clear as that. Speakers actually have a great deal of choice as to where they place emphasis (using stress and intonation) and may also use structure to

---

*See Chapter 2 for a description of contrastive intonation. For a more detailed treatment consult Kuiper and Allan (1996).

indicate a divergence from the neutral information structure described above. All deviations from this norm are significant and therefore meaningful. This section will concern itself with structural changes of this type, but note that many of the examples will be meaningfully equivalent to those using contrastive stress patterns, as in the following sentences:

> You **must** *go to school today.* (You cannot refuse to go.)
> **You** *must go to school today.* (Not me . . .)
> You *must go to **school** today.* (Not to town, like you did yesterday.)
> You *must go to school **today**.* (Not tomorrow.)

To begin with the normally early occurrence of the verb, a speaker may delay the verbal element of a clause by using a series of adverbials to set the scene of the action:

> *All day long, in the sweltering heat of midsummer and with no water to quench her thirst, she worked in the vineyards.*

There is often a symbolic meaning to such structures, which by delaying the onset of the main elements of the clause (i.e. subject and verb *she worked*), create a frustration in the hearer similar to that felt by the protagonist of the sentence. In this example, the three adverbials make us long for the start of the obligatory elements of the clause in much the same way that the subject must have longed for a drink.

There are other ways of delaying the verbal element, most obviously by using a very long, and often unwieldy, subject:

> *The man in the long coat with large eyes and a clay pipe is my uncle.*

Unless you deliberately want to bore your hearers so that they stop listening, you are likely to choose another way in to this information, perhaps by opting to split it into two sentences so that all the interesting bits can be in focal positions at the ends of clauses:

> *You see that man in the long coat with large eyes and a clay pipe? He's my uncle!*

Long subjects can, however, cause the listener to be drawn into the clause because they are dying to know what it is that the speaker will say about the subject:

> *A very tiny figure, wrapped in a dark blue cloak and carrying a tiny bag,* came in.

There are a number of ways in English, apart from using stress in the voice, of placing focus on any element that requires it, so that it can be seen as new and important. One of these is to introduce the impersonal pronoun *it* as the subject and use the complement position after the verb *be* to highlight whichever part of the clause needs special emphasis. A clause such as 'Stephen gave the teacher an apple' could then become any of the following:

> *It was Stephen that gave the teacher an apple.*   (Focus: subject of the original)
> *It was the teacher that Stephen gave an apple to.*   (Focus: direct object of the original)
> *It was an apple that Stephen gave to the teacher.*   (Focus: indirect object of the original)

The result of highlighting elements in this way is to subordinate the rest of the clause elements in a relative clause (beginning *that . . .*) following the highlighted element. This increases the difference of emphasis, making the highlighted element highly focal and the rest of the original clause relatively unimportant and causing it to be interpreted as 'given' or 'shared' information. Other possibilities for changing the focus include the use of the passive form:

> *The teacher was given an apple (by Stephen).*

This places the focus on the apple and demotes Stephen to an optional adverbial, which is ineligible for focus unless the voice is used to produce contrastive stress. Another, rather awkward structural change which produces changes in focus is the use of fronting. This simply entails putting a clause element at the beginning of the clause, altering the normal given-new information load:

The teacher, Stephen gave an apple (to).
An apple, Stephen gave the teacher.

The effect is very similar to the use of impersonal pronoun, *it*, though unusually it seems to place the focus on the first clause element. This may be because it operates almost as a separate clause.

What is most interesting to textual analysts is to see how variations on the normal information structure patterns of English can be used in texts to great effect. There are many texts where the relative emphasis on different elements has great significance for meaning of the text. For example, many newspaper texts use subordinate clauses or nominalisations to undermine the importance of elements or make assumptions that they would not want questioned by the readers. For example, in the late summer and autumn of 1995, there was a severe water shortage in parts of Britain and this was most worrying in Yorkshire where many homes were threatened with interrupted water supplies. The local papers in Yorkshire filled many column inches with discussion of this problem and one editorial in the *Yorkshire Evening Post* (29 November 1995) contained the following extract, discussing the recently privatised water company, Yorkshire Water:

This is capitalism from the world of Alice in Wonderland, a bizarre inversion of the normal workings of market forces.

This sentence, like many of those in its surrounding text, makes assumptions that it would like its readers to accept, namely that the *normal workings of market forces* are not bizarre. By focusing on the sentence's claim that the 'current' situation is *capitalism from the world of Alice in Wonderland,* the text naturalises the assumption that *capitalism* and *the normal workings of market forces* are right and natural.

Activity: information structure
Look closely at the following pairs of sentences and observe their information structure. What effects do the structural changes have on the information structure of these sentences?

Suddenly, at three o'clock, without waiting to say goodbye or wonder whether he was doing the right thing, he left the house for ever.

He left the house for ever suddenly, at three o'clock, without waiting to say goodbye or wonder whether he was doing the right thing.

The old problem of not wanting to appear too cocksure, but knowing that you're right even though the others are confident that they'll win was making him more and more hesitant.

He was becoming more and more hesitant because of the old problem of not wanting to appear too cocksure, but knowing that you're right even though the others are confident that they'll win.

Identify the focus of the following sentences:

I'd like a new computer for Christmas.
It will be seven years next April, since I saw her.
Money was all I ever got for my birthday.
Sally sent me the newspaper cuttings.

Discussion

The first pair of sentences has a string of adverbials which either precede or follow the main, obligatory clause elements, subject (*he*), verb (*left*) an object (*the house*). In the first sentence they delay the onset of the real information and by causing the reader to wait unusually long they create a tension and expectation, reasonably fulfilled by the abrupt and final nature of the main part of the clause. The second version does not make a drama out of the leaving, but seems to focus on the adverbials which one might expect to lead on to more consideration of the reasons for him leaving.

The second pair of sentences has an overlong subject (*The old problem of not wanting to appear too cocksure, but knowing that you're right even though the others are confident that they'll win*) in the first sentence which is moved into an optional adverbial in the second sentence. The first version could be seen to be symbolically representing the man's hesitancy, by delaying the essential part of the clause. Nevertheless, it is complex and inelegant, and the second version has a more 'normal' information structure, introducing the main elements first and then apparently explaining them in the adverbials.

The focus of each of the sentences shown above is shown below in italics:

I'd like *a new computer* for Christmas.
It will be *seven years next April*, since I saw her.
Money was all I ever got for my birthday.
Sally sent me *the newspaper cuttings*.

Notice that the adverbial *for Christmas* and the delayed subject *since I saw her* are both at the ends of their respective clauses, but are not focal because the adverbial is optional and because the subject is effectively repeating the substance of the pronoun *it*. The third sentence has a fronted focus, *money*, whilst the last example is a relatively straightforward example with the direct object *the newspaper cuttings* taking the focus and being new information.

4.5 Locating Meaning in Sentences

So far we have been concerned with isolating different strands of meaning in order to examine their contribution to the text with no interference from the other aspects of meaning. This is clearly a rather false exercise since we hardly ever have to respond to a word's meaning without some context surrounding it – and it is impossible to create a structure with no words.

This section, therefore, begins the process of seeing how the strands weave together into the fabric of a text. In particular we will investigate the interaction of word-meanings, as described in Chapter 3, with the structures that form the subject of this chapter.

There are many texts in the modern world that enjoy the word-play available as a result of multiply ambiguous words in English. Poetry, advertising and casual conversation all involve the punning use of polysemous words at some time or another. For example, advertising in women's magazines will be found using phrases like *Cotton on to cable* in promoting a cotton cable-patterned sweater. This exploits the idiom *cotton onto* (meaning 'find out about') as well as mentioning the material used to make the sweater.

Despite the rich possibilities of word-play, many of the words we come across in our daily lives are actually being used in a single sense, although many of them have other senses too. How do we know which sense of a polysemous word is relevant in a particular context? To begin with, we may be influenced by the other vocabulary in the context. Texts are usually dominated by a small number of interlocking lexical fields and sometimes these field of words help to disambiguate a polysemous word for the reader/hearer.

An article headed 'Unholy Mess for Vicar's Daughter' in a local paper leaves us with only one possible interpretation of the word *marry* and the idiom *tie the knot* with its subheading: 'Shock as She Marries Bigamist'. In the context of words like *bigamist* and *wedding*, we fail to even remember that *marry* can have a more general meaning of *match up* as in the sentence 'If we can marry the uprights to the ridge poles, we might finally get this tent up!' Similarly, the context leaves us with no option but to interpret *tie the knot* as a casual synonym for *wed* or *marry*, even though in an article about Houdini-style escapology we might have understood it more literally.

The structural context of a polysemous word will usually make clear which word-class it belongs to and this in turn will often make clear which sense is relevant. The positioning of *picture* in the following sentence firstly characterises it as a verb, and secondly leads the reader to the most likely interpretation as a verb meaning *imagine*:

> *Picture a sunny beach with palm trees and a bar serving Bacardi and coke . . .*

This explanation seems too obvious until you realise that out of context the word *picture* will almost always conjure up the noun meaning 'a rectangular object that you hang on the wall'.

An even more frequent interaction between word-meaning and structure occurs when texts foster or create relationships between words which would not be recognised as relationships out of context. All of the sense relations described in Chapter 3 were based on relationships that exist independently. But the relationships that can be created by a text are far more important and often far more powerful. Take the following passages from a children's book called *The Worst Witch All at Sea* by Jill Murphy:

'Well, I wish she'd let us in on the secret,' said Enid crossly. 'She's been really strange for weeks – sort of vague and not quite with it.'

A shriek of laughter rang out from Ethel, who had overheard.

'Do forgive me for stating the obvious, Maud,' she said, 'but Mildred Hubble is permanently vague and not quite with it. If I were you, I'd start worrying if she was suddenly alert and getting A plus for everything!'

First Enid explains exactly what she means by the word *strange* in this context: *sort of vague and not quite with it*. This creates a temporary, context-bound synonymy between *strange* and *vague*. The horrible goody-goody, Ethel, reacts by denying the synonymy set up by Enid: *Mildred Hubble is **permanently** vague and not quite with it*. By claiming that Mildred is always vague, she is asserting that this is *normal* behaviour for Mildred and cannot therefore also be seen as *strange* behaviour. She underlines her opinion by giving her own version of the opposition that is relevant to the context: *I'd start worrying if she was suddenly alert . . .'*. For Ethel, then, the relevant sense relation is one of opposition between the *vague* that is Mildred's normal behaviour and the *alert* that she apparently never is.

The general point here is that whilst we would probably not think of *alert* as the opposite of *vague* if asked out-of-context, we accept the proposition made by Ethel that these conditions are opposites in human beings. The 'joke' that is being played out between these schoolgirl witches is that another context-bound, but quite acceptable sense relationship of synonymy between *strange* and *vague* is being denied as far as Mildred Hubble, the worst witch, is concerned. The obnoxious nature of Ethel is underlined again and again, as in this extract from the lips of Miss Hardbroom, their form teacher:

If only you all had such organised brains as Ethel Hallow, Form Two. Ethel could make a rubbish tip look like an army barracks – even her cat knows how to arrange itself with taste.

If you were asked for the opposite of *rubbish tip*, I doubt that you would come up with the term *army barracks*. However, the comparison is an entirely apt one and for the purposes of this story, we understand that it is the orderliness and tidiness of the barracks that are the opposing feature.

One further example of a created 'opposition' can be seen in the following extract from Joanna Trollope's novel *The Men and the Girls*:

> Julia sat in the sitting-room, and reread Hugh's letter, for the eighth or ninth time. It was hardly a comforting letter. It was full of reproach, it seemed to Julia, reproach thinly disguised as self-reproach. (p. 245)

The juxtaposition of the two sentences beginning with a parallel 'It was . . .' is one common device to alert the reader to the impending comparison of the differing parts of the structures. In this case it is a negative comparison and therefore creates a temporary opposition between *comforting* and *reproach*. It is also possible, of course, to use parallel structures in this way to create not opposites but synonyms:

> It was *a very important day*. It was *a new beginning for all of them*.

Here, and for this context only, the phrases in italics are intended to mean the same. The second phrase explains in what way the day was important, and presumably refers back to something that has happened previously, by implying that the past is going to be left behind.

This contextual creation of semantic relationships both defies the notion of langue and to some extent relies upon it. We are only in a position to read 'new' pairs of synonyms and opposites, or even new types of lexical field, because we have some experience or understanding of what synonymy, oppositeness and other lexical relationships mean. Note that the syntax is very important in the new context-based lexical relationships, since it leads us to the relationship by structural means. For example, the last example given provides two sentences with parallel structures and an identical subject + verb combination; *It was*. The complement of each of these sentences is bound to be read as referring to the same thing as a direct result of the similarity of the structures. The effect is entirely different if a different structure is used for each sentence:

It was a very important day. They thought they would have a new beginning.

Whilst the *new beginning* still seems to be starting on the *very important day*, there is a separateness about the two that is absent from the earlier version.

Parallel or balanced structures are very often the vehicle for created opposites as well as synonyms, as in: 'He was a *gentleman, not a chauvinist.*' These two words are not opposites in my vocabulary, since I would argue, with other feminists, that the chivalric habits of *gentlemen* are similar to, and feed those of *chauvinists*. However, there could be a person who argues against my opinion by claiming that the two are opposed, one being 'kind' to women (e.g. by opening doors or standing up to greet them) and the other being unkind (e.g. by expecting household chores to be done by them). The sentence quoted above, would contextually create this argument by placing the two words into positions where opposites are expected.

Whilst the interaction of lexical and structural meaning is a very important feature of human language, there are other ways of embedding meaning into clause structure in such a way that the hearer/reader is invited to accept the assumptions of the text's producer almost automatically.

It is philosophers that have been most interested in the domain of meaning that lies behind the words of texts. Complex theories of truth-conditional semantics have tried to account for the propositions that are made by particular utterances and the other meanings that underlie them. We shall endeavour to avoid the confusion that some students feel when confronted by arguments of logic.

The main assertions that a sentence or clause makes are often known as the 'propositions' of the sentence. These are the things that the sentence is claiming, and are logically known as the 'entailments' of the sentence. The test for entailments is that if the sentence turns out to be true, the entailments should also be true, but they would be false if the sentence is false. The following sentence can serve as our example:

Thunderstorms can generate gamma rays that are detectable in space. (*New Scientist*, 28 September 1996, p. 20)

If it is true, this sentence entails the fact that gamma rays detectable from space are produced by thunderstorms. This is not very interesting, but it is important. If we make the sentence negative, the entailment no longer applies. There are other meanings, however, called 'presuppositions', which are more consistent than the entailments, and are to a certain extent more hidden. They are to be found in the noun phrases *thunderstorms, gamma rays* and *space* as well as the adjective *detectable*. Whilst we might question the entailment with sentences like 'Are you sure?' or 'How do you know?', we are likely to act as though gamma rays, thunderstorms and space exist and as though gamma rays are detectable in non-space situations. These matters are constant, whatever the force of the sentence.

Presuppositions are always consistent, almost irrespective of context. They are the assumptions upon which the utterance in question relies for its relevance and truth. For example, the utterance 'Will you get some milk while you're at the shops?' presupposes that the addressee is intending to go to the shops, that there are some shops nearby which sell milk and more generally that there is a person who can be addressed as 'you'. None of these presuppositions can be untrue without invalidating the whole of the utterance. So if you say this sentence when you are on your own, you must either be addressing yourself, think there is someone in the room or be suffering from a mental illness. Similarly, if you know the person concerned is going not to the shops, but to the golf course, the sentence becomes completely unusable.

Some presuppositions arise from the words used in the utterance. There is, for example, a group of verbs known as 'factive' verbs which have subordinate clauses as objects. These subordinate clauses (usually beginning *that* . . .) are necessarily true if the sentence is to work at all:

My son discovered that I was getting him a bike for Christmas.
The teacher knows that I haven't done my homework.
I hope you realise that the old lady needs daily help.

These sentences presuppose *that I intended buying a bike, that the schoolchild has not done her homework* and *that the old lady needs daily help* respectively. If you have in fact have done your homework, you might use another, non-factive verb: 'The teacher suspects . . .', and this would leave the question of whether the work had been done entirely open. Apart from special groups of words like the factive verbs, presuppositions can occur as a result of very innocent grammatical features. Take, for example, the definite article, *the*. Its use will almost always rely upon the existence of the referent concerned, where the use of an indefinite article, particularly in combination with a negative verb, allows for its non-existence:

Jane ate the cake.   *Jane did not eat the cake.*
Jane ate a cake.   *Jane did not eat a cake.*

In the first pair of sentences, the use of *the* means that irrespective of whether *Jane* ate it or not, there was indeed a cake she could have eaten. The second pair of sentences only presupposes the presence of a cake in the positive version where Jane eats it!

Activity: sense relations in context and presuppositions
Choose pairs of apparently unconnected words from the same word-class (i.e. both verbs, nouns or adjectives) and create a context in which they can be read as synonyms or opposites. You may find yourself creating metaphorical connections where the words are very different from each other. Here are some pairs to get you started, though you could ask a friend for ideas to practice this technique:

nouns   **verbs**   **adjectives**
cloak, happiness   *sing, calculate*   *frosty, huge*

The following sentences have presuppositions which are constant, even when the sentence is negated. Find the presuppositions and try to decide which aspect of the structure embodies their presupposed nature.

When I got to the party, Jane had already left.
That horrible smell has been there since Dad cleared the drains.

Discussion
The pairs of words would probably have to occur in parallel structures to be convincing as synonyms. The following example uses two noun phrases as its basis:

There was her happiness: a cloak to protect her from the unexpected.

These noun phrases are 'in apposition', which means that they perform exactly the same function in the clause, but are simply two different ways of referring to the same person or thing. A common use of apposition is in newspaper reporting where the people in the stories are often introduced by their names and their position or job:

Jan Gibson, spokesperson for the STG collective . . .
Mr Bun, baker to the Queen . . .
The Lord High Admiral, Horatio Nelson . . .

Apposition automatically confers equivalence on the two noun phrases, so that we look for correspondences between them. We therefore read the noun phrase containing the word *cloak* as metaphorically representing the happiness of the previous phrase.

The second pair, *sing* and *calculate,* are not so easy to bring into a sense relation. They might work as opposites in a context such as the following:

I can't just sing the answers, I'll need to calculate them.

This context seems to create a new meaning of *sing* which implies that it is an easy matter, and opposed to the more difficult process described by *calculate.* The new meaning of *sing* fits quite well with the more common *sing out* which is often used to describe the way that children in a schoolroom might produce answers to the teacher's questions.

The final pair, the adjectives *frosty* and *huge,* would need a metaphorical connection to produce any sense relation between them. It seems most likely that they will be oppositions, because *frosty* sounds small! The most likely meeting place for these words is the area of human emotion and behaviour:

My aunt was frosty, whereas my uncle was huge: a warm, friendly sanctuary.

This may not be the most impressive of literary texts, but the context does appear to lend the words some connection they would not have out of context.

The presuppositions in the two sentences given above are as follows:

When I got to the party, Jane had already left
I exist
There is a person called Jane
There was a party
I went to the party
Jane had been at the party

That horrible smell has been there since Dad cleared the drains
There is a smell
The smell is horrible
There is a person called Dad
There are drains
Dad has cleared the drains

Notice that some presuppositions are more interesting than others and some are downright boring! However, the importance of presuppositions for textual analysis is to recognise what the originator of a text is choosing to put into the presuppositions, which are normally assumed by the receiver without argument, and what is put into the entailments, which are open to question. The following sentences, for example, place different parts of the meaning into the presuppositions:

When you've finished your tea, I'll show you the book.
If you finish your tea, I'll show you a book.
Although I showed you the book, you haven't had any tea.

There is some tea presupposed in the first two sentences, by the use of the possessive *your*, but not the last. In the first and last sentences, the definite article causes us to presuppose the existence of the book, whereas the second sentence uses an indefinite article, *a*, and this refers to no particular book. The last sentence also presupposes the showing of the book by putting it in a subordinate clause, instead of the main clause where it is the entailment of the first two sentences.

5

Textual Meaning

5.1 Connections

The last chapter showed some of the ways in which structural properties of texts could contribute to their meaning. Most of the discussion in that chapter related to sentence-level structures and was concerned with the area of traditional grammar or syntax. However, there are many aspects of meaning that are the product of wider textual features and these form the subject of the current chapter.

In widening out slightly from sentence structure, we come across the sentence connectors, or cohesive features, that form links between sentences in a text. These features are fairly regular in English, although not as structured as syntax, and they alert the reader/hearer to the fact that the text is more than just a random series of sentences with no connections between them.

Apart from this general 'meaning' of cohesiveness, the connectors give other, more specific, information. Most typically, they indicate when parts of a sentence have the same referents as parts of an adjacent sentence. For example, the definite article in English is often used to indicate that the referent is the same as the one already indicated in the previous sentence:

> *A large dog came running up to the child. He patted the dog's head and smiled.*

Here the definite article makes a link backwards to the dog which was introduced (by the indefinite article, *a*) in the previous sentence. Most cohesive links refer backwards in the text, for logical reasons: first a new referent is introduced and later it is referred to again. This backward reference is known as 'anaphoric reference' and is much

more common than the forward-referring 'cataphoric' reference
which refers to something first and only explains precisely what it is
later. If you imagine that the following sentences form the opening
of a short story or novel, you can see that the *it* referred to in the first
sentence is only given a clear referent in the second sentence:

> *It came through the open window. Jane had never seen a squirrel so
> close-up before.*

The effect of cataphoric links between sentences is to delay some
of the information needed to interpret part of the first sentence. For
this reason it is used to create suspense and heighten interest and is
not used when organisation or clarity of information is the highest
priority.

There are a number of categories of standard cohesive connector
in English, the most common being the category of substitution. In
this very wide category, the word or phrase occurring in the first
sentence will be replaced by a pronoun or paraphrase in a later
sentence. In this example, we assume that the *young man* has already
been introduced in the story:

> *The young man stopped under a street lamp to look at the map. He
> couldn't work out where he had gone wrong. And he a geography
> student too!*

Here there is a chain of references to a single person who is referred
to as *the young man, he, he,* and *a geography student* respectively. When
we look at a text containing references to a number of different
people, it becomes plain that we need to keep making clear who is
being referred to at any one time, whilst using pronouns where
possible to avoid lengthy repetitions:

> The Social Security Secretary, Peter Lilley, was accused last night
> of planning a return to the Poor Law after he proposed local
> variation in benefits as a way of further cutting his department's
> expenditure. The minister signalled the end of uniform, national
> social security provision introduced almost half a century ago. He
> said there 'can be advantages in some circumstances in devolving
> responsibility to a local level'. (*Guardian*, 10 January 1995, p. 20)

This extract from a news article has so far only introduced one character, Mr Lilley, but it has already felt the need to return to a fuller form, *the minister*, after using two pronouns (*he* and *his*) referring back to the noun phrases in apposition which form his first appearance in the story.

Many of the items that can premodify nouns, including articles and demonstratives as well as enumerators, may form part of a cohesive link. We have already seen the potential of definite articles for referring backwards in a text. The same kinds of connection can be made by other determiners and enumerators:

> *There were three types of fabric in the shop. These fabrics were all synthetic and brightly coloured. The first fabric was a polyester in oranges and greens. The second one was a swirling red patterned viscose. The third was a pink and yellow paisley crimplene.*

Here the three *types of fabric* in the first sentence are identified again by the demonstrative *these* and the ordinal numbers *first, second* and *third*. There is also some substitution in the use of *one* and an examples of ellipsis (see below) in *the third*, where the word *fabric* has become so predictable that it would be tedious to repeat it and may even obstruct the meaning of the text.

Ellipsis is an unusual form of cohesive tie, because it involves missing out an item rather than adding it. It has a cohesive effect because ellipsis is only used when a word or phrase is completely predictable in the context. The effect is that the reader/hearer knows what is missing from knowledge of a previous sentence and the missing information is automatically filled in. Ellipsis normally only happens when a word or phrase has been repeated a number of times in quick succession as in this extract from *Winnie-the-Pooh*:

> So Eeyore stood there, gazing sadly at the ground, and Winnie-the-Pooh walked all round him once. 'Why, what's happened to your tail?' He said in surprise.
> 'What has happened to it?' said Eeyore.
> 'It isn't there!'
> 'Are you sure?'
> 'Well, either a tail is there or it isn't there. You can't make a mistake about it, and yours isn't there!'

'Then what is?'
'Nothing.'

The nature of children's literature is that it is repetitive and deals with small, self-contained worlds. In this passage, the only participants are Pooh and Eeyore and the only topic of discussion is the whereabouts of Eeyore's tail. The increasing predictability of the words leads to the shorter and shorter comments that each participant makes, until the end of the sequence, when Pooh's utterance consists of a single word, *Nothing*, which implies a much longer utterance such as *There is nothing there*. Other ellipted words include:

Are you sure *it isn't there*?
Then what is *there*?

Another major type of cohesive device is the use of sentence adverbials to make overall connections between sentences. These connections may be chronological as in the following sentences:

Last winter I went skiing with the children. *In the spring* I took a short break in Paris with a couple of friends. And *in the summer* we had the usual villa in Tuscany with Jonathon's brother and family. Yes, I suppose we're lucky to have so many holidays.

Here the sentences reflect the order of the holidays and are understood by the hearer to be referring to adjacent seasons in order. Some sentence connectors make logical rather than temporal links:

You know you had it when you came in the house. *Then* you must have left it in the lounge or the kitchen.
Do you know why they treat you so badly? *Because* you have a low self-esteem, that's why!

And still others may set up an opposition between the sentences:

He had never said he loved her. *But* she was certain that he did.
She might go to the party. *On the other hand* she rather fancied an evening in.

These factors seem to indicate global warming. *Nevertheless,* they are within the range of 'normal' variation.

Finally, we should note that all of the sense relations that can hold between lexical items can be responsible for cohesive effects in texts. Most conventional texts are made up of a number of interwoven lexical fields and the occurrence of a superordinate term (e.g. *animal*) in one sentence and one of its hyponyms (e.g. *fox, toad*) in a nearby sentence is clearly cohesive:

> The *animals* chattered excitedly at the news. Some were thrilled by the prospect, some were doubtful.
> 'What is this place? asked *Fox.*
> 'It's called a Nature Reserve,' *Toad* answered.
> (C. Dann, *The Animals of Farthing Wood* [1993] p. 16)

Similarly, the use of opposites in adjacent or nearby sentences is a linking device. These will not only apply to conventional opposites, but may include 'invented' oppositions which work for this context:

> Some days she felt *happy*. On other days she was as *miserable* as sin.

It is even possible to exploit the reader/hearer's knowledge of collocation to create a cohesive link between different sentences. This is achieved by putting one half of a normally restricted collocation in one sentence and the other half in a separate sentence:

> They stared at the *fish*. It had been cooked hours before the *chips*.

Whilst it is the phrase *fish and chips* that forms the familiar collocation, the words are still close enough in these two sentences to evoke their more normal arrangement.

The description of cohesive devices given above is intended to indicate the range of ways in which sentences can be connected in texts. There is a wide variation in the amount and types of cohesion between texts of different kinds. For example, there is a general tendency for children's texts to be more highly cohesive than texts intended for adult audiences. The texts shown in Figures 5.1 and 5.2 are coded to show those parts of the text that seem to have some

Here are **the little pigs. They** are *at home*
with <u>Mummy pig</u>. **You** are getting big, says
<u>Mummy pig</u>. **You** have to go to look for *a*
new home. Yes, say **the little pigs. We** can
look for *a new home*. <u>Mummy pig</u> gives **the**
little pigs some apples and some cakes.
See that the big bad wolf can not get **you**,
says <u>Mummy pig</u>. **The little pigs** go to
look for *a new home*. **They** see <u>a man</u>. <u>The</u>
<u>man</u> has <u>some straw</u>. **One little pig** says,
Please give **me** <u>some straw</u>. **I** want to make
a new home.

Figure 5.1 *Three Little Pigs* (1967, pp. 4–8). Key: underlining = Mummy; italics = new home; bold = little pig(s); double underlining = straw; dotted underlining = the man.

How do *I* account for **Smolka** and **his**
daring? **He** has <u>a mother</u> who works. *Mine,*
remember, patrols the six rooms of *our*
apartment the way a <u>guerrilla army</u> moves
across <u>its own</u> country-side – there's not a
<u>single closet or drawer</u> of *mine* <u>whose</u>
contents <u>she</u> hasn't a photographic sense
of. **Smolka's** <u>mother,</u> on the other hand,
sits all day by a little light in a little chair in
the corner of **his** father's store, taking
seams in and out, and by the time <u>she</u> gets
home at night, hasn't the strength to get
out <u>her</u> Geiger counter and start hunting
for **her child's** . . .

Figure 5.2 Philip Roth, *Portnoy's Complaint* (1971, p. 194). Key: underlining = mother; bold = Smolka; italics = narrator; dotted underlining = guerrilla army; double underline = closet/drawer.

formal or semantic link that contributes to their cohesiveness. It is noticeable that the children's text has more ties than the adult text.

Even within the range of adult texts, there can be a more or less concentrated occurrence of cohesive devices. For example, the written language is usually received and read in the absence of the writer, so it is important that the information is clear because it is difficult to ask the author what is meant by a particular word or phrase. The spoken language, by contrast, allows any confusion to be cleared up in the course of the conversation:

> Then she said to me, 'I hope you don't mind me saying . . .' *Who* said that? Oh it was Sheila, last Saturday when we met in Sainsbury's.

The other frequent difference between the written and the spoken language is that many conversations take place between people who share a great deal of knowledge, usually local knowledge about people. Thus it is much less important to make sure that the referent of any pronoun, for example, is clear. This fact becomes most obvious when you 'listen in' to a conversation like the one quoted above, perhaps on buses and trains. The cohesive structure of conversations between close friends will tend to be very concentrated, but often ambiguous to everyone except the participants, because pronouns will be used more often than names, but with a number of potential referents.

We tend to react strongly if a text has an inappropriate level of cohesion. A text with very few people as referents should, for example, use pronouns as long as they are unambiguous. When the name or other denoting phrase is repeated too often, the text becomes over-heavy and one begins to wonder whether it really is the same person being referred to:

> *The man* on the bus is my uncle. *The man* on the bus just jumped off while it was still moving. *The man* has run up the road.

Instead of assuming that it is the same man being referred to, we either think of this as being written in the style of rather old-fashioned children's reading books or we wonder whether there is more than one man involved.

Another type of 'loose' or non-cohesive text is where there is very little connection of any kind between the constituent sentences:

The salmon jumped early that year. I had been to London to visit the queen. Sandy's jumper was bright green.

Accomplished readers of modernist fiction will immediately assimilate such a text since they are used to being disoriented by their favourite authors. What comes naturally to human beings is the desire to make connections, even when none are evident. So we begin to build hypotheses about what the connections are. We assume, for example, that the past tense of the second sentence places the visit to London in the same 'year' as the first sentence. The lexical contrast between 'salmon', with a rural connotation, and 'London', the largest conurbation in Britain, causes us to assume that the narrator lives in the country, but made a journey to London. The complete change of topic in the third sentence only connects with the second because it sounds childlike. The second sentence refers to a well-known nursery-rhyme:

Pussy-cat, pussy-cat where have you been?
I've been up to London to visit the queen.

The *non-sequitur* in the third sentence may be just the kind of thing a child would skip to, not having learnt the 'rules' of conversation. The assumption that we know who *Sandy* is and would be interested in her/his jumper is also childlike. Alternatively, we may wonder whether the narrator is 'thinking aloud' and by introducing 'Sandy' is indicating that the story will centre on this person. Finally, we may refer to our experience of reading other similar novel openings and wonder whether, like James Joyce, this writer is evoking childhood memories. Or we may wonder whether it is rather like the opening of Faulkner's novel, *The Sound and the Fury*, indicating an adult with brain-damage whose perceptions are childlike. Or it may even be like Golding's *The Inheritors*, representing the hypothetical thought-processes of prehistoric human-like creatures.

The cohesiveness of a text, therefore, cannot be completely captured by a scientific description since it will depend partly on the reader/hearer. The human tendency to look for sense, even where there appears to be none, often causes us to see cohesion in apparently random sequences of sentences. The large majority of texts are much more mundanely cohesive and make their connections clear and understandable.

Activity: cohesion

Try to put the following (unordered) sentences into order, according to their cohesive ties. Notice those orderings that are possible, if stylistically unusual, and those which seem highly unlikely in any context.

1. So I refuse.
2. I have no job at the time, and if I give the money he want there's not much left.
3. But his wife is a bad one – now she walk in my room and say she must have cash.
4. One bright Sunday morning in July I have trouble with my Notting Hill landlord because he ask for a month's rent in advance.
5. When I tell her no, she give my suitcase one kick and it burst open.
6. My best dress fall out, then she laugh and give another kick.
7. The man drunk already at that early hour, and he abuse me – all talk, he can't frighten me.
8. He tell me this after I live there since winter, settling up every week without fail.

Discussion

These sentences come from the opening page of a short story by Jean Rhys. The style is fairly conventional and gives the setting (sentence 4) first: *One bright Sunday morning in July*. This sentence establishes a first-person narrator (*I*) and a third-person landlord which many of the following sentences refer to as *he* thereafter. We can tell that certain pairs of sentences go together by their opening words. For example sentence (3) opens with *But*, which indicates that this sentence will disagree with the previous one. Sentence (3) discusses the landlord's wife and how bad she is, so in order to create a contrast, we need to find a sentence indicating that the landlord himself is not too bad. Sentence (7) shows that despite his threats, the landlord does not scare the narrator, so this clearly precedes sentence (3). Similarly with sentence (5), which clearly follows some kind of question or request from a female person. The only sentence which fits this description is sentence (3), so it must precede sentence (5).

Although this exercise is quite easy to do, it is in making explicit the clues which lead us to reassemble the text that we are made more fully aware of the cohesive structure of the text which cuts across sentence boundaries.* The full list of sentences in their original order is: 4 8 2 1 7 3 5 6.

5.2 Speaking or Acting?

We have been concerned so far with aspects of meaning that are in some way 'carried' by pieces of language, whether those pieces be as small as phonemes or as large as texts, or one of the other levels between these two extremes. Whilst this chapter remains concerned with aspects of meaning that are actually carried by the texts concerned, there will simultaneously be an increasing tendency to place those texts in their situational or social context. The context of any language text is important to its meaning, but the larger the stretch of language, the more difficult it becomes to discuss the text and the context separately. Some of the more wide-ranging aspects of context will be saved up for Chapter 6, but for now we will consider aspects of language texts that begin to place them into their situational context a little more than we have done so far.

One theory that has strongly influenced the way that we view the relationship between language and context is known as *speech act theory*. Originating from the work of Austin (1962) and Searle (1969), speech act theory distinguishes between the act of speaking (or indeed writing, though speech is usually taken as the exemplar for this theory) and the actions being performed by the act of speaking. Thus we may say *I'd love an ice-cream!* and depending on the context we may be performing a number of different actions such as requesting an action (*please get me one*), agreeing to a proposal (*yes please*) or even making a statement of grievance (*you all know I'm on a diet and can't have one*).

---

*This exercise is similar to one in Simpson (1992), though others may have used the same exercise.

Because the context is so important in interpreting the speech acts involved in any utterance, we will return to them in more detail in Chapter 6. For now let us consider the general distinction between speaking and acting. Speech act theory arose partly as a response to the kind of linguistics that for a number of years had been analysing language as though it occurred in a vacuum and without any context. The effect of this kind of analysis, useful though it was in many ways, was to over-simplistically assign meanings to texts as though they were in a one-to-one relationship. So the early attempts to analyse grammar and semantics would assign a meaning to a sentence, rather than assigning a meaning to a sentence in its context. The glaring problem with this approach was that any utterance, taken in a different context, could mean something different.

Linguists spent a great deal of time discussing the meaning of sentences such as *John is easy to please* in order to compare their meanings with sentences with apparently similar structures, but different meanings such as *John is eager to please*. The problem is that *John* is the grammatical subject of both of these sentences, but seems to be more active in the second and fairly passive in the first, where he is not doing the pleasing. These discussions threw some light on the relationship between structure and meaning, but inevitably ignored the fact that just one of these sentences could have a wide range of meaning by itself.

Imagine a family where one person has to give up their bed for a couple of nights for an elderly visitor. One member of the family might try to make sure they keep their own bed by 'volunteering' another member. This speech act of effectively offering someone else's services could be achieved by the second sentence *John is eager to please*. John could, of course, deny his eagerness if he is present, but the speech act ('what about John?') has nevertheless been performed.

A different situation might result in the same sentence causing a different speech act to be performed. This time John is observed by his friends flirting with a girl he has just met. She finishes her drink and John leaps up to buy her another one. The sentence (*John is eager to please*), out-of-earshot for John, this time conveys between his friends their amusement at his efforts to impress and performs a commenting type of speech act. The denotation of the sentence does not differ in these two situations, so it is not a case of grammatical or semantic ambiguity. It is simply that the reason for using the sentence and the effect it has, i.e. its speech acts, are different.

It should be made clear that the distinction being drawn here between the utterance and the act is not the same as saying that form and meaning are in some sense separable. The whole of this book is aimed at demonstrating that meaning is bound up with every aspect of linguistic form and it is the complexity of their relationship that lends the English language its richness. Speech act theory aims to explain a particular aspect of that relationship, between the utterance (locution) and what it does (illocutionary force). Although they can be distinguished for descriptive purposes, these are really two intrinsically connected aspects of linguistic texts, since the illocutionary act is brought about by the act of speaking (or writing).

Less closely connected, but still important in the context is a third aspect of this relationship which is rather beyond the scope of this section, but will be mentioned here since it arises from speech act theory. This is the effect, unintended or not, of any utterance, known as perlocutionary effect. Whilst the illocutionary force might be attributed in some way to the speaker's intention, the perlocutionary effect is rather less under the speaker's control.

For example, if a speaker says *It would have been easier to finish the work with more people* to a colleague who'd been absent from work, the illocutionary act might be a complaint about the hearer's absence. If the hearer is the boss, the illocutionary act might be a complaint about management and staffing levels. In either case the hearer might feel either aggrieved or guilty, depending on circumstances, personality and so on. These secondary effects on the hearer, whilst they might be the ultimate aim of the speaker, cannot be illocutionary acts since they arise from the perspective of the hearer and are thus not under the speaker's control.

Before we move on to other aspects of conversational texts, let us consider a small but important group of utterances where the utterance and the act are more closely connected than usual. These cases, known as perfomatives, occur where the utterance itself is a performance of the act concerned, not just the cause of the act. They usually contain one of the group of verbs known as performative verbs which both name and enact the action that they describe. There are, for example, a small number of formal occasions when people in positions of authority may perform a speech act by using one of these verbs. These are occasions like weddings when an officiating religious leader might say *I now pronounce you husband and wife*. If this sentence is said by an authorised person in the appropriate circumstances, the couple become married. Clearly, if the sentence is said by a child to two of her friends in a dressing-up game, it does not have the performative effect. Other narrowly formal performatives like this include the sentencing of prisoners by judges using the verb *sentence* and the occasions when famous people open fêtes and fairs by *declaring* them open or name ships whilst wasting good champagne.

In addition to these socially prescribed performatives, it is possible in any context to make explicit the speech act you are aiming for by using an appropriate verb from the performative class. Instead of using a roundabout way of apologising such as *I didn't mean to* or even instead of the more straightforward *I'm sorry*, you might decide to say *I apologise*, thereby apologising in the act of speaking the words. Similarly with other speech acts such as requesting, stating, querying, etc. These performative utterances sound very formal and would most often be used in a fairly formal setting such as a business meeting.

Activity: speech acts and performatives
For the following sentences, invent situations when the speech act being performed is different, although the surface meaning of the sentence remains the same:

> *How many times have you been there?*
> *I'm talking to Maria.*
> *Whose biscuit is that?*

For the next set of sentences, add a phrase or produce a paraphrase which makes the performative aspect of the utterance explicit:

> *Coming to the club with me tonight?*
> *Have you got a spare couple of chairs?*
> *I don't believe you.*

Discussion
The first sentence, *How many times have you been there?*, could be a

straightforward request for information. Perhaps a friend has just told you that she is planning a holiday to Spain and you know she has been there before more than once. On the other hand, the situation could be that you are asking the way to a shop or restaurant in a city. The person who has been asked knows that you have been there before, more than once, and is incredulous that you apparently cannot remember the way. The speech act in this case is one if comment, paraphrased by 'is your memory that bad?'.

The second sentence, *I'm talking to Maria*, could be a plain statement of fact, answering a question, or it could be a complaint that the person addressed is interrupting a conversation. It would often apply in family situations where a child interrupts a parent or carer and in reply receives the speech act which indicates that they should not interrupt.

The third sentence, *Whose biscuit is that?*, might simply request information on the ownership of a biscuit. More likely this sentence would occur in a situation where the speaker covets the last biscuit on the plate and yet does not want to appear greedy. He or she indicates the fairness of their own actions by asking if anyone has a prior claim on the biscuit. The speech act could, therefore, be paraphrased as 'can I have the last biscuit?'.

The performatives for the second set of sentences might be added as follows:

I am inviting you to come to the club with me tonight.
I am requesting that you lend me a spare couple of chairs.
I am calling you a liar.

Notice that the performative versions are much more formal than the originals. The last example, in particular, illustrates the fact that the apparent speech act may sometimes be disputed. The original version would often be followed by the response *Are you calling me a liar?* to which the answer might be *No, it's just that I'm so surprised.* This exposes the speech act as being an expression of surprise rather than labelling someone a liar.

5.3 Answering Back

Much of the discussion of meaning in this book up to now has assumed that the text(s) being described and analysed originate from one speaker or writer. For many of the types of meaning already encountered, it is irrelevant whether they occur in texts produced by one person or by a number of people. Thus sound-symbolism, the structure of noun phrases and the cohesive effects of a text are all meaningful however many writers/speakers are involved. Although there are differences of style and effect in different media, many of the meaningful aspects of language covered so far can occur equally well in spoken and written language and in a variety of contexts.

There are some features of spoken conversation, however, that are meaningful in themselves and do not occur in written language, or indeed in one-way spoken language such as news broadcasts or public lectures. These features form the subject matter of this section as well as cropping up again in sections 5.4, 6.5 and 7.1.

When two or more people are talking, there are features of the text which are associated with the way in which the conversation is managed by the participants. There are many questions we could ask about the flow of conversation. Who begins a conversation and how? Who gets to talk and how do you hold the floor once you have started? When is it appropriate to interrupt and how do you do it? In this section we will look at some of the basic patterns observed in the course of conversation in English.

To begin with, how do conversations start? Much, of course, will depend on the relationship between the people involved and the situation they find themselves in. Because they are wider issues than those being considered here, these questions will be considered in Chapter 6. Nevertheless, there are some general features of conversational openings that can be observed. One feature that is present in conversations both between strangers and between people familiar to each other is the use of non-controversial and impersonal topics as a way of establishing an opening. For example, the English are famous for using the weather as a neutral topic for finding some common ground, though the topic might just as well be something in the immediate context. The pictures in a doctor's waiting room or some significant news visible on the front of a train passenger's newspaper might provide enough of a topic for an opening move.

Obviously, if we interpret some conversational opening utterances in terms of the speech act theory introduced in the last section, we will find that in addition to the local speech act such as requesting information or asking for agreement, there may be a wider speech act intended, such as initiating a conversation. Having exchanged a few comments, speakers can begin to establish whether developing the conversation further is likely to be worthwhile.

One of the most useful models for examining the structure of conversations is the adjacency pair. There are a great many exchanges in conversations in English that can be described in terms of pairs of utterances, the second of which is determined to some extent by the first.

Openings of conversations obviously often contain a pair of greetings such as the following:

Hello Jane!
Hi there, Louise.

In telephone conversations, there may be a pair of utterances establishing who the participants are:

Is that Peter?
Yes, is that Simon?

Similarly with endings, which are conventionally made up of a pair of 'goodbyes' or their equivalent:

Well, I'll see you later.
Yes, see you.

In fact, much of the conversation between the opening and the closing is also made up of adjacency pairs and sequences of such pairs. Many of our utterances have a built-in expectation of a particular kind of response. Take, for example, an invitation such as the following:

Why don't you come round on Thursday for a cup of tea?

The expectation is that the hearer will respond by accepting or declining in the immediately following utterance:

Thanks, we can can catch up on the rest of the news then.

or:

Sorry, I've promised to do Mum's shopping for her on Thursday . . .

It is, of course, open to speakers to respond in another, unexpected way to the first part of an adjacency pair, but the fact that they have done so will be significant to the first speaker. Let us change the response to the invitation to tea on Thursday:

Hey! That's a nice skirt – is it new?

Clearly the response is inadequate and the first speaker will be making judgements about why her invitation was ignored. Is the second speaker trying to indicate that their friendship does not extend as far as drinking tea together? Is there something secretive going on on Thursday that cannot be discussed? The point for us is that the very avoidance of an expected response is meaningful to both participants. The next section will look more closely at the meanings of responses in conversation, but let us return to considering adjacency pairs.

Other kinds of pairs that commonly occur include congratu-lations, which are usually followed by thanks, and accusations, which may be followed by denials or apologies. The following pairs illustrate these types respectively:

Brilliant catch!
Thanks – I thought I was going to miss it.

Thanks a lot for doing the washing-up!
I'm sorry, I didn't have time before I left.

Notice that the accusation in the second example above is appar-ently a speech act of thanking, but the situation (in which the washing-up is clearly still to be done) allows both speaker and hearer to interpret the utterance as a sarcastic accusation of not having done a job that should have been done.

Although adjacency pairs are not the whole story, there is a remarkable quantity of conversation made up of these pairs, particularly when they occur in sequences. One feature of such sequences is that there may be a pair of utterances which set up the expectation of another adjacency pair to follow. For example, if you are going to invite someone to your house on a particular day, you might want to minimise the risk of being rejected by establishing first whether or not that person is free on the day you have in mind. In the following pair, the first speaker wants to know if the hearer is free so that she can invite her round:

What are doing on Friday evening? Are you working?
No, for once I haven't got anything on at all.

There are a small number of choices at this stage, for example, the first speaker might be looking for a favour (e.g. baby-sitting) or just showing her concern at the hearer working too hard. Given that they are quite close friends and have not seen each other for a while, the hearer is probably safe in assuming that some kind of proposal or invitation will follow. Her admission that she is entirely free is a good sign to the speaker to press ahead with the invitation:

Great! Why don't you come round and we'll have a take-away pizza and some wine?
OK. Shall I come about eight?

The 'pre-sequences' that introduce other adjacency pairs are usually unambiguous in that the hearer will be able to guess whether it is an invitation or a requested favour that will follow. If they are unsure which it will be, they might hedge their answer to avoid being asked something they might want to refuse:

What are doing on Friday evening? Are you working?
I was going to go out with Sheila, but I'm not sure whether she's free . . .

This kind of response leaves the way open for the second speaker to change her plans if the following proposal sounds pleasant, by claiming that Sheila is probably too busy anyway. Alternatively, the second speaker could appeal to the first speaker's sense of fair play by saying that she really ought to check with Sheila first.

Another possibility with pre-sequences like this is that the first speaker will anticipate the ambiguity of her utterance and try to allay the fears of the hearer first:

> *What are you doing on Friday evening? It's OK. I'm not after a baby-sitter!*

Or, if the follow-up pair is indeed going to be a requested favour, then the speaker might try not to raise the hopes of the hearer:

> *What are you doing on Friday evening? I'm afraid I'm after a favour . . .*

In addition to pre-sequences which are the precursor to another pair, there may be pairs of utterances inserted between the first and second parts of an adjacency pair. This is particularly true of requests and fulfilments of requests like the following exchange in a shopping transaction:

> *I would like to buy a portable CD player please.*
> *Here you are, Sir.*

This exchange looks ridiculous because our knowledge of the world informs us that there will be a number of choices to be made in buying this kind of electronic equipment. If the first speaker had asked for a small brown loaf, the pair would have been perfectly acceptable. Nevertheless, how would the original request actually progress? Most probably, there would be a number of interim pairs of questions and answers between the first and second parts of the pair above:

> *I would like to buy a portable CD player please.*
> *How much would you like to spend?*
> *Not more than about £170.*
> *Do you mean a personal CD player like a Walkman?*
> *No, just one that I can carry.*
> *They all have radio and cassette facilities as well . . .*
> *Yes, that's fine, but it must play CDs.*

And so on until the customer is satisfied and the assistant hands over the goods with the second part of our original pair: *Here you are, Sir.*

Activity: adjacency Pairs

Write a conversation between two people, using only adjacency pairs. First, choose the people and their setting by answering the following questions:

- Who are the people? (i.e. age, gender, name, background)
- Where are they? (e.g. at work, school, on a bus, in the street)
- What is their relationship? (e.g. parent/child, boss/employee, friends)
- What is happening? (e.g. a parent telling a child off, boss praising employee's work)

You will need to make other, more detailed decisions as you write the conversation, but try to make it sound as natural as possible, even though you are being asked to constrain your writing to adjacency pairs. Do not forget that some pairs of utterances come embedded in others, so you might want to layer your pairs in this way.

Discussion

Instead of a discussion of this activity, here is an example of an invented conversation made from adjacency pairs alone. Notice how the second part of each pair is usually followed by the first part of a new pair from the same speaker:

- *Hi there, Martin.*
- *Wotcha mate, fancy a drink?*
- *Not now, I'm late already. Are you going to Janet's party later?*
- *I might do, but I don't know. Are you free tomorrow night?*
- *Why, what are you after?*
- *Nothing, I just thought we'd go round Rob's house and play some music.*
- *All right then, I'll see you tomorrow. Bye.*
- *See you later.*

5.4 Whose Turn Next?

Although much conversation is made up of adjacency pairs, longer exchanges involve some very complicated turn-taking procedures that cannot all be predicted from the adjacency model. Alongside the pairing of speech acts dealt with in the last section, there are many other options for taking the floor in a conversation as well as for giving the turn to someone else, keeping the floor and giving the speaker support. We will consider the significance of these turn-taking moves next.

The model of turn-taking that we will use here was first developed in Sacks, Schegloff and Jefferson (1974). This model first of all established that a speaker's turn could consist of a single word, a phrase, a dependent clause or a full sentence, and that hearers would be ready for a transition of speaker after these units were completed. Let us see some examples of different length turns:

What did you have for lunch today?
Some sandwiches and a yoghourt.
Bought from the canteen?
Yes

The four utterances in this exchange are, in order: sentence, phrase, dependent clause and word. Whilst a speaker may, in fact speak for longer than a full sentence, Sacks *et al.* suggested that participants in a conversation are always ready for a turn-change at these boundaries and, to that extent, they are always potentially the place for a speaker change. Thus they proposed the term 'transition relevant place' to describe the boundaries where all participants recognise a potential turn-change and where in fact most turn-changes do happen. Having recognised the usefulness of the transition relevant places, Sacks *et al.* considered the mechanisms by which speakers take or keep the turn at these boundary-points. They proposed three procedures by which the next turn would be allocated.

The first and most powerful mechanism is for the current speaker to choose the next speaker. This overrides other procedures because the choice is made well before the transition relevant place. For example, a speaker that chooses to use the first part of an adjacency pair will necessarily be counting him or herself out of the next turn since the second part of such a pair must be provided by another speaker. Usually the speaker is addressing the first part to a particular hearer, even if there are a number of participants. For example, the following question would probably be indicated to the intended hearer by the use of eye contact or nodding in the direction of the intended recipient:

Where did you get your shoes from?

The next speaker is selected by this device and all participants are expected to abide by the current speaker's choice. If the current speaker does not select another speaker by using a structured pair of this kind, then it is open to any of the hearers to self-select as the next speaker. This second mechanism is a free-for-all where speakers have to get in very quickly since the first one to speak is the rightful owner of the turn and other speakers are expected to give way.

If neither of the first and second options for speaker-selection occurs, then the current speaker may opt to continue the turn by beginning another unit, whether it be word-length or sentence-length or somewhere in between. If no one self-selects immediately, the speaker who wishes to will continue very quickly so that other participants do not take the floor as a second chance.

Natural conversation is managed by the participants themselves, and has no outside agent giving people turns according to any extraneous rules such as strict rotation as in a game of cards or according to social status or age. Sacks *et al.* call this feature of conversation 'local management' and also comment on the fact that conversational turns are managed 'interactionally'. This means that each stage in the conversation is influenced by what immediately preceded it and thus each turn can influence what follows it.

It seems a little surprising to realise how much of the conversation that English speakers are involved in is conducted according to the turn-taking rules outlined above. Whilst there are sometimes breakdowns and mistakes in the way that the turn is passed from one speaker to another, it is generally the case that speakers try to orient themselves towards the rules and may apologise or try to correct themselves when they are perceived to be breaking the rules. For example, a speaker who continues to speak after a transition relevant point may find themselves talking over another participant who has self-selected at that point. The first speaker will usually give way by falling silent and if this does not happen, other participants may complain. Similarly, a self-selecting speaker might anticipate a transition relevant point too early and sound as though he or she is interrupting the current speaker. Again, this will normally give rise to an apology or a complaint.

Although I have used the word 'interruption' in the last paragraph, in fact conversation analysts only use this term very strictly for speakers failing to observe the rules of turn-taking altogether. For example, it would apply to someone who wilfully started speaking during the middle of a turn when no transition relevant point was in view. There may be good reason for this kind of interruption to happen, for example in an emergency when the usual niceties of social interaction are suspended. The term interruption is therefore reserved for such transgressions, and the term 'overlap' is used for mistakes or slight inaccuracies in the application of the rules when two or more people are speaking at once.

'Staged' conversations, such as television or radio interviews differ from the language used in face-to-face interaction between speakers. In addition to the meanings associated with the sounds, words, phrases, sentences and text structure of the utterances, these exchanges also have meanings supplied by the very ebb and flow of the conversation.

It is noticeable, for example, that politicians, particularly successful ones, will not 'give way' to speakers who are interviewing them on television or radio. They are aware that their image with voters will be stronger if they can keep the floor and make other participants look weak and hesitant in comparison to them. Such speakers are exploiting our knowledge and experience of the 'rules' and conventions of conversation in English. Some interviews are deliberately set up with one participant having the power to cut in on the other participant, so that although in the studio it may sound like an ordinary conversation, a dominant microphone will allow hearers to hear only one speaker at a time. An example of this occurs in Britain on the early-morning news programme on Radio 4, *Today*, where the interviewer's voice can often override any politician who is using the interview to get an overlong exposure to radio audiences.

To return to 'natural' conversation, when we talk to other English speakers, we use and respond to many stimuli, in addition to the transition relevant places we have already identified, which indicate when there is an opportunity to change speakers, interrupt, keep talking or fall silent. These stimuli are sometimes vocal/auditory and sometimes supplied by body language.

For example, we may see the current speaker look directly at another participant and show that s/he is willing to give up the floor to that person by allowing the intonation to fall to low pitch levels. Alternatively, the speaker may respond to another participant who is trying to get in by looking pointedly away and keeping pitch levels in the mid to high part of her range.

There are, of course, also many ways of indicating turns directly through the language content and structure itself. As we have already seen, you may invite other speakers to join in by using the first part of an adjacency pair such as a question that requires an answer:

What do you think, Jane?

And there are many very straightforward ways of selecting the next speaker explicitly:

I'd love to know your opinion, George.
OK – it's your turn now!

There are also text-based ways of interrupting:

Hold on! You can't mean that . . .
No – no. There was never any question . . .
Let me get a word in . . .

Although speakers in informal conversations very often speak over each other for short periods, there is usually a clear distinction between the legitimate ending of a turn and the purest form of interruption that takes place when the speaker has shown no sign of giving way. Many speaker transitions are characterised by both speakers talking at once for a few words and then the new speaker taking over.

What are the signs that speakers 'read' in order to operate effectively as participants in conversations? They include an understanding of intonation at the discourse level which will enable speaker/hearers to use and interpret the sequences of tone units that indicate the different stages in a 'turn'. Although we can identify the 'meanings' of falling versus rising tones as attached to clauses or sentences (see section 2.3), they may also be sequenced in such a way that the hearer is aware of how far through the turn the speaker thinks s/he has got. For example, the following sequence of clauses may occur as one speaker's turn in a family conversation about what to have for tea:

Look, I've got some sausages, or we could have egg and chips . . . peas too if you want

The intonation could indicate a trailing off by the speaker who has no further suggestions by ending with a low rising tone on *want*, or it could be much more active in seeking the help of other speakers by using a high rising tone which may indicate a question and thereby demand an answer.

Body language may accompany and emphasise these meanings, or replace them if the intonation is neutral or ambiguous. Thus you might imagine the speaker using a half-hearted shrug of the shoulders to accompany the first, trailing off, interpretation and raised eyebrows and eye-contact to communicate the second, more actively engaged meaning.

Body language has a special role in the management of face-to-face interaction. It can be used by all participants to indicate their interest in the current speaker, their engagement with the subject under discussion and their desire to take a turn, either at a suitable point or by interruption.

It is easy to imagine the kinds of body language that indicate the positive, engaged attitude. The listener will typically be leaning forward, toward the current speaker, often looking directly at the speaker, though looking away intently might also indicate con-centration. The desire to take over the floor will often result in some fidgeting, more intense staring at the speaker and sometimes gestures that try to cut the speaker's flow.

Participants in conversations often also indicate orally their engagement with the subject and their support for the speaker by vocalisations, often called 'hearer support' that show agreement. These are sometimes represented in the written language by *mm* or *uh-huh* or other more inventive combinations of letters.

If we consider the speaker him/herself for a moment, we can see that body language is also used to add meaning to the discourse when you have the turn to yourself. The types of body language used in close conjunction with speech can be divided into those movements, postures and gestures which replace specific words or phrases, known as 'emblems', those which emphasise or echo the language that is being spoken, which are called 'illustrators', and those which have a role in the flow and turn-taking of conversation, known as 'regulators'. This last group is relevant to this section, since they help to create the conditions for turn-taking in conversation. For example, speakers keen to take the next opportunity for speaking often lean forward and look intently at the current speaker. If you are desperate to speak, you may start to gesture before the transition relevant place, so that other participants will be aware that you are about to speak. Sometimes, paradoxically, speakers look away from the current speaker just before they are about to take up the floor. This appears to be a way of withdrawing support for the current speaker in an attempt to make her or him ready to relinquish the turn at the next potential transition point.

We have already considered one model of conversational analysis that recognises the adjacency pair as a very important structuring devise for conversation. Another model of conversational practice that is very useful in our search for the location of meaning represents the general principles that regulate English conversations by a series of maxims. This model, first expounded by Grice (1975), claims that speakers operate under the constraint of a basic co-operational principle which dictates that participants should aim to fulfil the immediate requirements of the conversation. The general principle is given substance by four maxims.* These maxims are:

- Quantity – say enough but not too much.
- Quality – tell the truth and have evidence for what you say.
- Relevance – say only what is relevant to this point in the conversation.
- Clarity – use language that is as clear as possible to your hearers.

The first maxim, concerning quantity, puts the speaker under

---

*Other writers (e.g. Geis, 1982) have since listed different numbers of maxims, though they cover the same ground as those proposed by Grice.

pressure to say the right amount about the current topic. So, when a girl who is wondering what to wear asks her mother what the weather is like today, she expects a level of information appropriate to her needs such as:

It looks dry, but they said it might rain later.

In this context, it would be inappropriate to say too little:

Normal.

Similarly, we would not expect to have an overlong reply:

The wind is in the east, there's a small patch of blue over the park though the rest of the sky has a layer of nimbus cloud and there are puddles in the lane indicating that it rained in the night . . .

The second maxim, of quality, indicates the hearer's expectation that the speaker will speak 'in good faith' by stating only things that are true or for which there is some evidence. Although people do, of course, lie from time to time, thus flouting this maxim, it is significant that the notion of telling lies depends on the existence of the maxim of quality. If we were not expecting people to tell us the truth, then their lies would not be believed.

The maxim of relevance claims that speakers who are acting under the co-operative principle will try to make their contributions relevant to the current topic and the last speaker's turn. Thus a speaker might follow a comment about a restaurant meal in the following way:

This lasagne is really hot!
My pizza's cooling down really quickly.

The last maxim, of clarity, sounds rather obvious, since it requires the speaker to make their contribution as clear as possible. This needs some sensitivity to the other participants and might require taking into account their age, education, first language and so on. If you were talking to a toddler of two or three years old, you would probably avoid sophisticated vocabulary and formal structures in favour of simpler language. Instead of saying:

I wonder if you would mind retrieving your plaything from the cat's throat.

You would be more likely to shout:

Take the dolly out, now!

All utterances require the speaker to aim for maximum clarity, although most care has to be taken when there is some kind of linguistic difference of background or ability between the speaker and the listener.

The importance of Grice's notion for our purposes is that he proposed that in most cases when people are conversing they assume that other participants in the conversation are operating according to the co-operational principles. This means that when the maxims are flouted, the hearer has to make sense of the situation by accommodating the apparent flouting and assuming the speaker is, indeed, behaving co-operatively.

If a speaker clearly flouts the maxim of quantity by talking too much, the hearer has to decide why this is so:

A: *Shall I wash up the breakfast things first?*
B: *Yes – I didn't have time this morning. You know how late we got up – Jonathon wouldn't do his piano practice and Sheila couldn't find any clean clothes and then Clair rang to see if I could pick her kids up this evening and by the time I got back to the kitchen it was almost time to leave for school.*

In this example, A might have simply required a *yes*, but B decides to interpret the question as asking in addition why the washing up had not been done earlier. Having made this interpretation (of a nag) B could have said *Yes – I didn't have time this morning* but instead she or he decides that it isn't a fair nag and so gives rather too much in the way of justification for her/his failure to wash up.

Another example of clear flouting, this time of the maxim of quality, comes from a child who is known to have smacked her little brother:

A: *What did you do to him to make him cry like that?*
B: *I just made a funny face.*

Children soon learn that straightforward lying is often found out and punished. They also pick up the adult habit of avoiding a direct lie by flouting the maxim of relevance instead:

A: *What did you do to make him cry like that?*
B: *Oh look at the cat Mummy!*

Changing the subject is a very common way of indicating to the hearer that you are flouting the maxim of relevance because there are things you would rather not say. Sometimes the intention is more to protect the other participants than the speaker:

A: *What did you think of my new boyfriend then?*
B: *Did he tell you I saw him in the bank yesterday?*

Many of the meanings that seem to take place almost in the spaces between the words, rather than in the sentences themselves, are actively negotiated between the speakers and depend on both shared background knowledge and on the current situation as well as the turn-taking and co-operative principles described in this section. Section 5.5 introduces more discussion on these context-based aspects of meaning.

Activity: turn-taking and co-operative maxims
If you have access to a cassette recorder, try taping two or three minutes of a conversation between you and one other person. Transcribe the tape, showing where the speakers overlap in talking and then look at where the speaker changes took place. Were they mainly at clause boundaries or phrase boundaries? Were there any interruptions, as opposed to overlaps? Did the person in the listening role give any vocal support to the speaker? Look again at your transcription and work out whether all of the utterances were conforming to the Gricean maxims. If not, which maxim was apparently being flouted and how was the situation resolved? If you are unable to find examples of such flouting, look at the following pairs of utterances and identify the co-operative 'problem' there. In

some cases, it will be not a flouting at all, but an apparent lack of co-operation which simply requires some reasoning to work out.

A: *Did Bob tell you he was leaving? He says he's got a better paid job, I gather.*
B: *And I'm going to win the lottery on Saturday!*

C: *What day did you say you'd come and look at the boiler?*
D: *Well, I've got the children Monday and Tuesday, I can't leave Leonard alone on Wednesday, because he only gets meals on wheels two days a week now. So it'll be Thursday before I even think about it. Did you say it wasn't working at all?*

E: *I've been looking everywhere for a hat to go with this outfit. What do you think?*
F: *I think it'll be fine when you've got the whole outfit on, because you can't really get the effect in your jeans.*

Discussion

Speaker B is apparently flouting the maxim of relevance, but since no one can predict the lottery winners, s/he is also not adhering strictly to truth. This means that A has to interpret B's comments as both relevant and relatively truthful. If A assumes B is being ironic by referring to the unlikely circumstance of winning the lottery, it becomes relevant by implying that it is no more likely that Bob has got a better-paid job.

Speaker D is embarrassed about not being able to fulfil some expected favour for C. Since it is clearly quite urgent (a broken or malfunctioning boiler), she has to make her reasons sound very convincing. In doing so, she flouts the maxim of quantity and tells C far more than s/he needs to know about her week's activities. This kind of response rarely has the desired effect since it irritates more than it soothes.

Speaker F is lying, or flouting the maxim of quality, to save the feelings of E. However, in doing so, s/he also flouts the maxim of quantity by talking through circumstances in which the hat might be reassessed.

5.5 Storytelling and Persuasion

There is a case of polysemy in English that can have an important effect on children in school playgrounds. A six-year-old was outraged to have been told not to *tell stories* when she approached a playground supervisor for help following a minor physical assault on her by another child. Although the supervisor was probably ill-advised to dismiss any accusation of bullying in this way, the child concerned was angered not because her complaints were being ignored but because she thought she was being accused of lying. The supervisor, however, had intended the phrase *telling stories* to mean *grassing* or *getting your peers in trouble with authority* rather than *telling untruthful tales*.

This polysemy is instructive because it reminds us that we have a complex cultural relationship with the notion of *stories*. Just as we tend to believe that news reporting is 'factual' in some categorical way, we also tend to think of narrative as a stereotypically fictional. However, there are many types of narrative, in both spoken and written media, and most of them cannot be satisfactorily categorised as either truth or fiction. Most novels are based on some kind of truth, although this is often a psychological truth rather than historical fact. Many biographies are fictionalised to some extent, especially where there are salacious details to be embroidered upon in order to increase sales of the book! Similar effects take place in spoken discourse. A piece of interesting gossip about a friend may be embellished more by one friend than by another and the details may be relished more by one hearer than another.

Whatever the actual 'truth' value of a story, story-tellers have a range of stylistic choices open to them, and the decisions they come to about their style can have an important effect upon meaning. For example, the teller has to decide who is going to tell the story. In the case of a novel or short story, the writer may choose a character and tell it through their voice:

As I went towards St Marks' Bridge, where slow water drowned this summer's leaves, she accosted me, grinning, tugging with both hands at the ends of her red-spotted kerchief . . .
(Doris Lessing, 'Lions, Leaves, Roses . . .', from *The Story of a Non-Marrying Man* [Penguin, 1979] pp. 1–7)

Alternatively, the writer or storyteller may choose the 'omniscient narrator' who is a fly on the wall in all situations relevant to the story:

> Once, Long ago, Lion, Goat and Tortoise met at the edge of the forest. They were all very hungry. They had been hunting all day and had caught nothing. Tortoise called the others and said, 'Listen, my friends. When we hunt alone we catch nothing but if we hunted together we might be more successful.'
>
> (Loreto Todd, 'Tortoise, Goat and Lion: The Price of Wisdom', from *Tortoise the Trickster and Other Folktales From Cameroon* [Routledge and Kegan Paul, 1979] p. 23)

A third option is to vary the narrator from character to character as Virginia Woolf is famous for doing in her ground-breaking novels. Here are two openings of adjacent paragraphs showing different narrators whose internal feelings show through in a way that is not always true of omniscient narrators, even though it is a third-person narrative:

> There they are! he thought. Do what you like with them, Clarissa! There they are! And second by second it seemed to him that the wife of the Major in the Indian Army (his Daisy) and her two small children became more and more lovely as Clarissa looked at them; as if he had set light to a grey pellet on a plate and there had risen up a lovely tree in the sea-salted air of their intimacy (for in some ways no one understood him, felt with him, as Clarissa did) – their exquisite intimacy.
>
> She flattered him; she fooled him, thought Clarissa; shaping the woman, the wife of the Major in the Indian Army, with three strokes of a knife. What a waste! What a folly!
>
> (Virginia Woolf, *Mrs Dalloway* [Grafton, 1976] p. 42)

The writer/speaker also has to decide what sense of involvement the reader will have on reading/hearing the story. If the recipient is to be drawn in it may help to use the first person, and a well-known way of lending your story a sense of immediacy is to use the present tense. In the following section of a private letter from a teacher of poetry to his colleague, as well as using the present tense and the first person, the writer refers to shared cultural knowledge in the form of the *Archers* (a radio soap opera in Britain) and the Grundys (a family, including Eddie, that appears in the soap and represents a rural underclass):

> I'm working with a playwright – one of the Archers writers, but she won't reveal anything of the latest scripts which she posted off yesterday. The students are writing villanelles today, and I will press for a literary revelation at the Grundy's. Listen out for Eddie's sonnet sequence.

If narrators are largely interested in involving reader/hearers in their story and persuading them of its truth (psychological or factual), then there are many other texts in English culture that have different, more persuasive, aims. These texts may call on many of the meaningful properties we have already discussed at all linguistic levels to create the desired effect. There are, however, other properties of texts which have not so far been introduced, but which are most noticeable when they have a persuasive function – or (if there is no conscious intention) a persuasive effect.

One of the devices often used for such effects is the three-part list. Whether there is something deeply psychological about the number three, or whether it is a throwback to earlier times when human beings perhaps counted in simple terms of one, two and many, is speculation. However, the three-part list connotes completeness and is used in many political and other persuasive texts to indicate that all aspects of the issue have been covered:

> A linked series of traffic-free paths, protected on-road sections and minor roads, which together make a *safe, attractive, high quality* network for cyclists throughout Britain.
> (Sustrans promotional leaflet for the National Cycle Network)

Here the writer has indicated that the cycle routes will be perfect by using three modifiers before the noun 'network': *safe, attractive* and *high quality*. Although we could extend the list by thinking of other important areas of concern such as *easy to maintain* or *accessible*, a longer list begins, ironically, to look unfinished, because it leads the reader to think of what might have been left out – or unconvincing because it is trying too hard to show that it has thought of everything. The three-part list by contrast tends to remain unchallenged by the reader.

Many of the most persuasive aspects of texts are to be found in the semantic basis of the utterances or sentences themselves. In Chapter 7 I argue that a weak version of the Whorfian hypothesis might be accepted as explaining the creation and evolution of 'reality' – or cultural and social meanings. The hypothesis would claim that languages (and the cultures that use them) 'privilege' some categorisations of the world over others and that these categories, through common usage and habit, *tend* to structure the world in a particular way for that language's speakers.

Now, if we accept both the weaker version of the Whorfian hypothesis and the fact that speakers each have their own *idiolect* of the language, then we will have to accept the notion that each speaker's 'reality' is therefore slightly different from everyone else's. In addition, if we add the dimension of time to this model, we can see that these partially overlapping 'realities' will also be changing and evolving through time, since the speaker's experience of language will change throughout his/her life. If all language experience is part of the context in which language constructs our individual 'realities', then each time we engage in a communicative act, actively or passively, we are potentially having that reality changed and sometimes changing another's reality by the use of language.

If, in addition to this model, we assume that there is a difference of power between the participants in a communicative act (spoken or written), we find that instead of the language of both participants influencing the 'reality' of the other equally, it is the text-world of the more powerful person that influences the less powerful and alters, however minimally, the 'world' the other sees.

It is important to remember that power differentials may occur between people for a number of more or less complex reasons. Whilst it is easy to pursue the line that men are more powerful than women (and I would not disagree with that as a generalisation), it is clear that this does not apply to all men and women in all situations – take a female boss and male employee, for example, or a rich wife and poor husband, or a female doctor and male patient. Similar points could be made about the power of doctors over patients, bosses over workers, teachers over pupils, and parents over children. While the first of each pair has the most obvious and often institutionalised power, the second may take power initiatives in certain situations. Thus we have the patient that refuses to be intimidated by the questioning of the hospital consultant, but doggedly asks questions of her own; or the schoolchild that asks the teacher 'Why are we doing this?' If you have ever been the more powerful one in any of these pairs, you may know that the balance of power is often situationally determined and can alter from moment to moment.

If we assume, for a moment, that the simple model is accurate – that in any one speech or writing situation, there is a more and a less powerful participant – then how does the language contribute to the new 'reality' that the powerful participant is trying to impose on the powerless one?

All of the resources of the language can be used in powerful and persuasive ways to achieve this aim. However the semantic base of an utterance or sentence is central to the process of persuasion. As we saw in section 4.5, every utterance or sentence has associated with it one or more *entailments* and most sentences also have a number of associated *presuppositions*. The entailments of a sentence are those things that *must* be true if the sentence is true, but will be negated when the sentence is negative whereas the presuppositions are always true.

The different layers of meaning represented by entailments and presuppositions could, and often do, have different levels of persuasive power. For example, it is logically possible (even silently) to question the truth of an entailment, since that is one of the things being asserted by the utterance:

A: *The railways will be more profitable and efficient under private ownership.*
B: *Do you really think so? What evidence do you have? etc.*

The questions at B query the truth of the sentence and its entailment. But what cannot so easily be questioned is the presupposition that the railways *will be* privatised. Since I am writing this section at just the time in Britain when the privatisation of the railways is being pursued vigorously by an unpopular Conservative government and opposed by a Labour opposition who expect to be in power very soon, the *actual* truth or otherwise of the presupposition is difficult to assess. However, it is useful to those who are in favour of privatisation to build the expectation of it happening into the assumed or presupposed background of the sentence.

What happens if we build this sentence's entailment into a sentence but as a presupposition this time? One way of achieving this is to put into the subject noun phrase any material that you do not want questioned:

> A: *The profitable and efficient privatised railways will be in the ownership of a body of shareholders.*
> B: *Will they be floated on the stock market? Won't some of them be in single hands?*

Notice that the questions that this utterance allows you to ask are aimed at the new entailment about ownership, not at the presuppositions:

> *that the privatised railways will be profitable and efficient*

How is this achieved? In this case the required message (i.e. the one that is not to be questioned) has been placed into a Subject noun phrase:

> *the profitable and efficient privatised railway*

with the three adjectives (*profitable, efficient* and *privatised*) used alongside each other as though they naturally go hand in hand. A much simpler example shows that it is more effective to insult people by using premodifying adjectives than by using adjectives as complements:

> A: *Look at the fat man in the corner!*
> B: *Do you mean by the door?*

is more insulting than:

> A: *Look at that man in the corner. He's fat.*
> B: *No he's not.*

The analysis of language (discourse) *within a particular context* is often known as 'pragmatics'. Sometimes the language alone, even with all its layers of meaning, does not give us enough information to be able to decode it. In such situations, we may find that the semantic base (including the entailments and the presuppositions) of the utterances will not be a reliable guarantee of the meaning. For example, apparent *non-sequiturs*, like those which appear to break the Gricean maxim of relevance, may require some background knowledge to understand. Take the following example:

A: *What is this sock doing on the stairs?*
B: *I see you have put your shoes in the shoe cupboard.*

It requires both participants jointly to produce the meaning here – and it is produced by the apparently irrelevant remarks of B (who is getting back at A for a perceived 'nag') and the efforts of A to understand such apparent disregard of the conversational rules. Thus A (who always complains loudly about stray items of clothing being found about the house) will realise that B has countered with a nag about his own sloppy habits with regard to putting away his shoes. Notice, incidentally, that B's utterance also flouts the maxim of truth as it is a sarcastic reference to the fact that A has *not* put his shoes away.

Meanings such as these, jointly produced by speakers with shared knowledge of both the situation and some background, are known as *conversational implicatures*. They differ from semantic entailments (which can be questioned) and presuppositions (which cannot) in that they can be denied or ignored by either the speaker or the hearer.

Our happy couple* in the example above, have expressed their differences by acknowledging equal fault. Other possible ways of defusing potentially explosive conversational openings such as this are for B to make explicit the implicature that she 'reads' from A's utterance:

---

*Note that for the purposes of illustration, I have chosen to give A and B different genders, which may or may not be read as stereotypical. Of course, any people of any age or gender who share living accommodation are subject to the same pressures on their relationship as a result of tidiness or lack of it!

B: *Why do you think it's my job to keep everyone's socks under control?*

A might then reject B's interpretation of the initial 'nag':

A: *I didn't say it was . . .*

Alternatively, B might decide to ignore the implicature and answer A's question literally:

B: *Waiting for you to pick it up and put it in the wash, of course . . .*

Activity: narrative choices and pragmatic information
Read the following extract from the local paper in Leeds, Yorkshire. It takes a fairly personal view of one of the many lottery stories that have arisen in the first eighteen months of the British national lottery:

> In Britain's hour of need there was never a shortage of brave young men volunteering to fight for King and Country. Hundreds of thousands sacrificed their lives, and tens of thousands who survived were maimed for life.
>
> But now those who selflessly stepped forward in defence of the Realm – only to return with shattered limbs and torn bodies – need a little bit of help. And it looks as though they'll have to fend for themselves.
>
> In their hour of need they have made a modest request to the National Lottery Charities Board for £80,000. That's the cost of replacing their 24-year-old coach that takes them on summer afternoon outings. But their appeal for a grant is about to be rejected . . . because the new coach won't do enough miles every year.
>
> (John Thorpe's Yorkshire Diary, *Yorkshire Evening Post*,
> 7 December 1996, p. 6)

Find some examples of entailments, presuppositions and implicatures in this passage. Remember that entailments can be negated by negating the sentence, presuppositions are always true and implicatures can be denied, even without negating the sentence. Consider the narrative choices that have been made in this passage.

Does the writer's voice and viewpoint intrude into the story? If so, how is this shown?

Discussion

The first sentence proposes that *there was never a shortage* and this entailment would be negated by excluding the adverb, *never*. What there was no shortage of was *brave young men volunteering to fight for King and Country*. This noun phrase forms the presuppositions of the sentence and includes the 'facts' that the men were *brave*; that they *volunteered*, rather than being drafted or in some way shamed into going to war; and that they fought *for King and Country*, rather than for their families and friends. The reader may, or may not agree with all of these presuppositions, but they are nevertheless being asked to accept them as part of the argument of the text.

Similar presuppositions can be found throughout this text, and in case the reader had hesitated over the *King and Country*, the writer appeals to a slightly more community-based motivation for fighting, although couched in equally old-fashioned language: *defence of the Realm*. This passage also includes some implicatures. For example, in the third sentence, we find the columnist saying:

> But now those who selflessly stepped forward in defence of the Realm (. . .) *need a little bit of help.*

At this stage we are unaware of the implicature to come, but it is being prepared by the emphasis on the great sacrifice made by the men concerned in contrast to the *little* size of their need for help now. When we later learn that they are asking for £80,000 for a new coach, we are already prepared to accept the presupposition that this is a *modest request*. Thus the implicature that the National Lotteries Charity Board is mean, or in some sense too rule-bound to see the sense of granting this *little bit of help* rings through the article, even though it turns out later that as yet no letter has been received saying that the grant will be turned down. Of course, this is part of the purpose of the whole article: to shame the Lottery Board into granting the money or to claim responsibility for the change of heart when they do.

Although this kind of column is often written in the first person, this one does not use the pronoun *I* at all. Instead we are led to believe it is the 'voice' of the writer concerned by the use of informal language and contracted forms of verbs, which make it sound like spoken style:

> e.g. *a little bit of help/it looks although they'll have to/That's the cost/the new coach won't do*

In addition, it is the emotive and largely clichéd nature of much of the vocabulary which indicates that this is more than a factual report of a failed lottery bid:

> e.g. *hour of need/King and Country/maimed for life/fend for themselves/ summer afternoon outings*

It is usually much harder to discuss and describe the persuasive techniques of a passage that you agree with, than one which you take issue with. You might try this exercise on another pair of passages, where you have sympathy with the viewpoint of one and not the other. Two different newspaper editorials might provide an easy comparison, particularly on a day when they discuss the same news item. Notice the difficulty of looking dispassionately at the presuppositions and implicatures of the one that is more to your taste.

6

Contextual Meaning

6.1 Style and Manners in Interaction

As we saw in Chapter 1, language is only one of the systems of signs used by human beings to communicate with each other. We use colour to indicate danger (red) and mourning (black or white, depending on cultural context), and we use symbols to show when an answer is correct (✓) and when it is incorrect (✗). These are quite conscious uses of an alternative to language, though language is often used alongside them.

There are other, less conscious, ways in which we communicate with each other by symbolic means. These other systems may be exploited consciously, but are very often subconscious expressions of who we are, or think we are, or would like other people to think we are!

Although they are not, strictly speaking, part of the English language, these symbolic systems often work very closely with the linguistic systems. In just the same way that Chapter 2 showed how regional accents and even voice quality can affect the meaning of a message, so the general appearance and clothes of a speaker can communicate meaning, whether intentionally or not.

We draw conclusions from the dark suit and expensive tie of a business man, about his conformity to the 'dress code' of his career. We may notice the difference between a receptionist and a shop assistant, even when they are on their lunch breaks, by the smart suit of the former and the uniform of the latter. We might avoid walking too near to people dressed in a manner that signals aggression, such as cropped hair and big boots. We may categorise people according to whether they wear short skirts, leather jackets, gold chains, over-large jumpers, etc. And, of course, we may or may not be right in the assumptions based upon these categorisations.

So the posh woman in the smart blue suit and large hat might turn out not to be the snob he had assumed. And the young woman with dreadlocks and a dirty calf-length skirt ending in tassles may not be the lazy layabout they thought. Nevertheless, like all stereotypes and oversimplified clichés, these assumptions are based partly on experience and function to allow us to operate in a very complex social world where we meet new people all the time.

The linguistic parallel of dress-sense is the kind of language we choose to use in any particular situation. There are two issues here. One the one hand, we may choose to use language that is socially seen as inappropriate to the situation in which it occurs. On the other hand we may (choose to) use language that gives us an 'image' in very much the same way that our clothes tell other people something about us.

Taking appropriateness first, we could imagine examples where people were out to shock, embarrass, impress or even just to make a statement about their identity or their attitude to the current situation. For example, a young person going for a job interview would be expected to use all the polite forms and relatively formal language as in the following opening exchange:

Receptionist: *Good morning, can I help you?*
Candidate: *Yes, my name is Amy Hughes. I'm here for an interview with Mr Wright.*
Receptionist: *That's fine. You're a little early. Would you like a coffee while you're waiting?*
Candidate: *Yes please. Milk and no sugar thank you.*

A candidate who arrived and behaved in the following way would be interpreted as not knowing – or not caring about – the usual forms of address and politeness in English:

Receptionist: *Good morning, can I help you?*
Candidate: *Yea man! I'm Amy, but my friends call me 'aimless'. I'm here to see a geezer called Wright. Get him on the blower would you?*
Receptionist: *You're a little early. Would you like a coffee while you're waiting?*
Candidate: *Yeuch! Can't drink that stuff man!*

There are many issues surrounding appropriateness and language. After all the English-speaking world is vast and culturally diverse, so that different styles may be appropriate for different speakers. Nevertheless, it remains true that people can communicate information about themselves by choices that go against the prevailing cultural expectations, either unwittingly or consciously.

To take one further example, imagine a fairly well-to-do middle-class and middle-aged woman entering the scene of a rave (party) – perhaps to search for a missing child:

Woman: *Excuse me, I wonder if you have seen a girl with long blonde hair recently?*
Dancer: *Yo! There's a whole stack of long-haired dudes in here.*
Woman: *Of course, I'm sorry – I should have been more specific. She's wearing a pair of those big boots in bright red.*
Dancer: *DMs? . . .*

Without knowing whether the dancer takes against her for her accent and choice of formal and polite language, we can surmise that the dancer makes conclusions about the differences exhibited by the older woman. She doesn't know the name for Doc Martens (the fashion boot worn by many young people in England in the 1980s and 1990s). Neither does she use the same street language as the young woman. As well as dating her, this shows her lack of membership of the young people's 'club'.

The second way in which our language 'labels' us as people is in our choice of vocabulary and structures in a more general way. This can take effect in a number of dimensions, including age, geography, class, background, gender and education. The most common of everyday expressions can give away a lot of information about us. For example, the way that we say something is 'good' can indicate that we are quite old-fashioned (or old!), up to date, lower class, etc.:

That's absolutely spiffing/ace/brill/wicked/bleeding wonderful/bad.

Similarly, our vocabulary for referring to other groups of people may show us to be sexist, racist, politically correct, etc.:

She's a tasty girl/a nigger/a lovely person.

And we may choose to show different sides of our personalities to different groups of people. Thus some men might join in with the 'lads' when they describe women in demeaning ways (*look at the tits on that!*), but behave very differently in the company of women (*I think she's beautiful and intelligent*). This is not as hypocritical as it seems, though it does not mean that I excuse racism or sexism. However, in many ways we *are* different people in different situations. Most of us, after all, do put on a smarter outfit for an interview than we would wear at home. And language is just the same.

There are, of course, in addition to the linguistic 'clothes' we choose to wear, some features of our language that are almost in-built. These include regional and social dialects which work with accent (Chapter 2) to give the speaker an 'image' that hearers will interpret according to their own identity and background – or their prejudices. Although on the whole there is little we can do about these permanent features of our language, they do contribute to the message we communicate when we speak or write to others.

It is this aspect of meaning, above all, that illustrates the reader's or hearer's part in the interpretation of communication. If the reader/hearer comes from the same area as the speaker, and has a positive attitude towards his/her home, then the effect of, say, a Geordie dialect will be one of familiarity and comfort. If, by contrast, the reader/hearer either has a very sour view of the home area or comes from another area completely, it may be the case that the dialect has a very negative effect. There are some social and cultural meanings attached to dialects in Britain that are based on prejudice, but are nevertheless real for all that. Many urban dialects, such as those spoken in Birmingham or Liverpool, can be interpreted as indicating stupidity or lack of taste. Although as linguists we would defend all dialects (and accents) as equally valid, in the real world such stereotypes unfortunately have real meaning. Similarly, rural dialects whose vocabulary includes words foreign to Standard English may suffer from a stigma of being quaint but old-fashioned, or even backward.

Another contextual feature of meaning that is subject to regional and cultural differences is body language. Although it is not, strictly speaking, *part* of any language like English, there are some aspects of posture and gesture which seem to be more closely connected to language than others. If we saw a woman greeting a man at a railway station and could not hear what they were saying, it might well look very similar whether they were speakers of English, Spanish, German or Russian. On the other hand, it might not. Cultural differences in such standard settings as greetings can be very great. It was a ritual for a close Spanish friend of mine to kiss me when I arrived at her house when I hardly knew her, but as we got closer, the kissing became less frequent. I think the opposite would happen in my particular kind of British English society where I only kiss very good friends and then only when I have not seen them for a while or when they are going away.

Although we cannot claim that particular body language is intrinsically English, like the 'rules for speaking' and other contextual features of meaning, it can be so tied up with the language that it would be difficult to ignore its contribution to meaning.

Here we will only consider in detail the most language-based aspects of body language, passing over more quickly the less obviously communicative types. Notice that the distinction between communicative and non-communicative types of body language is not an absolute distinction and could never be so. Whilst some body language is very clearly equivalent to language and can be seen as a kind of substitute for language, at the other extreme, some body language is not only not intended as communication, but is not decoded as meaningful in any conscious way either. Despite this apparent distinction, most body language falls somewhere between these two extremes with intention being very difficult to prove and decoding often being at a fairly subconscious level.

Let us set aside, then, the kinds of body movements, facial expressions and gestures that only highly trained professionals such as psychiatrists would try to interpret and concentrate on those that are clearly understood by the average speaker of English.* Non-verbal behaviour may communicate significant information about emotions, speech, individual differences and interpersonal relationships, depending on the particular situational context. The areas of body language that tend to be involved in such non-verbal

---

*As I have already pointed out, the boundaries of body language behaviour are not the same as the boundaries of languages, thus there will be some English-speaking communities that do not recognise themselves in what follows as well as some non-English-speaking communities that do.

communication include: facial expression, gaze, pupil dilation, interpersonal distance, posture and gesture. They are, of course, very difficult to study, partly because of the difficulty of observing and notating the interplay of all of the different kinds of body language that occur together. Nevertheless, researchers have found some specific examples of apparently meaningful movements that can be observed fairly readily.

One of these is known as 'postural congruence' which refers to the mutual positioning of people who are talking together in a pair or a group. Research has shown that when there is good rapport (such as in a chat between a lively group of friends), the participants will often be seated in a mirror-image of each other's posture. Thus they will have opposite legs crossed or the opposite arm raised, etc. Bad rapport seems to be emphasised, if not communicated, by postural incongruence, i.e. by people adopting radically different positions such as one leaning forward and one leaning back or one with crossed legs and one with legs splayed out. There is apparently no clear 'meaning' for identical positions, though these anyway happen very much less than the others.

Posture as a form of non-verbal communication is in general much more radical in its messages than gesture. For example, if you see a friend standing under a hanging basket of flowers, completely unaware that they have just been watered and are likely to 'rain' on her, you will probably point to the basket at the same time as telling your friend about the imminent downpour. On the other hand, if you noticed instead that the hanging basket was hanging by a frayed rope that looked in danger of breaking at any moment, you would probably use your whole body (as well as the pointing arm/hand) to indicate the danger. Notice that the metaphorical use of the words 'posture' and 'gesture' reflect this difference in seriousness. Thus we may say that the government has made a 'gesture' towards clearing up crime, meaning that there has been little serious progress. If, however, we say that the government has adopted a 'posture' to eradicate crime, we may remain cynical about the outcome or motives, but we are nevertheless acknowledging the government's more widespread approach.

Whilst it is difficult to categorise non-verbal communication according to its physical properties, it has proved useful to look at different categories of function, in relation to language. Ekman and

Friesen (1969) suggested that linguistically relevant non-verbal communication (NVC for short) could be divided into three categories called 'emblems', 'illustrators' and 'regulators'. The emblems would be the most language-like of the NVC, having a direct translation into the local language. Thus nodding or shaking of the head is accepted to mean *yes* and *no* respectively in English-speaking (and many other) speech communities. Similarly, raised shoulders and outstretched lower arms with open hands will mean *I don't know* for many speakers, and a frown with a raised first finger in front of the face will mean *don't be naughty* to many children.

Other very common types of emblems are greetings and goodbyes which may be culturally specific to small speech communities within the English-speaking world, but would very generally include waves, handshakes and smiles. The Afro-Caribbean comunity, for example, have a number of different greetings, based on handslapping with formulaic spoken phrases such as *Gimme five!* Notice that the kind of greeting you give someone will depend very much on your relationship, where you are and how long since you saw that person. Thus you may hug and kiss your mother if you have not seen her for a few weeks, but it is unlikely if you only saw her five minutes ago. On the other hand, you would probably never hug your bank manager, unless s/he happened to also be your uncle or aunt. We also tend to adapt to other people's emblematic habits, so that white friends of West Indian people might adopt the *Gimme five!* type greetings.

Notice that these gestures and expressions often occur in a particular combination when they are used as emblems. Although they often occur simultaneously with speech, their equivalence with language means that they can be used in the absence of speech and this is particularly useful to overcome distance and background noise or to communicate with people with loss of hearing. Another very common use of emblems is as an insult. Insulting by gesture has the added advantage over spoken insults that it can be delivered at a distance, giving the insulted person less chance of catching the offender! The two-fingered sign, translating directly as *fuck off*, is the commonest of these insults, though there are many others, some of which are restricted to sub-groups of English speakers who share a particular code.

The second group of NVC communicators are called 'illustrators'. These occur simultaneously with speech and usually have the function of emphasising or underlining the points being made by the speaker. Thus a speaker who is angry and accusing a hearer of various misdemeanours might stab the air in the direction of the hearer for every 'crime' being described. These gestures would probably coincide with the stressed parts of each crime:

*You **always** criticize my driving, you **never** encourage me to do what I'm interested in and you glaze over **every time** I start to talk about my father.*

Other illustrators occur when we are trying to describe the shape or size of something, when we will use our hands to illustrate what we mean. Not all illustrators are so obviously iconic in this way, since we may use our hands to show regularity or order by using a 'chopping' motion with both hands together and we may use movements of our head to emphasise the moments of our speech that will also be vocally stressed.

Whilst illustrators seem to occur more in face-to-face interactions than in remote situations such as giving directions on the phone, nevertheless we still employ them even when we know that the hearer cannot see them. This implies that there may be an *en*coding as well as a *de*coding function to illustrators, i.e. speakers get some assistance in formulating their language from their own body and face movements. More complex tasks often show an increase in illustrators, implying that they have an encoding function in this situation.

The last group of non-verbal communicators is known as 'regulators'. These were introduced in section 5.4 as having the function of helping to guide and control the conduct and flow of the conversation, usually in accordance with the local 'rules for speaking' such as the no-overlap rule, or the conventions excluding interruption in many conversations. The regulators work in conjunction with vocal cues and indications such as the use of a long falling intonation pattern to indicate that the speaker is coming to the end of her turn, or the vocalisations that are used to support the current speaker and are often written as *uh-huh* or *mmm*. Like the vocal regulators, the non-verbal ones have different functions including the following:

Turn-yielding cues
These include the termination of hand gestures so that the sudden stillness of the speaker indicates her or his readiness to let another person speak. The speaker may also look pointedly at the person selected to be the next speaker, though this will often accompany a clear linguistic cue, such as a question.

Attempt-suppressing cues
When speakers are being interrupted but do not want to yield the turn, they may start gesticulating more intensively, to indicate that they are keeping the turn.

Back-channel
These are the non-threatening support mechanisms by which hearers show speakers that though they are not claiming the turn, they are nevertheless listening closely. As well as the vocal supporting phrases mentioned above, the hearers may nod or shake their heads, use facial expressions of interest and attention and even on occasion gesture their reaction to what is being said. Not all back-channel is supportive, though. The hearers may show boredom or lack of interest by looking away for long periods, or nodding or shaking their heads in disagreement rather than in solidarity with the speaker. In both positive and negative forms, however, back-channel is non-threatening to the speaker's right to the turn. Notice that the nodding and shaking of heads is ambiguous between emblems, where a very clear *yes* or *no* is intended and regulators, where either can be used to mean things like *how awful* or to show agreement with a negative:

> *That was an awful winter last year.* [hearer shakes head to indicate 'yes, awful']
> *You can't trust her.* [hearer nods head to indicate 'yes, I agree, you can't']

The other way in which hearers can use regulators is in indicating that they would like to take the turn from the current speaker. They might do this by turning their head away briefly from the speaker before turning back and trying to get the turn. Or they might begin to gesture quite actively to show that they have something to say.

There are, of course, enough types and variations of non-verbal communication to fill a book or two on their own. This section has attempted to introduce the most language-like types of non-verbal communicative behaviour, to demonstrate that language is the centre of a much wider network of symbolic meanings in human contexts.

Activity: linguistic style and non-verbal communication
Use the topic of greetings and goodbyes to focus on the different linguistic fashions people adopt. Try observing throughout a whole day the different people you come into contact with and how the differences in age, status, background, etc., affect the way that you interact with them. Notice whether, and how much, your own style changes in response to the people around you. Incidentally, you might also take note of the non-linguistic signs that you respond to in each person, such as their dress, hairstyle, vehicle choice, etc.

There are a number of non-verbal communication exercises that illustrate the contribution body language makes to interaction. Try, for example, sitting back-to-back with a friend and trying to discuss something of mutual interst, such as a television programme you have both watched, or some gossip that concerns a mutual friend! If there is a third person available, ask them to observe your body language, including leg and arm movements, head movements and whole body posture. Another exercise is to have a face-to-face conversation, but sitting on your hands. Ask a third person to observe what compensating body movements you make and when you have finished, discuss with the other person involved how you both felt, deprived of hand movements. In a larger group, you can ask different observers to watch for emblems, illustrators or regulators, or to concentrate on different parts of the body, including facial expression. Notice how difficult it is to notate the complex set of movements that make up body language as a whole.

Discussion
Your typical day of greetings and goodbyes might have included items like those shown in Table 6.1. Notice how many conversations do not seem to start and end with overt greetings and goodbyes. With people you know well, the dress and other non-linguistic clues are taken as signs of temporary and current states of mind, health and so on. With people you have only just met, the tendency is to

Table 6.1

Person	My greeting	Their greeting	My goodbye	Their goodbye	Non-linguistic trait
Bus-driver on new type of bus	City Square	68p	Thank you	Ta luv	flat cap – not smart as Yorkshire Rider buses – does it reflect standard of driving?
Colleague	Hi there! OK?	Hello. Yes, fine. You?	See you tomorrow	Yeh, s'pose so!	wearing suit – trying to impress someone? In for promotion?
Student	Come in, Susan. Sit down.	Can I have a quick word?	Right, let me know how it goes.	Thanks, I'll see you later.	Baggy dress – pregnant?

draw conclusions about long-term characteristics of personality and outlook. This is clearly unfair, but nevertheless true!

In trying exercises which prevent you using one type of body language, you may have felt deprived of that facility and frustrated as a result. The restrictions affect some people more than others. In some cases, people become painfully aware of how much the gesturing or eye-contact contribute to the encoding or turn-taking processed and find that the conversation is more stilted and full of silences as a result. The need for eye-contact when possible sometimes leads people who have done the back-to-back exercise to 'drink in' the other person's eyes for a surprisingly long time when they are allowed to turn round! This happens even when the participants are not very well known to each other.

6.2 When, Where, Who, Why and How?

Throughout this book we have been considering meaning as it appears to arise from texts and utterances, though the importance of the audience has also been reiterated a number of times. When we consider the social or cultural context in which any English text occurs, it becomes clear that some aspects of meaning are linked to features of the situation as much as, or more than, features of the text.

Let us first consider the participants. In a spoken conversation there will be at least two participants (ignoring for a moment those occasions when we talk to ourselves or to inanimate objects such as the washing machine!). The social background, education, occupation, regional origin, gender and possibly sexuality of the participants may influence relatively permanent aspects of their language. Many of these aspects have been discussed in other chapters. They have all, so far, been treated as affecting formal features of language, mostly below the level of the sentence. There are other linguistic consequences of having a particular background, which are discussed here.

The participants in any interaction will all be members of a number of 'speech communities'. The term 'speech-community' was first used by Dell Hymes (1972) who was working in a branch of linguistics arising from anthropology and which was interested in the ways in which people spoke to each other in different cultures. It seemed to Hymes and other researchers that some of the communities they studied had very different 'rules for speaking' from each other and from the American communities they were familiar with. Whilst the turn-taking and co-operative principles outlined in Chapter 5 may have some universal application, it may be that they are only typical of the data from which they were drawn.

Thus, devices for speaker-selection and Grice's maxims for co-operating might well differ in communities speaking languages other than English and, indeed, in some English-speaking communities too. There are some communities which have strikingly different rules for interrupting and tolerance of silences compared with English and English-speaking American cultures. We, on the whole, find silences uncomfortable and interruptions rude. Others may find silences polite or companionable and interruptions supportive or flattering.

Dell Hymes's notion of speech-community was based on observations of Native American groups whose culture differed very markedly from the dominant surrounding culture. He defined a speech-community as sharing the same rules for speaking and at least one linguistic variety. Later, a more complex notion of overlapping speech-communities was developed (notably by Savile-Troike, 1982) and this was found to be a useful way to model the linguistic habits of late twentieth-century human beings. On the basis of the Hymes version of speech-communities, most readers of this book would presumably label themselves as belonging to a community called something like 'British English' or 'American English'. I hope there will also be some Welsh-speaking readers who are simultaneously part of the Welsh speech-community and the British English one. There are also Italian, Gujerati and Swahili speakers who belong to English-speaking communities. The 'rules for speaking' may well differ for the different communities that a bilingual speaker inhabits. It may be that in speaking English, the speaker will use more overt politeness markers during transactions in shops or cafes than, for example, in Spanish, which appears to be much more economical and business-like on these occasions.

If bilingual speakers belong simultaneously to more than one speech-community, might other speakers also have similar multiple membership of groups defined by shared dialect, register or other specific variety? Someone who speaks a particular regional dialect as well as Standard English may find that they change not only their vocabulary, grammar and pronunciation when swapping between dialects, but also change their ways of interacting to match. Thus a regional dialect, such as Yorkshire English or Geordie (from the north-east of England) is associated with casual situations since it tends to use fewer politeness markers and may well have 'rules for speaking' that forgive interruption more readily than does Standard English.

The implication of this multiple membership of speech-communities for our concern with meaning is that the 'meaning' of a particular interactive behaviour, such as talking simultaneously with another current speaker, means different things in different contexts. Using an item of vocabulary associated with a particular trade or profession outside that community may well appear to mean something like *you are not part of this group* at the same time as conveying its literal meaning (for those who understand it). Thus a speaker (K) who belongs to a speech-community concerned with ballet, might attend a performance with colleagues (A and B) from the bank who have never been to the ballet before:

A: *Wasn't all that jumping exciting!*

K: *Yes, the grand jetés were really good and their entrechats were mostly excellent. (Addressing B) What did you think of the adage section?*

B: *I preferred the long, slow stuff myself.*

Whilst the conversation can limp on in this fashion, A and B might be justified in feeling a little irritated by K's inappropriate use of technical terms which they have never met. K is flouting Grice's maxim on clarity, which in this context 'means' that she is showing off. Since K's comments, including technical vocabulary, would be quite at home in the right community, it could also be seen as K operating with the wrong set of 'rules for speaking', which for non-specialist theatre-goers include the rule: 'Use general terms rather than technical vocabulary'.

Most of us, then, belong to a number of speech-communities, which might include some of the following, but might consist of an entirely different set:

pregnant mother
parent of toddler (or school-age child, college student, etc.)
carpenter/joiner, plumber, builder, plasterer, etc.
music-lover, theatre-goer
cook
cricket enthusiast (or soccer, American football, baseball, athletics, etc.)
political activist, pressure-group member, school governor, town councillor
doctor, lawyer, schoolteacher, priest, etc.
Hindu, Muslim, Christian, Buddhist, Jewish, etc.

There, are, of course, many more lists that could be added, until the whole complexity of modern life is revealed.

As well as the identity of the participants in any conversation, there are other factors which might influence aspects of the interaction to produce a complete social and textual context. Some of these factors have been introduced in earlier sections and chapters, but they are revisited here to enable us to see the overall picture of how texts fit into their wider context.

Dell Hymes introduced a mnemonic using the word SPEAKING,

to represent the different factors influencing the interaction in a conversation. There could be other, perfectly adequate ways of structuring the same information (i.e. other models), but we will accept Hymes's version as one useful alternative:

Situation (including setting and scene)
Participants (who the participants are and their relationship)
Ends (outcomes and goals)
Act sequence (what is said and how, i.e. form and content)
Key/manner
Instrumentalities (channel and form
Norms (of interaction)
Genres

What Hymes has labelled the 'Act sequence' is what we normally think of as the 'text', so it is clear that he was envisaging language as operating in a very rich context in which the other seven factors have a role. Let us imagine an interaction between a male stockbroker and his female secretary. Their gender, background and status differences will probably produce certain permanent linguistic characteristics, but we are concerned here with the meanings arising out of a particular conversation between them. When he enquires of her what she is doing at the weekend, she may interpret his question in a number of ways, including:

- A polite, but patronising enquiry from a boss who thinks he should demonstrate an interest in his 'inferiors'.
- An implicit request for her to take some work home at the weekend.
- An unhealthy or intrusive interest in her sexual or social life.
  A desperate plea for company from a lonely man.

And so on, depending on what happened last week or five minutes earlier, who her other bosses have been, whether she likes him, what she actually *is* doing at the weekend etc. Whilst all of these, and many more meanings may be 'read' in an utterance, and possibly acted upon, it is possible that the boss intended one of these meanings (Hymes's Ends: goal) and not the others. However, the secretary may misread the boss's goal and get hold of the 'wrong' meaning (Hymes's Ends: outcome). And more confusingly still, since human beings are notoriously self-deluding, he may have consciously intended one of these meanings and subconsciously intended another! He may, for example, have thought that it was appropriate for him as the boss, to demonstrate their shared humanity, despite the difference in power. Nevertheless, he may have other reasons, such as finding her attractive, for wanting to know what she was doing at the weekend. These more self-interested meanings may or may not be suppressed by him.

In addition to the participants and their relationship, there are other contextual features to be considered. Where did the interaction take place, for example (Hymes's **Situation**: setting)? And what else was going on at the time (Hymes's **Situation**: scene)? This invented interaction between a boss and his secretary would very likely have different 'meanings' associated with it if it appeared that the boss entered the secretary's office specifically for the purpose of asking the question rather than using it as a casual enquiry to relieve the tension in a lift.

Let us consider another example, this time between a parent and a teenage child. The parent asks: *What time did you get in last night?* The child, depending on his or her interpretation of the question might answer with one of the following:

Midnight, like you told me to. Why don't you trust me?
I had to wait ages for a bus, so I was a bit late.
Exactly 12.15. I remember looking at my watch and I didn't notice anything odd then.

The last response might occur when a family is discussing the likely timing of a burglary, whilst the first and second are more common negative and neutral interpretations of the question as being a check on the child's obedience to the rules laid down by the parent.

Clearly, the written language is different from the spoken one in a number of ways, but nevertheless the background of the writer and reader, their relationship to each other and their previous experience will all contribute to the reader's interpretation of the text. Thus a reader who has always believed in the honesty and integrity of published material, including newspapers, may interpret a fantastic and largely invented tabloid newspaper story as being a factual piece of news. On the other hand, a critical reader, aware of the political affiliations of the newspaper, may interpret the same story as an attempt to discredit the politician concerned for political ends.

So the perceived authority of a published text and the relationship between writer and reader of a letter or a note may be seen as contributing to meaning in just the same way as the power difference between a doctor and a patient or a teacher and a pupil. The place and circumstance of reading a written text are also important to the meaning. So, a love-letter read in the thick of a relationship will have a different meaning to one read, or re-read, after a bitter split between the writer and reader. Similarly, the reader of a novel about the Second World War will construct different meanings depending on whether they are directly affected by the events of that time (e.g. survivors and families of victims of the Holocaust) or view it as distant history.

The situational context of production and reception of a text or utterance is also relevant to its meaning or interpretation. The two processes are more separate for the written than the spoken language, but there are nevertheless important implications for both if we ask the question 'why'?

Why did a lover write that letter? Why did the recipient read it/throw it away/burn it when it arrived? Why did s/he read it again years later? Why did the novelist write a war novel? Why have I chosen to read it? Why did you ask me if I wanted a cup of tea? Why did her Mum phone to ask what the weather was like?

The answers to these questions might be straightforward, but will depend on many personal and contextual features. The novelist might have chosen a subject s/he knows a great deal about to exorcise deeply troubling memories. Or s/he may have thought it was time s/he learnt more about the war and settled down to some in-depth research. The reader might have chosen to read the novel to learn about the war in a relatively 'entertaining' way by choosing a fictionalised account rather than a history book, or might just have picked it up at the airport. Or s/he might be studying it as part of a 'literature of war' course.

The final question we might ask of the context in which a text is interpreted is 'how?' There is a very wide range of contextual features that could be subsumed under this question, but they share an interest in the 'manner' in which a text is received. At one end of the spectrum this is very close to the 'why?' question. For example, the novelist will approach the material of a novel in a manner that reflects the reason for writing it. Nevertheless, we could still in principle distinguish between a writer with experience or knowledge of the war who decided to write in the first person ('I') and a writer with similar background who decided to create some distance by writing in the third person ('s/he').

If we look at the spoken language, the question 'how?' again seems to address issues of stylistic choice, relating them to the contextual pressures on the speakers to make particular choices. In section 6.1 we looked at fashion and image in language as being partly a socially dictated phenomenon and partly an individual statement of image. The question of how we communicate in the spoken language (i.e. which stylistic choices we make) is also partly context-driven and partly individual choice. Thus we may not feel able to use our most natural language when talking about parts of our body to the family doctor because we know that the words we use are not technical and might make us seem childish or immature. On the other hand, we may decide for one of a number of reasons to challenge the perceived authority of the doctor and try to treat him/her as an equal by using more down-to-earth or colloquial terms than the formality of the situation seems to dictate.

Activity: speech-communities

The most useful way to conceptualise the interaction of simultaneous speech-community memberships is to think about your own array of speech-communities and work out how they affect your linguistic behaviour. Make a list of all the speech-communities you currently belong to, however large or small. Add speech-communities you have once belonged to, but perhaps 'grew out of' either literally or metaphorically.

Choose a particular conversation you have had in the last week and try to identify the characteristics of the context according to Hymes's SPEAKING acronym. Assess whether there could be more than one answer to some of the questions, according to whether you or the person you were talking to answered them, or according to whether you (or the other person) are being entirely honest about motivation or intention.

Discussion

My own current membership of speech communities is partly described in Table 6.2, with examples of linguistic features associ-

Table 6.2

Speech-community	Examples of linguistic features
University	*modularisation, semesterisation, CATs*
Linguistics	*bilabial plosive, Transformational Grammar, . . .*
London	*let the tea draw* (i.e. brew or stand), . . .
School (governor)	*LMS* (local management of schools), *standard number* (i.e. intake to school), *pupil number adjustment* (changes to budget in light of pupil number changes), . . .
Parent	*how many times have I told you?*, . . .
Ballet-goer	*pliés, pirouettes, assemblés, . . .*
Singer/music community	*crescendo, ritardando, da capo, . . .*
Spanish (as a foreign language)	*me hace gracia, que hora es, . . .*
French (as a foreign language)	*lundi, qu'est ce que c'est, . . .*

ated with the variety of language spoken in that community. With the exception of the foreign language communities, the varieties overlap to a large extent, apart from their specialist vocabulary. Note that membership of these groups can be temporary. Thus, although I was once a Girl Guide, it is twenty-five years since I had any contact with that particular speech-community and I am no longer an active speaker of their variety. I am unaware of whether they still talk about *patrols* and *pow-wows* and whether their leaders are known as *Captain* anymore! Similarly with speech communities that we are likely to pass through, such as the speech-community of carers of young babies. The only people who are constantly in touch with the language and rapidly changing technology of the baby world are those whose jobs require this knowledge, such as nannies and nursery assistants.

This afternoon I had a conversation with my mother about what she could buy my children for Christmas. If I analysed this conversation in accordance with the SPEAKING acronym, the analysis would look like Table 6.3.

6.3 Whose Meaning is it Anyway?

The traditional view of where meaning resides is that it is somehow 'in' the text. The readers or hearers are then more or less able to

Table 6.3

Contextual feature	As applied to this conversation
Situation	long-distance phone call, child needing attention in the background
Participants	myself and my mother
Ends	to decide on presents (goal) to leave the conversation in order to attend to child (outcome)
Act sequence	(transcription of call would fit here)
Key/manner	jovial (mother) perfunctory (me)
Instrumentalities	spoken language (channel), Southern English dialect (form)
Norms	British informal conversational norms
Genres	casual speech

interpret the text 'correctly' depending on their social or geographical background, period of history, knowledge or skill. This model of text meaning allows for different text-types that require different skills or background for successful interpretation to occur. For example, a written text of the Tudor period might contain words or phrases referring to items not so common nowadays like *codpiece* or *stock-fish* (unsalted, cured cod). Its successful interpretation, therefore, depends on the understanding of this historically restricted vocabulary. Similarly, a spoken conversation between friends might rely on the shared knowledge that forms the background of the friendship. Eavesdroppers will not know who *she* and *he* refer to in the following snippet:

A: *I told him that he was a fool to risk it.*
B: *And I'd heard her saying the same.*

However, what is not being questioned about text meaning in this model is whether there is, in fact, such a thing as successful interpretation – or 'full' interpretation. If we imagine the traditional model characterises linguistic meaning as a box of coloured beads, then the speaker/writer gets out a number of beads and arranges them in a tray with certain shaped compartments. The successful interpreter of the text will pick up *all* the beads and arrange them in an identical pattern in his or her own identical compartmentalised tray.

Whilst we may take this model of text meaning for granted on a daily basis, it has been questioned more and more persistently in the late half of the twentieth century by linguists, philosophers and literary scholars amongst others. In response to the work of people like Barthes and Bakhtin, meaning has recently been located nearer to the recipient's end of the transaction. The originator provides a text, possibly, though not always, with a clear meaning in mind. The argument is that the relevant meaning is the one that is received by the hearer/reader and it follows from this that interpretations differ with each individual receiver.

Let us return for a moment to the box of coloured beads. Under this new model, the speaker/writers get out a number of beads and arrange them as before. But it may also be that a few beads are spilt or escape unnoticed while the speaker/writers are busy arranging the beads they have chosen. It may also be that they decide to offer a range of optional beads that the reader/hearer may decide to choose or not. The interpretation involves the reader/hearer picking up some of the beads on offer, possibly including the spilt and the optional ones, but also possibly excluding some of those consciously chosen by the speaker/writers. The recipient may then arrange the beads in an identical, similar or completely different pattern, according to the shape and compartments of the trays available.

Of course, we might assume that the recipient whose resulting arrangement of beads is very far from the original is simply 'getting it wrong'. This model might well agree that 'being wrong' is in fact a rather extreme case of getting a different meaning from the text. But different from whose? It would no longer be the originator of the text who has the last word on its meaning. But we might hypothesise a kind of 'consensus' of meaning from which 'wrong' interpretations simply diverge too far. This 'consensus' would vary, of course, from place to place and from time to time. An interesting, though rather worrying example is the case of Salman Rushdie's novel *The Satanic Verses*, which presumably had a very different meaning for parts of the Muslim community who were outraged by it, than it did for other readers. The result of his alleged blasphemy was that Rushdie was put under a sentence of death by the then ruler of Iran and will probably live partly in hiding for the rest of his life.

The question that arises from Rushdie's story for this section is whether we can say that the blasphemy is not 'there' because Rushdie did not intend it. Given a liberal outlook which is horrified by the idea of death penalties, we may want to say *yes* and privilege Rushdie's own intended textual meaning. However, the same argument may not be well-received by the same people when a different text and a different area of sensitivity is involved. When people subscribe to a mild form of political correctness (as I admit I do), they are usually concerned not to offend or upset people belonging to traditionally oppressed groups like ethnic minorities, women or people with disabilities. But how do they answer the man who claims that using a term like *girl* to or about adult women is not intended to offend and therefore should not offend. Or the people who say they have always used the word *Paki* to refer to Asian shop owners and they really like them – *thank goodness they're always open when the supermarkets are shut!*

This kind of offensive language is rapidly becoming a new taboo in English-speaking societies. The phrase 'taboo language' is, strictly speaking, a contradiction, since *taboo* normally refers to subjects that societies do not mention. However, the anomaly is actually rather accurate because, throughout the human world, people have found linguistic ways of referring to the unmentionable.

Taboos in society change through time and reflect the values, politics and morality of the place and time. For example, though there are still taboos surrounding sex and bodily functions in Western society, they are not as strong as they were in Victorian Britain. Other taboo subjects may include death and disease, religion and race.

The taboo surrounding disease has largely faded during the twentieth century in Britain, but there have been fluctuations in the strength of a number of taboos during this period. For example, the 1950s saw a post-war backlash against many of the freedoms of action and expression that had occurred as a result of the mixing of sexes and classes in the war effort. Women were encouraged to return from the workplace to their traditional place in the home, and in middle-class families there was some success in convincing women that this was their true position. In her poem 'Litany', Carol Ann Duffy captures some of the taboos that grew up amongst the housewives of that decade:

_ An embarrassing word, broken

to bits, which tensed the air like an accident.
This was the code I learnt at my mother's knee, pretending
to read, where no one had cancer, or sex, or debts,
and certainly not leukaemia, which no one could spell.

(Duffy, 1993, p. 9)

We may no longer feel the need to spell words to do with sex,
money or disease, and I have not heard anyone call cancer *the big C*
for a long time, but this does not mean that there are no taboos in
our society. As we have become more relaxed about bodily issues,
other social pressures have arisen, concerning our attitudes to
groups of people different from us. It has already been pointed out
that the growth of political correctness in the second half of the
twentieth century reflects an increasing consciousness of how language can demonstrate our prejudices to our hearers and can hurt
those concerned. So we have become more aware of inequalities in
the way we name women as opposed to men, black people as
opposed to white people, people with disabilities as opposed to
people without disabilities and so on.

There are large areas of disagreement about whether it is desirable
and/or possible to change the English language to avoid this kind of
offence. However, the move to eradicate such prejudice seems to be
gaining ground in the last years of the twentieth century as some
major groups of people (most obviously in the middle classes) find
themselves less and less likely to use terms which might offend (e.g.
coloured, spastic, lady doctor) and more and more likely to overlook
sexual or body-related words which used to have a strong taboo
(e.g. *dick, fuck, orgasm, vagina*).

If the problems of political correctness illustrate the flaws in
adhering to either the textual or the recipient extreme of where
meaning is located, there may be a kind of compromise model that
can take into account both the originator's intended meaning and
the recipient's constructed meaning. We may accept that the creator
of a text has an idea of what the text communicates, but we also have
to be aware that this does not constitute the whole meaning of the
text, since different recipients will draw different meanings from it.
The meaning of a text is thus seen as flexible within a certain range
that is defined by the text itself. Paul Simpson (1993) puts it simply:

The stance adopted throughout this book has been that the producers of texts *do* mean things when they say things, but that the negotiation of meanings is, in the words of Bakhtin (1981) a *dialogic* process.

Although readers in particular do not literally engage the producer of a text in a dialogue about the meaning of the text, it can be seen that when readers construct the meaning of a text, they are producing and revising hypotheses about the meaning as they read. You may have had the experience of being part of a group where one person is telling a story about something personal that has happened to them (betrayal by a partner, defiance from children, dependence of elderly relations, etc.). If that story is close to an experience you have had, it may 'mean' something particular to you, since at the very least it reminds you of your own experience. At this stage you may become more involved in the conversation, leaning forward and looking animated, and trying to get a turn in order to relate your own tale. The same story will communicate in a completely different way to people with no similar experiences. It might simply not interest them and leave them taking in the 'factual' content without going beneath the surface. Or it may fascinate them in a morbid kind of way, to know what problems lie in store for people in such situations.

The same kind of reaction can happen with a written text. A similar kind of content might be found, for comparison, in a chatty magazine telling 'readers' stories'. Again, the meaning of the text will differ according to the reader's own life experiences. The only difference is that readers will hold an internal dialogue about the meaning of the text and its relevance to their own lives.

Activity: negotiation of meaning and taboo
Try a longer and more complicated version of the game known as 'Chinese whispers'. You will need a group of co-operative friends to agree to take part. The aim is to send a message, perhaps a short story or piece of news, round a circle and back to its originator to see how it changes in the telling. You could do this in a classroom or you could telephone the story round a group of people, asking receivers to 'pass it on' in their own words. Ideally you need to know what happens at every stage and each version should be tape-recorded so

that you have a complete record of the way in which the story changes. Another variation would be to ask receivers to take brief notes of the story (not verbatim) and you could collect the notes in and analyse them. When you have the complete sequence of versions, assess each adjacent pair of versions to see in what way the speaker has made an interpretation of the version s/he received and how this has resulted in a different version being passed on to the next receiver. The changes might be in any level of the language (i.e. from sounds to structures) or it might be in the emphasis or priority given to different pieces of information.

Taboo language is difficult to investigate by its very nature, since people are not easily persuaded to break taboos in order to talk about them unless they are not very strong taboos. One way of approaching this topic is to find out what people were told not to talk about or say when they were young. Normally, these taboos have been broken later and are therefore easier to speak about. Interviews with people from a range of different age-groups could be based on questions like the following:

- What words would you have been told off for saying when you were young? (if you don't feel able to say them still, can you hint at what they were?)
- Which words make you feel uncomfortable when you hear them said? (e.g. words describing bodily functions, sexual activity, people of various races or backgrounds, women or men, people with disabilities, death or disease, religious words)
- How would you tell someone that a mutual friend had died?

Discussion

The 'chain story' which you passed round a circle should illustrate that people will take different parts of any narrative to be important as well as making their own judgements about the content of a story. The impact of the last version being so different from the first version is part of the fun when this is played as a game, but in conjunction with the evidence of each pair of narratives, it should be possible to show that the very different stories which occur first and last are nevertheless joined by a string of stories that are arguably 'the same' as the ones each side of them. This is a graphic illustration of the fact that texts have open and flexible meanings, not prejudged and closed meanings.

Although it is difficult to collect research data on the taboos of our societies, it is much easier to notice anecdotal evidence, once we have sensitised ourselves to the topic. For example, I always notice which kinds of topic people are unable to discuss aloud and start to mouth the words as if that excuses their use. One elderly 'Auntie' I know is unfortunately prey to many illnesses and understandably these provide her main topic of conversation. However, she is psychologically of the generation that Duffy's poem refers to, when disease and bodies were unmentionable. So her sentences will sometimes be half-spoken and half-mouthed when words like *bowels* or *intestines* are unavoidable. It is not only elderly people who succumb to the mouthing solution to taboos. I notice in classes full of students much younger than me, there is a tendency to mouth the 'rude' words at first, until they establish that in this context the words themselves are under the microscope. It may be my presence or the apparent formality of the classroom situation that intimidates, since these same students readily admit to using the same words amongst their friends.

6.4 Ideologies, Common Sense and Texts

As we have already seen in Chapters 4 and 5, there are some aspects of textual meaning that underlie the words, either by being implied (implicatures) or by being assumed (presuppositions). Previously we have been concerned with sentence-level implicatures and presuppositions, but it is often the case that longer texts create the conditions for these 'hidden' meanings by a build-up of topic or expectations. In order to avoid unnecessary repetition or over-explanation, texts use not only cohesive devices, but they also take advantage of the potential of presupposition and implicature for conveying meanings in addition to the entailments themselves.

Most texts, then, use these features to add meaning to their apparent literal meaning. Many examples can be found which are innocent of any ulterior purpose, but simply enable the speaker/writer to be more concise than would otherwise be possible. It is, however, very difficult to draw a clear dividing line between such 'innocent' uses of presupposition and implicature and uses which have a more didactic or persuasive purpose or effect.* The last section argued that we can make no clear division between meanings that are intended by the originator of a text and those which a 'reader' draws from the same text. Whilst many presuppositions, for example, will be largely agreed upon by the community, this may remain nothing more than a consensus and cannot automatically be labelled 'truth'. It only needs someone with a different set of beliefs or opinions to read the text for the consensus to break down and seem like nothing more than one opinion among many.

The most readily available texts which can illustrate this point are news texts. Many people believe that the reporting of the news is one of the more unbiased and 'factual' uses of language. After all, newspapers can only report what actually happened, can't they? It is difficult to remember when you are engaged in reading a news report, but in fact the language used can have a huge impact on the way the story is received. At the more neutral end of the range, we have stories which concern international events that Britain is not closely involved in:

Russia announced last night a 48-hour ceasefire in Chechenia from 8 a.m. local time today and ordered rebels to stop resistance and disarm within the two days.

A statement distributed by the Itar-Tass news agency said the decision was prompted by Moscow's desire to give a chance for a peaceful solution to the Chechen crisis.

The prime minister, Viktor Chernomyrdin, faced with mounting international condemnation that threatens to cut aid to Russia and kill his attempts to stabilise the economy, was earlier reported to have ordered military commanders to arrange a 48-hour truce in Grozny. (David Hearst, *Guardian*, 10 January 1995)

In this extract from the start of an article about the crisis in Chechenia, the writer builds upon the supposed shared knowledge that most informed readers will have accumulated during the weeks leading up to this article. So the first sentence is dependent on a

---

*Note that as a result of locating meaning in the 'dialogue' between originator and recipient it is unnecessary to distinguish between intention and effect, although sometimes it may be more clearly one or the other.

number of presuppositions that we, the readers, are assumed to know – or accept – including the following: *There has been fighting going on in Chechenia.* – presupposed by the use of the word *ceasefire*. *The rebels are armed* – presupposed by the use of *disarm*. Of course, there is a great deal of further background being assumed, but not in the firm way that characterises presuppositions. Although this article may be seen as largely uncontroversial in its reporting, it could be noted that there are some assumptions being made that could be queried by a reader. For example, the structure of the final sentence quoted insists that readers accept the *reality* of *the mounting international condemnation that threatens to cut aid to Russia*. By placing this phrase in a subordinate clause as a kind of aside, the writer is assuming the following as fact:

> *Viktor Chernomyrdin is attempting to stabilise the Russian economy.*
> *There is mounting international condemnation, etc.*
> *This condemnation threatens to cut aid to Russia*

Whilst we may accept these presuppositions, they are nevertheless presuppositions. For this reason, it is very difficult to argue against them, even if you feel that there has, in fact, been very little condemnation, compared with, for example, the outrage about the fighting in Bosnia. The sentence is not asserting these 'facts', it is assuming them in order to make the main point, which is to report Chernomyrdin's apparent ordering of the ceasefire.

Of course, this use of subordinate clauses is widespread and unavoidable as a way of setting out the background against which the proposition of a sentence is being made. It is not desirable, and certainly not possible, to write texts full of sentences that make no presuppositions or assumptions. However, it is important to be aware that no text is 'untainted' in this way. It is also useful to be able to see what kinds of information a text is taking for granted in order to decide whether you agree with its assessment. The ideas or facts that are taken for granted by a text are often known as *ideologies*.

Critical awareness of the basic ideologies of texts has been fostered in recent years by 'Critical Linguistics', whose proponents argue that all texts take certain facts or opinions for granted and in many cases the opinions become so entrenched in the community that they are eventually taken to be common sense. This 'natural-ising' of opinion, they claim, should be exposed so that reader/hearers can think for themselves about whether they wish to accept the opinion as obvious or 'common sense' – or whether they might indeed reject it.

On the same day as the article about Chechenia was published, many newspapers had articles reporting the decision of Camilla Parker-Bowles and her husband, Andrew Parker-Bowles, to divorce. The scandal of her alleged long-term affair with Prince Charles had been headline news on earlier occasions, so many reports were able to make assumptions about the level of knowledge most readers would have. This extract from a commentary in the *Sun* newspaper illustrates the ways in which opinions can be reported as facts:

> Brigadier Andrew Parker-Bowles silently bore the humiliation of his wife's affair with Prince Charles for 20 years – until it all finally became too much.

Whilst the overwhelming view of the press on that day seemed to be that he was an innocent victim, those readers with some experience or knowledge of these matters, perhaps wondered whether there was another side to the story of the Parker-Bowles' marriage. These texts, however, steeped as they are in traditional family values, assume that the monogamy of traditional English marriages is sacrosanct and that the affair between Camilla and Charles must therefore be a humiliation to Andrew Parker-Bowles. By placing the *humiliation* into an object following the verb *bear*, the writer makes no allowance for the reader having a different perspective on the situation.

The tabloid press in Britain often bases its reporting on 'common-sense' assumptions like these. It may be assuming the agreement of its readership rather than trying actively to change their views or persuade them to adopt a certain outlook. However, the effect is often to offer regular readers a 'world view', built in to the pre-suppositions of the reporting rather than asserted as one opinion among many. As the last section argued, readers may well negotiate the meaning of the text, but it is more difficult to negotiate the common sense on which the text is based. The only way to deal with ideologies that you do not accept is to step outside the usual relationship between writer/speaker and reader/hearer and assert:

I do not accept the assumptions which underlie this text. This often happens, in particular in interviews with politicians who are wary of being tricked into admitting or accepting unpopular views.

Not all ideologies are built into texts as presuppositions. Many are much closer to implicatures, which are more elusive than presuppositions and if challenged, can be denied. An extract from a women's magazine illustrates the point:

> One thing that's certain is that there isn't just one thing that makes a girl sexy. Reading women's magazines, as I'm often wont to do, I realise you spend an awful lot of your time trying to work out exactly what makes a woman desirable to the opposite sex, searching for some kind of eternal secret of sexiness. Yet, sitting here, trying to define just what makes a woman alluring to us men, I can't come up with a magic formula for the perfect dream girl.

These sentences introduce an article in which Robert Elms, 'life and style commentator, author and TV presenter', gives the readers a male view of 'what makes a woman desirable'. Whilst I personally find the article patronising and insulting, other readers may genuinely respond to the reassurance he offers:

> Most women seem to worry about their weight, while most men find their attitude slightly mysterious. Very few of us would notice a few pounds either way and your paranoia is almost entirely self-generated. Yet there's absolutely no doubt that Roseanne carries more than a few extra pounds and still I find her sexy.

The interesting implication of this paragraph in the context of the article is that it implies that the main – or only – reason that women worry about their weight is because their *extra pounds* might make them less attractive to men. Even the expression *extra pounds* belies Elms's soothing tone – *extra* to what? There is clearly a mismatch here between what he denies is a problem on the one hand, and what on the other hand he implies is a 'norm' plus *extra*. The implication that all women are constantly on the lookout for new conquests – and always male ones – shows us that despite his protestations, Elms is really not up with the times:

> A little feminine vulnerability every now and then – to bring out the big strong man in us – spices up the dish, but at heart the truly confident girl will get me every time.

The use of the 'woman as food' metaphor is a giveaway here, implying that women are there primarily for the delectation of men. Similarly, the implication that in every man there is the 'strong protector' waiting to get out exposes an ideology of 'natural' gender differences which go back to prehistoric times. None of these assumptions is asserted directly, and many are not technically presupposed, but they are part of the text's meaning nevertheless.

Activity: ideology and common sense

Look at the following passage from *Peace News*. What are the common-sense notions that underlie the text and how are they realised (i.e. as presuppositions, implicatures, textual build-up of similar features)?

> The continued presence of US warships in the Persian Gulf has meant the constant transit of naval convoys from the US West Coast to the Gulf region, with stopovers in between for what is euphemistically known as R&R (rest and recreation). In Australia, these port calls are officially welcomed as a chance to show the flag and cement the ANZUS alliance, but above all to capitalise on all the dollars saved up by the crew sweating it out in the Gulf for months on end.
>
> A large proportion of US warships are now nuclear powered and for many years various protest fleets have taken to the water whenever a nuclear powered warship has anchored in an Australian harbour.
>
> (Peter. D Jones, *Peace News*, December 1996, p. 6)

Discussion

The context of any text may alert the reader to its likely attitude and particularly so when the publication it occurs in is as open about its approach as *Peace News*. This means that we read the word *continued* in the first sentence as implying that it is an umwelcome presence in the view of the writer. This sense is reinforced by the negative connotation of the word *constant* which describes the movement of warships to and from the United States and the Gulf. This word is normally found collocated with negative words like *difficulties* or *problems* and brings with it the sense of not being able to deal with the difficulties implied.

The reference to *R&R* does not spell out how the writer would label the activities of the off-duty American crew, but since the word *euphemism* means 'to give a more pleasant label' to something, we can only infer that the activities are more harmful and disruptive than *rest and recreation* suggests. The disapproval of such activity is ideologically connected with the main force of the article, which is to report on the protests against the presence of nuclear-powered ships in Australian ports. There is a further link with the ideological opposition to capitalism, which is embedded in the description of the local economy capitalising on *all the dollars saved up by the crew sweating it out in the Gulf for months on end.* The image of ports awash with money and presumably alcohol is implied by the reference to heat, and by implication to the lack of freedom for the crew to drink and quench their thirst whilst on duty in 'dry' areas such as the Gulf.

Unlike some of the earlier examples of clear uses of presuppositions, this text works through pragmatic shared knowledge (e.g. that the Gulf is 'dry') and implicature (e.g. that rest and recreation are not as harmless as they sound).

7

Meaning and Reality

7.1 The Whorfian Hypothesis

When I ask students to define 'language', they very often have the same three ingredients in their definitions. These are 'communication', 'ideas' and 'sounds'. They have thus picked out the medium (speech) in which much of our language emerges, and what is often considered to be the main function of speech: the communication of ideas. Notice that these two latter notions often go hand-in-hand, although they *can* exist independently. Thus we can communicate things other than ideas, including emotions. We can likewise encode ideas in language without necessarily communicating them. Talking to oneself might be deemed odd behaviour if it is witnessed, but it is one way we have of working out our ideas – for ourselves as much as for communication to others.

It is noticeable that in being asked to define language, people tend to focus on the stereotypical aspects, rather than, for example, the function of language that allows us to express our emotions or to buy groceries. We also idealise language as notionally successful in all of these functions, forgetting that there are many instances where language *fails* to communicate ideas, express emotions, etc. Another part of this stereotype of what language is like is the idea that language in some sense frees us to think and say ever more interesting and world-changing things. To some extent this is true; human society has built the complex civilisation that we have today partly because it had a complex language available to it. Because language gives us the capacity to talk or write about things happening in remote places and at different times, we are able to learn from each other and push forward the frontiers of human knowledge and understanding.

However, this rosy picture is not necessarily the only one that can be drawn. There are many who would argue that far from being a tool of freedom, language is a dictator, allowing us to see the world only through its structures and restricting us from 'seeing' new things that cannot be encoded in our language. The notion of language as oppressor arises out of the work of the linguist Benjamin Lee Whorf. He was working within the Saussurean structuralist tradition of linguistics, which saw language as a system, with all the parts of the system mutually supporting and defining the other parts.

If language was, indeed, such a system, it is argued, then the 'reality' that it represents is constructed in a particular way for that language. Also, since the speakers of that language learn to perceive the world around them through the language, their understanding of the world will necessarily be constructed by that language. Whorf and later his pupil, Edward Sapir, were interested in describing the linguistic systems of human societies very different from our own, including native Americans societies and some African communities. Whorf found that some of the ways in which we perceived the world, though fundamental to our society and our language, were entirely different in these societies.

The examples given by Whorf and others are quite difficult to understand, lending credence to his argument that we *should not* be able to understand them, constructed as we are by English. As we saw in section 3.4, languages like English and Spanish divide up the day and night into different numbers and sizes of units, with names that do not translate exactly. These customs affect us quite deeply so that we feel that our own way of perceiving the sections of the day are in some sense 'natural'.

This example of comparative divisions of the day is really very easy for English speakers to understand, though they might find in practice it takes a little getting used to if they lived in Spain for any length of time. The very fact that people can and do learn to speak foreign languages, in some cases to very high levels, is evidence against the strongest version of Whorf's hypothesis: that we perceive the world through, and only through, our language. If we model Whorfian (and indeed Saussurean) descriptions of language as a mosaic or a jigsaw, we find that different languages do seem to divide the picture up into different size, shape and colour pieces.

Although we are accustomed to seeing the world in a particular way, it seems we are not confined to using our own jigsaw, but may 'retrain' in the ways of perceiving by learning other languages, or other varieties of English. Each time we join a new speech community, we acquire new ways of looking at the world. This could involve, for example, learning to 'see' different ways of tackling and kicking by learning the terminology associated with soccer.

Although we may not want to accept a strong Whorfian account of how language relates to reality, this model of the relationship between language and perception of reality has been taken up by a number of groups who felt that it precisely explained their feelings about the language they speak and how it seems to restrict their ability to express themselves. It is no surprise that these are the same groups of people who feel themselves to be in some way socially and/or politically disadvantaged such as women, ethnic minorities, homosexuals and people with disabilities.

A more disturbing consequence of the general acceptance of language's ability in some sense to determine reality is the use of language to control and influence people politically. Thus the 're-education programmes' of the communist regimes of the first half of the twentieth century and the relatively right-wing 'market-led' economies to be seen in Western Europe since the 1970s share the desire to control the language people use. This is seen in operation in many small ways in the Britain of the late twentieth/ early twenty-first century. It is increasingly difficult to 'hear' the quotation marks surrounding the word *customer* when it is used in areas of work which used to be perceived as services rather than commercial transactions. People who used to be called *passengers* on public transport systems, *patients* in healthcare, *pupils/students* in schools and colleges are all beginning to be known, more or less seriously, as *customers*. And even the ironic use of the term acknowledges linguistically that society has changed its way of perceiving such services. Students tell me that when they work in fast-food restaurants, they have a set of formulaic greetings, questions and answers that they have to learn and repeat for every customer. Likewise, in universities academics are required to write their course descriptions in the approved (corporate) style, sometimes to the detriment of meaning and lucidity!

Of course, we may be confident that 'they' (our political or employment masters) are unable to control our minds in quite the way suggested by George Orwell's novel *1984*, which warns of political domination through language, but the theme of language as a powerful tool in political control has recurred again and again in literature since Orwell's warnings about totalitarianism. Suzette Haden Elgin (1985), for example, in one of the many feminist dystopian novels, *Native Tongue*, suggests a society where women subvert the political domination of men by inventing their own, feminist language, that the men are not able to understand. This could be read not as a futuristic fantasy, but as an allegory of what actually happens. It is true that most cohesive social groups, even families, evolve their own ways of speaking and even some unique vocabulary which gives the group an identity but may also illustrate that group's way of perceiving the world. Some would argue that women have in fact evolved ways of excluding men from their discussions and there is certainly evidence of slaves and their descendants using their own variety of English as a way of subverting the power of the owners/white people.

Some feminist theorists (see, for example, Spender 1980) would argue that the restriction placed on women's expression by the patriarchal language they are obliged to speak is so severe that women are unable to function through it. The argument is often based on a strong version of the Whorfian hypothesis. It claims that women's view of the world is so completely dictated by the patriarchal language from the first acquisition of symbolic language, that whatever their later needs, the language can only construct certain representations of them. Some writers (see Schultz, 1975) use as evidence of the strength of this trap the words that have been associated with women and have become 'tainted' by this contact. This process is known as semantic derogation, and is seen in the inequality of status of apparently paired terms:

male term	female term
husband	wife
manager	manageress
Lord	lady

The inequality of *husband* and *wife* is quite subtle; the phrase *my husband*, I would argue, being more often offered as a status symbol than the phrase *my wife*. The differences between *manager* and *manageress* are much clearer, with the former being more likely to be seen as a serious job (often in banking) and the latter probably assumed to be a relatively trivial post in a cake shop or a dress shop. The final pair are slightly out of date, but illustrate the difference between the elevated, aristocratic use of the title *Lord* and the democratic, but inevitably levelling view of all women as *ladies*.

There is plenty of evidence to support the claim that words associated with women will lose status and respect as a result of this association. Even the word *feminist*, created by feminists to describe their view of the current inequality between the sexes and their desire for equality, became for a while a 'tainted' word, associated with tabloid images of masculine, unconventional and therefore threatening women. This view of the Whorfian trap can lead us to despair, since it seems that whatever we do, even creating new words, can be used in the service of the dominant ideology.

Other similar processes of derogation can be seen in the stigma attached to disabilities and how they are named. Periodically the charities dealing with particular disabilities find that they need to change their names because the term once used neutrally to describe the disability has become derogatory and even a term of abuse. This was the case with adjectives like *spastic* and *mongol* which used to characterise people in an intrinsic way in phrases like *a spastic woman* or *a mongol child* and eventually replaced the human nouns altogether, losing all reference to their gender and age in the process: *a spastic, a mongol*. Recently these terms, which became terms of abuse as a result of their connection with the taboo of disability, have been replaced by nouns *cerebral palsy* and *Down's syndrome*, so that the people who suffer from them are described as *having* these conditions, rather than *being* the condition. The ability of life to infect language is perhaps most clearly illustrated by the developing trail of words and euphemisms referring to the toilet. Whilst nobody seems to object to this particular part of our culture's (every human culture's?) world view, seeing the toilet as an intrinsicallly negative thing, it is true that there can be no *nice* word to refer to the place associated with dirt and germs (see section 3.5 for discussion of the synonyms for *loo*).

Is the situation, then, really that hopeless? Can women never escape the patriarchal view of the world, people with disabilities never find acceptable ways of being referred to, toilets never be nice? The model we have been using in investigating the Whorfian hypothesis and its effects has taken for granted the langue/parole distinction that was outlined in section 1.4. You will remember that we began to dismantle this distinction, so deep-rooted in linguistic thinking since Saussure, that it illustrates a fairly strong Whorfian effect, i.e. as a consequence of its widespread acceptance for many years, it is difficult not to think of language as having an abstract system (langue) as well as a more messy daily usage (parole).

Nevertheless, we have to try and re-educate ourselves to see language as existing only in use, so that any abstract system we try to capture in grammars and dictionaries will only be seen as a snapshot of a moving picture, constantly affected by all the new texts being created all the time. Thus the codes that we use in different situations and as members of different speech communities are constantly under review, adapting and changing to changes in culture, technology and politics. This intertextual approach to language, where the 'system' is seen as in flux, though with a core of consensus making up the 'langue-like' centre, is one which allows us an escape route from the Whorfian trap. If language is adapting to new circumstances, and no one can deny that it is, then there can be no absolute dictating of reality by language. If people can learn new varieties, new dialects, new languages, to any degree of efficiency, they have to that same degree escaped the clutches of their first language. If language is nothing more than a collection of texts (both spoken and written, of course) with constant and repetitive reference between them, then the 'reality' that is being created by language is also being re-created (or changed) with each new text.

One of the reasons that feminists and other language activists have experimented so much with linguistic structures and meanings is precisely because they have not taken the bleakest Whorfian view of the power of language over perception. They must feel that the language is inadequate in order to want to experiment, but they must also see the hope of changing people's perceptions by the process of 'making strange' that is involved in experimenting. Not all commentators on political correctness have appreciated the subtlety of these actions. Whilst the invention of the term *herstory* is clearly tongue-in-cheek, deliberately mistaking as it does the etymology of the word *history*, it also highlights in a single word the male domination of the stories of human endeavour and civilisation that make up the canonical history curriculum in most industrialised countries.

There remains the uncomfortable reality that processes of derogation still continue in the language associated with society's less than fully-valued citizens. There are still many women who feel that the English language is not adequate to describe their bodies, their experiences, their emotions. Despite the model that allows us to change the way that language constructs reality, we still operate on a daily level on a kind of linguistic 'automatic pilot' which takes for granted the structures encoded in our current system.

Activity: Whorfian escapes
The following are some meanings for which there are no single names in English. Think of some examples of your own which seem to you to describe a very simple thing, set of things, feeling or action, but require quite complicated explanations in English:

- The appreciation of watching someone do something they are very skilled at. For example, someone riding a bike, conducting an orchestra, playing cricket, acting, bricklaying.
- The act of claiming the credit for someone else's work without apparent shame, even though everyone involved remembers whose work it was really.

Discussion
These ideas are quite easy to express in English and yet it takes a fairly large number of words, so we may assume that these precise meanings are not privileged as unitary or important in the English language. The novel *Native Tongue* (Haden Elgin) mentioned earlier illustrates, ironically, that although the women in the story feel the language they have available is inadequate (and we are presumably intended to read their story as applying equally to English), nevertheless the story, including their invented language, is told through English. This allows us to see that there is, despite the dominance of our language, a way out of the trap. Some of the meanings encoded in the new language in *Native Tongue* are very similar to my examples, above, though they tend to privilege meanings that might be ascribed to women:

radíidin non-holiday, a time allegedly a holiday but actually so much a burden because of work preparations that it is a dreaded occasion; especially when there are too many house guests and none of them help.

7.2 Meaning and Literature

If we accept that language does not ultimately structure our whole reality and that 'langue' is a convenient fiction rather than an absolute model of the language system, then the corollary is that textual meaning is partly in the hands of the reader/hearer. You may have proved this to your own satisfaction in the 'Chinese whispers' activity which was intended to show graphically how a chain of apparently similar texts can result in changing the meaning of texts quite radically. If the audience (hearer/reader) has come to take such an important part in theories of textual meaning, how does this affect our view of the meaning of what are traditionally known as 'literary' texts? Is literary language fundamentally different in the way that it means from other types of language? These two questions form the starting point for this section.

In the past, literary language has been seen as in some sense superior to or elevated above the ordinary, everyday language we use for shopping and other mundane activities. For a long time, the approach to literary language was to claim that it had certain features that were different from the norms of English and which were therefore said to be 'foregrounded' and consequently more noticeable than the more ordinary language that surrounded them. This model of literary language effectively picks out the 'literary devices' (such as metaphors, alliterative sequences, etc.) from their surroundings as though they were the jewels in a crown made of some rather ordinary material such as iron. The meanings of these devices, then, seemed to be in addition to or superimposed on the meanings generated by the levels of language (phonology, grammar, semantics) in the usual way.

There are a number of problems with this approach to literature and literary meaning. Most obviously, what we like to term 'literature' is not the only text type that uses the stylistic 'devices' traditionally associated with literature. Advertisers and journalists, for example, love to play with language in many of the same ways as poets and novelists. We will see a detailed example in section 7.4

where the pervasiveness of metaphor as a meaning-maker in different genres of texts is explored.

A second problem with approaching literary meaning and style through foregrounded aspects of style (and nobody doubts that they exist) is that it is very difficult to define the 'norms' from which the foregrounded passages stand out. Is it everyday spoken English, in which case there has not been enough descriptive work to define those norms? Is it, rather, some notion of standard written English? Still, there would be problems deciding which variety of written English would be taken as the standard. And why should, say, the language of school textbooks or *The Times* newspaper be the basis against which literary language is judged?

Although it is now much easier, with powerful computers, to establish some of the common features of any range of English styles,* this does not solve the 'problem' of defining foregrounding partly because foregrounding is a term covering a rather wide variety of textual features which have in common the fact that they stand out from their surroundings. This, of course, means that if the surroundings are consistently non-standard in some way (such as the language of poet e. e. cummings), a short passage of quite ordinary English might be foregrounded.

This discussion illustrates how we may accept the notion of foregrounding as one of the factors in literary (and other) texts whilst recognising that this does not necessarily mean that foregrounded passages are non-standard or in themselves identified as literary.

It is difficult to continue with this line of argument much longer without introducing the wider context into the picture. If certain passages of text *are* considered to be 'literary' by the culture in which they exist, then it is partly the foregrounded nature of these passages and partly the expectations of the audience that makes it so. Thus, the genre will influence a reader's reception of a poem, story or play and incline her to interpret foregrounded sections through some kind of aesthetic filter. The same material might have a very different effect if the reader was not aware of the genre first. Similarly, different times (centuries/decades) will provide readers with different aesthetic filters, allowing writers to be villified in one

*For example, the BNC (British National Corpus) consists of a computer corpus of 100 million words of spoken and written English from British sources.

century and fêted in the next. In the eighteenth century, for example, the seventeenth-century poet John Donne's work was not polite and genteel enough for the fashionable tastes although he later came back into favour. On a smaller timescale, readers may find that they are pleased by certain kinds of literary language at one time in their life and by others at other times. I enjoyed the novels of D. H. Lawrence very much as a teenager, but am not so pleased by them now. Such fluctuations may even occur on a weekly basis, depending on mood swings and other external events.

Whether or not we happen to value a particular style at any one moment does not alter the fact that there is much that stylisticians can say (and have said) about the language of literature. What they increasingly avoid, though, is the tendency to allocate meanings to structures or features on a one-to-one basis. Like word-meanings, stylistic meanings are not straightforwardly identified with a particular textual feature. Rather, there is usually a range of effects that can be gained by particular textual devices *in context*. The following examples come from a long poem called *The Schooner Flight* by Derek Walcott and an article in the *New Scientist* magazine respectively:

> I had a sound colonial education
> I have Dutch, nigger and English in me,
> and **either I'm nobody, or I'm a nation.**
> (Derek Walcott, *The Schooner Flight*, ll. 344–6)

Did we really choose what was most interesting or were our imaginations manipulated by the needs of agribusiness?
(Martha Crouch, 'Confessions of a Botanist',
New Scientist, March 1991)

In both of these examples, the text creates oppositions which would never be described as part of some theoretical 'langue', since they are specific to this context. Walcott encapsulates all of the complex arguments about the identity and status of Caribbean people, particularly those, like himself, who have both indigenous and colonial ancestors. By creating a pair of converse opposites, *nobody* and *nation*, he underlines the exclusion of West Indian people from notions of nationhood in the face of colonial and even post-colonial dominance from other *nations*.

The example from Martha Crouch's article illustrates the fact that the very same strategies are used in non-literary texts as in literary ones. This scientist has rejected the financial imperatives which she sees as driving research into molecular biology. In doing so, she wishes to oppose her earlier, idealistic motivations, which were largely to do with interest and enthusiasm with her later, more 'realistic' view that it was big business that was taking over her imagination.

Although the context (both linguistic and non-linguistic) is important for those features of style that would be picked out as foregrounded, it is even more significant for stylistic features that are harder to pinpoint, but are nevertheless present in a text. For example, the choice of tense to be used throughout a long passage in a novel or short story cannot exactly be seen as foregrounded, since it becomes the norm for that passage. However, the build-up of verbs in a particular tense may, in that particular context, have a specific stylistic effect which the analyst (stylistic or literary) would wish to comment on. Another passage with the same consistent tense might have another interpretation of essentially the same feature or it may have little or no significance in another text.

What is the place of the audience (reader/hearer) in this account of literary meaning? Whilst the representation above sounds as though the text and textual context provide the 'answers' to the meanings of literary (and other) texts, the reader will in fact bring to the interpretation of any text a range of preconceptions, knowledge and experience as well as a social background, education and more temporary features like alertness or tiredness. In addition, the reader might have one or more of a range of reasons for reading the text in the first place. These may include:

- A friend lent it to you to read on holiday.
- It is on the reading list of a course in English literature you are following.
- You found it on the train.
- You have been meaning to read it for ages.
- You felt you ought to read it, though you do not have much inclination for it.

These factors, combined with the formal textual features of the text will result in a unique meaning for every reader, though many of these 'readings' will overlap in a number of ways. This does not indicate that any linguistic text *can* mean anything at all, since there are constraints on the meanings of words, grammatical structures, etc.

The reason that there is in fact a great deal of agreement about what many of our everyday utterances, and indeed many literary texts mean is that there is a very complex network of consensus-based meanings from every level of structural features to the culturally derived 'rules for speaking' or 'rules for interpreting poetry' which incline us to certain ways of reading. Literary genres are not different in this from other genres of text, except in so far as our culture reveres the literary and sets it aside from other non-literary texts. In this cultural separation lies the 'meaning' of the literary work. All other features of the text may be read through this cultural filter, but otherwise operate in much the same way as other texts.

Notice that I have been stressing the consensual nature of much of the reading we do. This is not, of course, the only way to read texts and many literary theories and courses precisely aim to make the student try reading 'across' or 'against' the grain of the text in order to question our, and its preconceptions about issues such as the role and representation of women, the representation of formerly colonised areas of the world or the construction of working class people in the text. We will look at some of the better-known examples of this in the next section.

7.3 Negotiating Meaning

The last section mentioned the fact that some theories of literature (and indeed, of text) took reading of texts against or across the grain as part of their strategy for interpretation. In most cases, these theories are part of the reaction against the domination of the text (particularly written text) and the text-producer in the producing of meanings. The very fact that literary studies traditionally went on a search for the author's 'true' meaning illustrates the dominance of the notion that meaning resides in the word on the page.

We will return to the reader's end of the process later, but for now, let us consider how the model of meaning we are now using differs from the one taken for granted in the early chapters of this book. Although I have repeatedly hinted that the langue/parole distinction was no longer as fundamental to linguistic description as it had been, for descriptive convenience Chapters 2–4 behaved as though there were indeed an abstract 'system' (Chomsky's 'competence') which is drawn upon in 'performance'.

Let us imagine a concrete realisation of how the langue/parole or competence/performance models work. The Saussurean model might have the language, including words, meanings, structures, etc., in a big cupboard, which speakers and writers would raid when they wanted to put together an utterance. Everyone who spoke the same language would have roughly the same items in their cupboards. Sometimes, in uttering or writing, items would get dropped and break, or get in a muddle. But this would be seen as simply the imperfect use of a perfect system.

The Chomskyan model would look similar, although the items (such as words and meanings) would be in a computer memory and there would be a separate processing unit to put them together according to certain rules of grammar. Each person would be born with the processing unit and would gradually fill up their own memory banks with units from the language surrounding them.

How can we represent the model which has been emerging since Chapter 5 first introduced the idea that some 'rules' of language might be operated between participants in conversation? It is, perhaps, a little like a community (or even a commune) of people who all share various resources such as a food processor, a hairdryer and a step-ladder. When they wish to use one of the communal implements, they have to go and find out who had it last and ask to 'borrow' it. Whilst the item is never fully 'theirs', it is partly theirs, so they have owners' rights in the use of the implement, and may even use it for slightly unusual tasks, but also have the responsibilities of shared ownership. Thus the individual owner of a hairdryer who used it to dry the hamster after it fell in the bath would not think twice. This would probably also be an acceptable use of a communal hairdrier, though if the hamster's fur was found all over it by the next person, there might be some cause for complaint!

How does this represent the model of language we are now

working with? If language is a communally held resource, it belongs to us all, though we might all use it for slightly different tasks and in different ways. Our own use of a word is neither identical with our neighbour's (as in the identical stock cupboard model) nor entirely different from theirs (since we are borrowing the *same* resource). Because it is the same item that we are using, rather than an identical copy, the item will be affected by our use of it. It might be affected very slightly, like the minor amount of wear and tear on a hairdryer used to dry a single head of short hair. On the other hand the used might do something so unusual that it is dramatically changed. A poet might use a word in a way that no one has ever thought of before, but which 'infects' many of its uses ever afterwards.

What seems to be happening here is that we are replacing a 'system vs. use' model of language with a model that takes for granted the consensus-based nature of everything about our linguistic habits. The model can, incidentally, be developed to cope with notions of overlapping speech communities introduced in Chapter 6. Literary theorists have been working for some time with the notion of 'intertextuality', which, like this model, suggests that texts are not – and never can be – isolated from other texts. We do not derive the meanings of texts by looking in our 'cupboards' (or dictionaries, grammars etc.). We (re-)construct the meaning of a text by looking around at other texts, or by referring to our previous experience of other texts. The meaning of any text, therefore, is partly based on its connections with other texts, both contemporary and historical.

It is relatively easy to see how all literature might be said to be influenced by all other literature to a greater or lesser extent. Much of literary criticism has depended in the past on tracing the 'influences' of the writer, though 'intertextuality' would claim a much wider range of influence than was common in this kind of criticism. Is it possible to use the model of intertextuality to help explain what is going on in all linguistic material? Many writers would claim that it is:

Ultimately this means that virtually all language use enacts a creative tension between 'another's words' and 'one's own language'. The words we speak, write or otherwise record are never wholly our own. And yet, crucially, in the moment of use they are turned towards our own ends, whether these ends are overt or covert, conscious or unconscious. (Pope, 1995)

Here, Pope is explaining Bakhtin's notion of intertextuality, as applied to the novel. Pope is paraphrasing (and indeed indirectly translating) Bakhtin's own words, and then choosing to use the idea for a wider concept of intertextuality as applying to texts beyond the novel, and even beyond literature. I, in turn, am using Pope's words, to introduce intertextuality as Pope means it, but in a very different context and as an explicit alternative to the Saussurean or Chomskyan models of language. This specific aim, of course, was not Pope's concern.

Apart from 'intertextuality', Bakhtin highlighted what he called the 'dialogic' nature of much literary practice. He was most interested in the constant renegotiation of linguistic meanings by novelists, though the notion of 'dialogism' has come to refer much more widely to the fact that all language use involves negotiation between speaker/writer and hearer/reader. In some very clear cases, you can 'see' the negotiation taking place:

As I was writing the outline for this section and thinking about negotiation of meaning, I was interrupted by a phone call from a friend who had a Canadian upbringing. Our conversation went like this:

L: *I forgot to ask you something the other day. Did Dave tell you I rang last night?*
Me: *No – he probably forgot because Sam was sick.*
L: *Oh dear, what's wrong with him?*
Me: *He just threw up, so he's off school today.*

Whilst this conversation was going on, I was aware that my friend and I were using the word *sick* differently. She interpreted my use of the word to mean 'generally unwell', whereas I meant that he had vomited. She therefore asked for more details, which seemed strange, since I felt I had already said what was wrong. However, it alerted me to the difference of meaning and left me searching for a synonym for *sick*. I felt mildly uncomfortable using the more casual (and more colourful) *threw up*, but would have felt very stiff and formal saying *vomited*.

The negotiation in this example illustrates the co-operative principle at work, with both participants working towards an agreed meaning despite the minor barrier of coming from different English-speaking communities. The dialogic model of meaning, however, also allows for a very different kind of negotiation whereby the reader/hearer deliberately resists or remakes what is 'given' in a specific text. As Pope says of this kind of practice:

> In cultural studies there is also a developed sense of the value of *counter-* and *alternative* (or 'aberrant') *decoding*: reading against or across the grain of the text so as to produce a response which is revealingly at variance with the dominant reading apparently expected of an 'ideal (i.e. submissive) reader'.
>
> (Pope, 1995, p. 186)

Whilst this idea of reading against/across the text can occur in any context and with any text, there have been groups that have developed techniques of radical reading to a high level, usually for an openly political purpose. These are, unsurprisingly, groups of people who feel powerless or marginalised in the society that surrounds them and therefore include feminists, gays, racial minorities and in some cases also workers.

Whilst for practical reasons we might not want to base our social structures on the notion that any text can mean anything, notice that the development of a new and more flexible notion of 'where' meaning resides has been at the root of some of the liberating and 'consciousness-raising' movements of the twentieth century.

Let us take the feminist example to illustrate the dynamic 'negotiation' of meaning that has arisen from this movement. Feminism is best-known as a stereotype whereby women who seem to want to look like men try, without apparent humour, to overturn long-standing linguistic practices such as calling women Mrs when they are married and Miss when they are not. The questioning of this practice of identifying women as (sexually) 'taken' or 'available' has been partly a question of radical reading. Where traditionalists might argue that 'Mrs' was a sign of respect, feminists argued that the sexual availability of women was of concern only to themselves and their immediate family, as it is for men. Much more playful have been the attempts to rename areas of human activity which appear to privilege men. The term *herstory* for the history of women was not originally intended as a serious replacement for the word *history* (though some have tried to promote this view) – and no one ever suggested that the *his-* was historically a masculine pronoun. The tabloid papers and other popular media affected to see all such playfulness with language as intense and rather serious feminists overstepping the mark – who are they to play about with 'our' language?

In fact, the truth was that feminists had discovered that if you did not like the meanings apparently encoded in the texts making up society around you, you could challenge them. Equally, if you suspected that the texts were sexist (or racist or biased in some other way) but could not put your finger on how or why, radical reading would help to expose the underlying meanings. Pope points out that Bakhtin's notion of 'carnival' was anarchic in a very literal sense, since it 'celebrates a repressed or suppressed culture of playful, holiday a-normality, grotesquery and positively charged "non/sense"' (Pope, 1995, p. 188). It can, however, also show how arbitrary are the semiotic systems of human languages and thus undermine meanings that seem to be overly important in human societies – such as the inferiority of women.

Another textual practice that feminists have used in this spirit is that of 'reclaiming' words that have been used of and against women, most specifically words referring to female body parts. Thus some women will use the word *cunt* to refer to their vagina in the attempt to drain from the word its ability to shock and thus deprive the language of an insult which demeans women. Reclaiming has also been the practice of some black groups who have used the word *nigger* about themselves. Notice in both of these cases that the reclaimed words would still be interpreted as insulting if they were used by people outside the group concerned.

Activity: negotiating meaning and intertextuality
After reading the following passage once or twice through, put it aside and paraphrase it fairly freely in your own words. You may decide to change the details of the story a little, or you may change the genre in which it is written.

It was on a dreary night of November, that I beheld the accomplishment of my toils. With an anxiety that almost amounted to agony, I collected the instruments of life around me, that I might infuse a spark of being into the lifeless thing that lay at my feet. It was already one in the morning; the rain pattered dismally against the panes, and my candle was nearly burnt out, when, by the glimmer of the half-extinguished light, I saw the dull yellow eye of the creature open; it breathed hard, and a convulsive motion agitated its limbs.

(Mary Shelley, *Frankenstein* [1818] chapter V, p. 57)

Compare your own version with the one given here. What aspect(s) of the text did you emphasise or draw attention to? Were they different from the original? Did you update the language or give it a nineteenth-century flavour? Did you keep the first-person narrative or recast it as an omniscient narrator? If you have seen a number of different films derived from the Frankenstein story, was your version influenced by these visual texts? If you were influenced by film versions, were they recent/old, serious/humorous? And was your attitude one of fear/amusement or another emotion?

If you stayed rather close to the original and would like to be more flexible in your response, try rewriting the passage again, perhaps using a different perspective such as that of the monster, of a cat or mouse in the room, or a neighbour overhearing the goings on.

Discussion
When I tried this exercise with a class of students, many of them chose to make the monster a woman. This is interesting as we might conclude that gender issues are at the forefront of their thinking. One of the most unusual rewrites was in the style of a detective novel and was striking in the way that it was devoid of the emotion that the original is steeped in.

7.4 Chickens and Eggs

Let us assume that we can accept a weak version of the Whorfian hypothesis, indicating that we often and typically operate through the 'reality' constructed by our language, accepting that it is possible both to resist this influence and that 'language' is a fluctuating, consensual concept anyway. Let us also widen our view a bit here, to include other symbolic and semiotic systems, such as visual ones, since they also have an effect on our perceptions of the world. A disturbing example comes from the world of fashion where the repetition of images of painfully thin girls reinforces the 'truth' that female beauty is childlike and very thin.

In addition to our version of the 'language equals reality' model, we need a way of explaining the fact that despite the power of language over perception, changes do take place over time and in response to new communicative needs as well as political pressures. It is not longer quite so unacceptable to call yourself *Ms* instead of *Miss* or *Mrs*, although there is some resistance among older or more conservative people. Similarly, there is less pretence of debate in the tabloid press about the shocking suggestions emanating from the women's movement, that some women might prefer not to be called *Chairman* or would object to being included in the pronoun *he*. There is the 'backlash', of course, with 'lad culture' taking a stand against feminism, but this should not overshadow the linguistic changes that have been achieved in the interests of constructing a fairer reality for women.

Other changes have included those mentioned earlier which saw changes in the naming of mental handicaps or disabilities. In section 7.1 I argued that the taboo surrounding all of these issues (from female equality to disabilities) was so strong that any word used to describe them would in time become 'infected' by the taboo. We cannot assume that this is the only or most accurate model of what is going on, because language change and history in general contradicts this view; attitudes to people who are in some way different do change for the better.

Let us consider the model of meaning we are left with if we assume that langue and parole are at best a convenient fiction. In that case, the 'system' of language is a very temporary affair, constructed out of nothing more stable than precedent. In the case of language, precedent means other texts. Thus the meanings of words, sounds, grammatical structures or text structures exist only because there have been innumerable earlier occasions when they occurred with the same, or almost the same meanings. The analogy with the criminal law system in England and Wales is a useful one. Instead of having laws to cover every conceivable future crime that will be committed, we have a number of general laws, coupled with a history of all the judgements and sentences that have been given in the past. When a barrister goes to court to prosecute or defend an accused person, she will argue the case partly on the grounds of other decisions that have been made in the past. Of course no two crimes are ever completely identical, just as no two utterances are identical, since situational aspects of meaning will ensure that there are always minute differences of meaning. Nevertheless, we can make sense of utterances and texts on the basis of our previous experience of other similar texts, in just the same way that barristers and judges use similar cases to argue their point of view.

If the meaning of a text *is* a complex set of references to myriads of other texts, then the set of references will differ for every reader, for the writer and probably for every occasion of reading. There remains a relatively stable 'core' of intertextual references that most readings of a text will agree on, and these will most likely be those that turn up in general critical readings and essays about literary works. Other and additional meanings will depend on the reader and the occasion of reading and will reflect theoretical viewpoints (Marxist, feminist, post-colonial, etc.).

How does this model work for non-literary texts? I would suggest that it operates in a very similar way and explains why sometimes we misunderstand other speakers or disagree with their meanings. We may have sets of references to other texts (i.e. similar linguistic experiences to the current one) which nevertheless differ from those of the person we are talking to. These are usually trivial and do not hold up communication in any serious way. Sometimes they are more problematic and leave us struggling to make sense of each other's utterances. The example in section 7.3 is a case in point. When a speaker uses her experience of Canadian English to interpret the word *sick* as meaning *generally unwell* rather than the more British *vomit*, she is relying on the longer and more over-whelming precedents that she has experienced. If, however, she has lived in England for a while and has a conflicting set of precedents where it means *vomit*, then she may use situational evidence (i.e. it was an English woman speaking) to construct the alternative (correct) meaning.

If we return for a moment to the langue/parole distinction, which still permeates much linguistic description, we can see that the problems with the model are much the same as those for the Whorfian hypothesis. Neither adequately explains or allows for the facts of language change and language differences such as those between speakers of overlapping dialects or varieties of English.

The problem of *sick* in Canadian and British English would be difficult for either of these more static models to deal with. The Whorfian model would have the Canadian speaker constructed to 'see' the world as having a general concept called 'sick' which means 'generally ill' and other specific forms of sickness including vomiting. These two varieties of English, which are in fact so alike in many ways would seem incomprehensible to each other in a Whorfian world. The langue–parole model would have different 'systems' for each variety and the actual conversation where both systems were in operation would be seen as odd or maverick rather than a negotiation between two speakers with slightly differing sets of precedents to refer to.

One textual practice that contributes to our developing and changing consensus about linguistic meaning is that of metaphor. This book opened by pointing out that speakers of any language, and specifically English, were prone to using language in a non-literal way. Since that chapter, we have discussed many different ways in which people can mean things without saying them literally: by tone of voice or intonation, by adopting particular levels of formality, by using Standard or non-standard forms of English, by choosing words with particular connotations, by implying the presence of words through their common collocates, by presupposition and implicature.

In addition to all of these, and sometimes as an additional layer to these non-literal uses of language, there are many ways of using metaphorical structures to create meaning, and these are as common in our daily language as they are in literature. Lakoff and Johnson (1980) explore at length the sets of metaphors that are embedded in our language and lives so deeply that we are sometimes unaware that they are metaphorical. These include, for example, metaphors such as **'time is money'** which cause us to talk about *spending two weeks in France, wasting our time waiting for someone, saving a weekend for you to come and stay* and so on. In addition to these deep-rooted metaphors, we use and extend metaphors creatively a great deal, and not just in creative writing. Some of these changes are politically motivated and may be quite far-reaching such as those discussed earlier in relation to the commodification of services such as education, transport and health. The metaphor in these cases is something like **education/health/transport is a product for sale in a commercial market** and causes all sorts of new language to cluster around the central concept, which makes these services sound like oranges for sale from a street vendor:

the **delivery** of new courses
accumulation of credits
the **queue** for operations

A specific example of this process happened in Britain in the mid-1990s when the supply of water was privatised and what had been a public service became a commercial enterprise. There was a severe water shortage in Yorkshire in 1995 and the local press (*Yorkshire Evening Post* and *Huddersfield Examiner*) had many column inches devoted to the topic for a few weeks. The language used in these reports was overwhelmingly constructed within the **water is a quantifiable and moveable commodity** metaphor. Although no one would deny that we can indeed measure water and move it around, the notion of commodity means that the measuring and movement are geared toward commercial ends rather than needs.

As well as the post-monetarist metaphors where everything becomes a product and all human interaction becomes a commercial transaction, there are other relatively recent metaphors which might be considered to have changed our ways of looking at things in an enlightening way. One such metaphor is **machinery and big organisations are computers**. Although machinery, large institutions and public service departments have been around much longer than computers, we have begun to use some of the language which grew up around computers to explain our confused and vulnerable relationship with these intimidating bodies. Thus we may talk about local government departments or new microwave cookers as being *user-friendly* or *user-unfriendly*.

Activity: metaphors for change

Look at the following newspaper article or some recent press reports of a news story with which you are familiar:

For a man who professes to be the champion of the information revolution, Tony Blair could not have received a better lesson in the consequences of arming the nation's youth with access to cyberspace. Last night, the Labour Party's Internet site was being stripped in a desperate attempt to fend off a determined onslaught by an American hacker which started on Saturday. In the space of two attacks, the site was transformed from a slick exercise in the future of political communications to the laughing stock of the World Wide Web.

(Stuart Millar, *Guardian*, 10 December 1996)

Which metaphors are drawn upon in the reporting? Are the metaphors well-established in English? (Can you think of a number of other, similar expressions, based on the same overall metaphor?) Are there any metaphors that appear to be quite recent or created in this context? Do they seem to be likely to become established or more widespread?

Discussion

This short passage is apparently built very largely on the metaphor of war. Whilst Blair is said to be keen on *arming* young people with computer skills and equipment, the hacker is seen as an assailant on the Labour Party who they need to *fend off* and who is mounting a *determined onslaught*. The hacker's activities are also described as two *attacks*.

The metaphor of war is very commonly applied to both politics and business, so this is not particularly striking. What is perhaps more interesting is the representation of computer links like the Internet as being spaces, and in particular, being akin to land, which is capable of being owned, accessed and invaded in the same way. The term *cyberspace* lays down the basis of this metaphor, but it is supported in addition by *access* and *site*. These seem to me fairly recent, but already well-established aspects of the perception of the Internet. Although we know that there are no places associated with these *sites* and that we cannot physically *enter* them, nevertheless, we have become so accustomed to the concepts of 'virtual reality' that it is now very difficult to think of another way to talk about using the Internet. In addition, the notion of space and movement has been part of the metaphor surrounding communications since the telephone took over from written communications. By analogy with the letter, English retained the notion of *sending* a message although there was no transfer of place involved. These early space metaphors made the acceptance of *sites* and *access* on the Internet very much easier to assimilate, although the metaphor has taken the logical further step of conceptualising the person communicating as travelling, rather than just sending messages. Hence you might hear an Internet surfer using phrases like *I've got into the NASA site* or *Why don't you go to his web page?*.

A final dimension of the metaphors underlying this short passage similarly takes the software to have a physical construction, but in this case it is like an engine: *Internet site was being stripped*. This appears to be a shortened version of the verb *strip down*, a process usually carried out on car engines to find out what the problem is, although some readers might argue that it could refer to wallpaper or clothes being stripped off. Oddly enough, these metaphors, of land which needs defending and of a constructed mechanical object, seem to sit quite happily next to each other. I predict, however, that the land metaphor is more long-lasting and powerful, since it has ageless emotional appeal as well as a more 'natural' base.

It cannot be reiterated too many times about all the kinds of meaning discussed in this book, that they are only ever a part of the whole picture. It is necessary, if we are to learn anything about the way that language works, to divide the material into manageable layers and chunks. But the division is only a useful model and should always be supplemented by the knowledge that all the different aspects of linguistic meaning operate together in real situations.

Further Reading

References for the extracts included in this book and other texts quoted are to be found after the Further Reading list. This list of further reading is intended to be enticing rather than intimidating and for that reason is kept short and restricted to books that are written in a relatively readable style. For simplicity and ease of access, all of the further reading is taken from the following seven texts:

Blake, N. (1990) *An Introduction to the Language of Literature* (Basingstoke: Macmillan).
Fasold, R. (1990) *Sociolinguistics of Language* (Oxford: Basil Blackwell).
Fiske, J. (1990) *Introduction to Communication Studies* (London: Routledge).
Freeborn, D., P. French and D. Langford (1993) *Varieties of English* (Basingstoke: Macmillan).
Jeffries, L. (1993) *The Language of Twentieth Century Poetry* (Basingstoke: Macmillan).
Kuiper, K. and W. Scott Allan (1996) *An Introduction to English Language* (Basingstoke: Macmillan).
Wardhaugh, R. (1985) *How Conversation Works* (Oxford: Basil Blackwell).

Readers who would like to take their studies into meaning further would find a more technical, but thorough treatment of many of the same issues in Saeed, J. (1997) *Semantics* (Oxford: Blackwell).

Chapter 1
1.1 Kuiper and Allan (1996) ch. 1 and Fiske (1990) chs 1 and 2.
1.2 Fiske (1990) ch. 5.
1.3 Fiske (1990) ch. 3.

Chapter 2
2.1 Jeffries (1993) ch. 3.
2.2 Freeborn *et al.* (1993) chs 3–5.
2.3 Kuiper and Allan (1996) ch. 4.
2.4 Jeffries (1993) ch. 3.

Chapter 3
3.2 Kuiper and Allan (1996) ch. 5.
3.3 Kuiper and Allan (1996) ch. 6.
3.4 Kuiper and Allan (1996) ch. 6.

3.5 Kuiper and Allan (1996) ch. 6.
3.6 Kuiper and Allan (1996) ch. 6.

Chapter 4
4.1 Kuiper and Allan (1996) ch. 6.
4.2 Kuiper and Allan (1996) ch. 5.
4.3 Kuiper and Allan (1996) ch. 7.

Chapter 5
5.1 Blake (1990) ch. 7.
5.2 Fasold (1990) ch. 6.
5.3 Wardhaugh (1985) ch. 3.
5.4 Wardhaugh (1985) ch. 3 and Fasold (1990) ch. 5.
5.5 Fasold (1990) ch. 5.

Chapter 6
6.2 Fasold (1990) ch. 2.
6.3 Fiske (1990) ch. 9.
6.4 Fiske (1990) ch. 9.

Chapter 7
7.1 Fasold (1990) ch. 2.
7.2 Blake (1990).
7.3 Fiske (1990) ch. 9.

Bibliography
Austin, J. (1962) *How to Do Things with Words* (New York: Oxford University Press).
Brazil, D. and M. Coulthard (1975) *Discourse Intonation* (University of Birmingham, monograph).
Chomsky, N. (1965) *Aspects of the Theory of Syntax* (Cambridge, Mass.: MIT Press).
Cole, P. and J. Morgan (1975) *Syntax and Semantics: Speech Acts* (New York: Academic Press).
Crystal, D. (1969) *Prosodic Systems and Intonation in English* (Cambridge: Cambridge University Press).
Ekman, P. and W. V. Friesman (1969) 'Categories, Origins, Usage and Coding: The Basis for Five Categories of Non-verbal Behaviour', *Semiotics*, vol. 1, pp. 49–98.
Fillmore, C. (1968) 'The Case for Case', in E. Bach and R. Harms (eds), *Universals in Linguistic Theory* (New York: Holt, Rinehart and Winston).
Grice, P. (1975) 'Logic and Conversation', in P. Cole and J. Morgan (eds), *Syntax and Semantics: Speech Acts* (New York: Academic Press) pp. 41–58
Gumperz, J. and D. Hymes (1972) *Directions in Sociolinguistics* (Oxford: Basil Blackwell).
Hjelmslev, L. (1953) 'Prolegomena to a Theory of Language', trans. F. J. Whitfield, *International Journal of American Linguistics*, Memoir 7.
Hymes, D. (1972) 'Models of the Interaction of Language and Social Life' in

J. Gumperz and D. Hymes (eds) *Directions in Sociolinguistics* (Oxford: Basil Blackwell) pp. 35–71.

Jeffries, L. (1993) *The Language of Twentieth Century Poetry* (Basingstoke: Macmillan).

Kuiper, K. and W. Allan (1996) *An Introduction to English Language: Sound, Word and Sentence* (Basingstoke: Macmillan).

Lakoff, G. and Johnson, M. (1980) *Metaphors We Live By* (Chicago: University of Chicago Press).

Lyons, J. (1977) *Semantics 1* (Cambridge: Cambridge University Press).

Miller, G. (1961) *Language and Communication* (New York: McGraw-Hill).

Nida, E. (1975) *Componential Analysis of Meaning* (The Hague: Mouton).

Palmer, F. (1976) *Semantics: A New Outline* (Cambridge: Cambridge University Press).

Pope, R. (1995) *Textual Intervention* (London: Routledge).

Quirk, R., S. Greenbaum, G. Leech and J. Svartvik (1972) *A Grammar of Contemporary English* (Harlow: Longman)

de Saussure, F. (1959) *Course in General Linguistics* (Fontana Collins).

Sacks, H., E. Schegloff and G. Jefferson (1974) 'A Simplest Systematics for the Organisation of Turn-taking for Conversation', *Language*, vol. 50, no. 4, pp. 696–735.

Sansom, P. (1994) *Writing Poems* (Newcastle: Bloodaxe).

Savile-Troike, M. (1982) *The Ethnography of Communication* (Oxford: Basil Blackwell).

Schultz, M. (1975) 'The Semantic Derogation of Woman', in Thorne and Henley (1975) pp. 64–75.

Searle, J. (1969) *Speech Acts* (Cambridge: Cambridge University Press).

Simpson, P. (1992) 'Teaching Stylistics: Analysing Cohesion and Narrative Structure in a Short Story by Ernest Hemingway', *Language and Literature*, vol. 1, no. 1, pp. 47–67.

Simpson, P. (1993) *Language, Ideology and Point of View* (London: Routledge).

Spender, D. (1980) *Man Made Language* Routledge and Kegan Paul

Trier, J. (1934) 'Das sprachliche Feld. Eine Auseinandersetzung', *Neve Jahrbücher für Wissenschaft und Jugendbildung*, vol. 10, pp. 428–49.

Whorf, B. (1957) *Language, Thought and Reality* (Cambridge, Mass.: MIT Press).

Sources

Alvarez, A. (ed.) (1962) *The New Poetry* (Harmondsworth, Middx.: Penguin).

Baldwin, J. (1985) *Notes of a Native Son* (Pluto Press).

Beckett, S. (1976) *Footfalls*.

Buckeridge, A., Jennings books (Basingstoke: Macmillan).

Dann, C. (1983) *The Animals of Farthing Wood* (London: Red Fox).

Duffy, C. (1993) *Mean Time* (Anvil Press).

The Enormous Turnip (Ladybird Books, 1980).

Faulkner, W. (1929) *The Sound and the Fury*.

Field, S. (1985) *Out of Wedlock* (London: Mills and Boon).

Golding, W. (1955) *The Inheritors* (London: Faber and Faber).

Guardian, 10 January 1995, 10 December 1996.

Haden-Elgin, S., *Native Tongue* (The Women's Press).

Kuzwayo, E. (1985) *Call Me Woman* (The Women's Press).

Lane, R. (1977) *Himalayan Moonlight* (London: Mills and Boon).

Larkin, P. (1945) *The North Ship* (London: Faber and Faber).

Lessing, D. (1979) *The Story of a Non-Marrying Man* (Harmondsworth, Middx.: Penguin).

Milne, A. (1926) *Winnie-the-Pooh* (London: Methuen).

Morrison, B. and A. Motion (eds) (1982) *The Penguin Book of Contemporary British Poetry* (Harmondsworth, Middx.: Penguin).

Murphy, J. (1994) *The Worst Witch all at Sea* (London: Puffin).

New Scientist, March 1991, September 1996.

Peace News, December 1996.

Raine, C., (1982) 'An Inquiry into Two Inches of Ivory', in B. Morrison and A. Motion (eds), *The Penguin Book of Contemporary British Poetry* (Harmondsworth, Middx.: Penguin).

Redgrove, P. (1962) 'Old House', in A. Alvarez (ed.), *The New Poetry* (Harmondsworth, Middx.: Penguin).

Roth, P. (1971) *Portnoy's Complaint* (Corgi Books).

Scupham, P. 'The Old Pantry', in B. Morrison, and A. Motion (eds), *The Penguin Book of Contemporary British Poetry* (Harmondsworth, Middx.: Penguin).

Shakespeare, W., *King Lear*.

Shelley, M. (1818) *Frankenstein*.

Strong Jeremy (1989) *The Karate Princess* (London: Puffin).

Sustrans promotion leaflet

Three Little Pigs (Ladybird Books, 1967).

Todd, L. (1979) *Tortoise the Trickster and Other Folktales* (London: Routledge and Kegan Paul).

Trollope, J., *The Men and the Girls*,

Walcott, D., *The Schooner Flight*.

Woolf, V. (1976) *Mrs Dalloway* (London: Grafton).

Yorkshire Evening Post, 29 November 1995, 7 December 1996.

Glossary

accent The way in which people speak, including the pronunciation of words and intonation, but not including choice of words or grammatical structures. Usually, but not necessarily (e.g. in the case of RP) associated with the region in which the speaker grew up or has lived for a considerable time. ⇒ RP, dialect, intonation

active verb phrase A verb phrase such as *will have eaten* or *must be playing* which has no passive auxiliary, but which can be changed to a passive by the addition of the passive auxiliary, *be*: *will have been eaten* and *must be being played*. ⇒ passive verb phrase, auxiliary verb

adjacency pairs Pairs of utterances said by different participants in a conversation where the speech act of the first requires the second utterance to perform a particular speech act in response. For example, questions require answers: *What's the time? Six o'clock*, and greetings require greetings in response: *Hello George!, Hi there, Sam!* ⇒ speech act

adjective Words such as *bad, blue, happy* which either premodify nouns as in *the happy music* or occur as complements after verbs like *be* as in *The music was cheerful*. They are sometimes formed from nouns by the addition of a suffix: *careful, flashy, warlike*. ⇒ premodify, complement, suffix

adjective phrase A phrase, rather than a word, performing the same range of functions as single-word adjectives: *the very sad music, the music was really loud*. Usually consist of an adverb premodifying the head adjective. ⇒ adjective, adverb, premodify, head

adverb Words such as *joyfully, later, home* which usually function as a clause element describing the manner, time or place of the event described by the sentence: *Later they all ran joyfully home*. Many adverbs are formed by adding the *-ly* suffix to adjectives as in *candidly, wonderfully*. ⇒ clause, adjective, suffix

adverbial The name of the clause element formed by adverbs, but also sometimes formed by prepositional phrases: *In the morning we walked to the boathouse*. ⇒ clause, adverb

affix Derived words often have a morpheme added to show that they have changed. These may be prefixes, such as *unkind, disruptive*, or suffixes, such as *helpful, sweeper*. Prefixes and suffixes are jointly known as affixes. ⇒ morpheme, prefix, suffix

affricate A 'manner of articulation' of consonants where there is a complete closure in the mouth, as for plosives. Unlike plosives, however, the articulators open slowly and the result is not an explosion of air, but a fricative phase where the narrow opening allows the air to escape, but noisily. The two affricates in English are /tʃ/ and /d/.

agent Nouns derived from verbs, often by the addition of a suffix *-er,* may denote the person (or animal) performing the action of the verb. Thus a *baker* is someone who *bakes* and a *trier* is someone who tries hard. They are agents of the action. In the context of a clause, the agent may be the subject of the verb: *The donkey kicked me.* However, subjects may not be agentive in their participant role: *Susan was hurt by what you did.* ⇒ suffix, subject, participant roles

alliteration When two or more words close together in a text begin with the same consonant: *muck and magic, bring and buy.* A similar effect is gained even when the consonants are not all at the beginning of words: *limpid pool of liquid.* It is important to remember that alliteration is primarily a sound effect; written consonants which share a sound may therefore be used alliteratively: *surreptitious celebrations.* An extension of alliteration is the use of consonantal sounds which share their manner of articulation as in *nauseating miasma* where there is a mixture of nasal sounds: bilabilial /m/, alveolar /n/ and velar/ŋ/. ⇒ nasal, bilabial, alveolar, velar

alveolar One of the 'places of articulation' of sounds, involving a closure between the tongue and the alveolar ridge (just behind the front teeth). Examples of alveolar sounds in English are: /t/, /d/, /n/. ⇒ Other places of articulation: bilabial, velar

anaphoric reference When there is a connection between two sentences in a text (cohesion), there will usually be a full version in one sentence and a referring item in the next sentence: *The man next-door hates cats. He threw a stone at one yesterday.* As in this example, the normal order is for the full version (The man next-door) to occur before the referring item (*He*) and this is known as anaphoric reference. ⇒ Opposite: cataphoric reference

antonymy Although we often use this word to mean 'opposites' in everyday English, linguists use it to refer to a particular kind of opposition, known as 'gradable antonymy'. ⇒ opposites, complementaries, converses, directional opposites

auxiliary verb The subtler modulations of meaning carried by verb endings (inflections) in some European languages are carried instead in English by the auxiliary verbs. These occur before the main verb, and indicate whether, for example, the action is continuous: *he is playing* or whether it is possible, but unlikely: *Sheila might come tomorrow.* ⇒ inflection, continuous, participle

back-channel The supportive noises and body language made by hearers who are not challenging the speaker's right to he floor.

bilabial A place of articulation of consonants in which both of the lips are involved. English bilabial sounds are /b/, /p/, /m/ and /w/.

bound morpheme A morpheme which cannot stand alone but has to be attached to a free morpheme or another bound morpheme: e.g. *in-,* *-ation.* ⇒ free morpheme

cataphoric reference A form of textual cohesion whereby the 'ties' point forward in the text. ⇒ anaphoric reference

clause element The five basic clause elements are subjects, verbs, objects, complements and adverbials. All clauses should be analysable into a string of these elements.

closed system A small group of words which are mutually dependent on each other and where a change to the meaning or scope of one item affects all the others, e.g. grammatical systems such as the pronouns.

cohesion A label for the many different ways in which sentences in texts refer to each other and interlink to ensure that the text is not simply a random series of sentences.

collocation The range of words which a given word will occur with. The most interesting collocations are those which are arbitrarily restricted. ⇒ restricted collocation

complementarity A relationship of opposition between words which are mutually exclusive in their meaning, e.g. you cannot be both *male* and *female*.

componential analysis The process of analysing word meanings into components so that overlapping meanings can be compared. ⇒ semantic feature

compound A word made up of two or more free morphemes, e.g. *corkscrew*.

connotation The part of a word's meaning which relates to its use, rather than its referents, e.g. *tummy* is a word that has connotations of children.

consonant A sound which is made by the articulators moving together and away from each other so as to cause a particular quality of sound. ⇒ fricative, nasal, plosive

conversational implicature Those aspects of meaning which are not logically implied or entailed by the utterance, but which nevertheless would, in similar circumstances, usually be assumed to follow. ⇒ entailment, presupposition

converseness A relationship of opposition which describes words which focus on different perspectives of the same action, e.g. *buy/sell*, *husband/wife*. ⇒ complementaries, directional opposites, gradable antonyms.

countable noun A noun which treats its referent as a countable unit, e.g. *chair(s), idea(s)*.

deixis/deictic The property of some words to shift their reference according to who uses them and where they are in space/time, e.g. *I/you*, *this/that*.

denotation The part of a word's meaning which deals with reference, rather than use. ⇒ connotation

diphthong A vowel sounds which involves a movement from one position to another and sounds like a slide between two vowels, e.g. /ʊə/, /aʊ/.

directional opposite A relationship of opposition between words which reverse the effect of each other, e.g. *button/unbutton, break/mend*.

entailment Entailments are true if the utterance is true. They follow logically from an utterance, but are not presupposed by it.

free morpheme Morphemes that can stand alone: *cat, dog, think*.

fricative A manner of articulation of consonants in which the articulators are brought close together, although not so form a complete closure. The resulting narrow gap allows the air from the lungs to escape, but with an accompanying whistling or breathy noise. English fricatives are: /f/, /v/, /θ/, /ð/, /s/, /z/, /ʃ/, /ʒ/.

given information Shared knowledge which the speaker and the hearers (or writer and readers) are aware of, or assumed to be aware of.

gradable adjective An adjective which can be graded, often by the addition of an intensifying adverb before the adjective: *very **difficult***.

gradable antonymy A relationship of oppositeness whereby the two terms name the ends of a scale, e.g. *big/small, heavy/light*.

homonym A word-form which is related to two or more completely unrelated meanings, e.g. *bank/1* and *bank/2*.

hyponym A word which has a relationship of inclusion with another, more general, word, e.g. *a retriever* is a specific kind of (or hyponym of) *dog*. ⇒ superordinate

icon A semiotic sign which is completely arbitrary in its connection with its referent. ⇒ index, symbol

idiolect The variety of a language which is unique to each speaker, though it overlaps with many other speakers' idiolects.

impersonal pronoun English *it*.

indefinite article English *a/an*.

index A semiotic sign which has a connection (though it is not a representation) of its referent, e.g. a table-setting is indexical of food. ⇒ icon, symbol

instrument A participant which is used by another participant to achieve the action of the verb, e.g. *He hit the nail with **a hammer***.

intertextuality The tendency for all texts to have meaning partly as a result of and through their relationships with other texts.

intransitive verb A verb which does not have an object, e.g. *He **died***.

langue A structuralist model of human language would include a 'core', known as the 'langue', which would hold the common and regular features and items of the language. ⇒ parole

linearity One of the properties or 'design features' of human language. The units of language cannot occur simultaneously, they have to follow one another.

mass noun Nouns which treat their referent as a mass substance, rather than as a collection of countable units, e.g. *air, water, survival*. ⇒ count noun

morpheme, morphology The smallest unit of meaning, the constituent of word-structure.

nasal A manner of articulation of consonants where the soft palate moves away from the back of the pharynx and allows air to escape through the nasal cavity. English nasal sounds are: /m/, /n/, /ŋ/.

nominalisation The process of changing an action into an item by representing it as a noun, e.g. *The **shutting** down of coal mines*.

non-segmental Those features of the voice (including intonation and stress patterns) which are not tied to the sequential units of language, such as sounds, morphemes and words. ⇒ segmental

obligatory clause element Those clause elements which are necessary for the grammaticality of the clause. Usually including Subjects, Verbs, Objects and Complements, but only sometimes including Adverbials.

observer's paradox The problem of observing human behaviour without the observer's presence interfering with the behaviour under scrutiny.

onomatopoeia The direct symbolism by sound of the sound a word is supposed to refer to, e.g. *boo-hoo.* ⇒ sound-symbolism

open class Classes of word (noun, verb, adjective and adverb) which have a large and changing membership. They form a much looser mutual dependency than the closed systems of grammatical words. ⇒ closed systems

orthographic Of, or relating to the written language.

paradigmatic The relationship between items which can replace each other in particular 'slots'. ⇒ syntagmatic

parole The everyday performance of language, including imperfections and innovations. ⇒ langue

patient A participant role which is affected by the action of the verb, e.g. *Susan dropped the plate.*

performatives Verbs which are acted by being spoken, e.g. *I pronounce you guilty as charged.*

phoneme, phonology The systematic study of speech sounds (phonemes) in a particular language.

plosive A manner of articulation in which some part of the oral cavity causes a complete closure so that the build-up of air from the lungs causes a sharp burst of air when the closure is released. English plosives are: /p/, /b/, /t/, /d/, /k/, /g/.

polysemy The phenomenon of words which have two or more related meanings.

postural congruence The tendency of participants in a conversation to mirror each others' bodily positions.

pragmatics The study of linguistic meaning in its textual and situational context.

prefix A bound morpheme which precedes the free morpheme to which it is attached, e.g. *in-flexible.* ⇒ bound morpheme, free morpheme

prepositional phrase A phrase consisting of a preposition and a noun phrase (e.g. *in the bus, on the street*) which can either follow the head of a noun phrase (e.g. *the boy on the corner*) or may act as adverbials (e.g. *Put it in the bag*).

presupposition Those features of the meaning of an utterance which remain true even when the utterance is negated.

product A participant role which labels those things which come into being as a result of the action of the verb, e.g. *I made a cake.*

relative clause A subordinate clause which follows and modifies the head of a noun phrase, e.g. *the old dog that died last week.*

restricted collocation The tendency for some words to occur in a very restricted set of contexts, although the reasons for this restriction may appear to be arbitrary.

RP (Received Pronunciation) The prestigious accent of English in England, associated with the south-east of the country and with the ruling-classes.

segmental Associated with the sequential units of language, such as sounds, morphemes and words. ⇒ non-segmental

selectional restrictions The semantic restrictions on normal combinations of words, e.g. the verb *think* normally expects a human (or at least animate) subject. This is not a grammatical phenomenon, since breaking selectional restrictions does not cause ungrammaticality, e.g. *The table thought it would fall over.*

semantic derogation The process whereby words associated with 'difficult' or taboo areas of meaning take on some of the negative connotation of their meaning. Often used to describe the way that words associated with women become less powerful as a result.

semantic feature An element of meaning which a number of word-senses share, e.g. ± animate

semantic field A group of words which share the core of their meaning and between them cover an area of meaning.

sense relations Relationships, such as synonymy and oppositeness, that hold between word-senses in a linguistic system. ⇒ synonymy, system, oppositeness

sibilant A sub-group of fricatives which share a well-defined whistling sound and in English include /s/, /z/, /ʃ/ and /ʒ/. ⇒ fricative

sign Any unit of communication (e.g. a word) which is part of a symbolic system such as human language.

sound-symbolism The association of a meaning with a particular combination of sounds in a range of words, e.g. *snide, sneaky, sneer* all share some 'nasty' element of meaning as well as beginning with *sn-*. ⇒ onomatopoeia

Speech Act Theory An approach to the meaning of language which stresses the use made of language, rather than the literal meaning of the combined words. Emphasises what we *do* with language, rather than what we *say*.

speech-communities Overlapping social groups of people who share a variety of language because of shared background or shared interests.

stress A term used for both word-stress, where words longer than one syllable have one syllable which is more prominent than the others, and sentence-stress where one syllable in a clause normally carries extra emphasis.

structuralism The name for the model of language which arose from the work of Ferdinand de Saussure. Structuralism emphasises the systematic and arbitrary nature of human language. ⇒ system

subject pronoun The set of pronouns which are used in subject position in English are *I, we, you, he, she, it, they*. The object pronouns are *me, us, you, him, her, it, them*.

suffix A bound morpheme which follows the free morpheme it is attached to, e.g. femin-*ism* ⇒ boun d morpheme, free morpheme

superordinate A word that shares a core of meaning with other, more specific words and which serves as a generic term for those more specific words, e.g. *flower* is the superordinate for *rose, anemone, daisy*, etc. ⇒ hyponym

synonymy A rare equivalence of meaning between words. Partial synonymy is much more common in English.

syntagmatic The relationship between linguistic units, such as sounds or words, which are combined in a linear sequence to make larger units. ⇒ paradigmatic

system A term used in structuralist models of language to describe the interdependence of the units of language. Members of systems are defined in relation to other members, rather than by reference to the world outside the system

tail The syllables (both stressed and unstressed) which follow the head of a tone unit and continue the pattern of intonation started there. ⇒ tone unit

tone unit The range of an intonation pattern, such as a fall or a fall-rise. Most neutrally, but not inevitably, corresponding to a clause.

transition relevant place A point in the speaker's text when other participants in the conversation will recognise a potential opportunity to take the floor. Usually corresponds to a grammatical unit.

transitive verb A verb which has an object, e.g. The woman *ate* my cake. ⇒ intransitive verb

velum/velar The soft palate, behind the roof of the mouth (palate). A number of English sounds are articulated here: /k/, /g/, /ŋ/.

voiced A speech sound that is made when the vocal cords are drawn together and are taut as well as almost touching. The air from the lungs comes up through the larynx and causes the vocal cords to vibrate. ⇒ voiceless

voiceless A speech sound that is made when the vocal cords are apart and therefore cannot vibrate. ⇒ voiced

vowel Unlike consonants, vowels are sounds made with no full or partial closure of the articulators in the mouth. Instead, the mouth is formed into a particular shape and the vibrations from the larynx are amplified and given a particular sonority as a result of the shape of the oral cavity. ⇒ consonant

Whorfian hypothesis Named after Benjamin Lee Whorf, the hypothesis claims that the world we perceive is to a greater or lesser extent (depending on how strong a version of the hypothesis we espouse) structured by the language we speak. This is in contrast to the popular view of language simply reflecting a given 'reality'.

Index

adjacency pair 172–6, 177
adjective 130–1
adverb 131–3
adverbial 136, 160
anaphoric reference 157
antonymy 102
apposition 154
appropriateness 199
arbitrary 17, 18, 24, 37

binary features 89
body language 200–7
bound morpheme(s) 80, 86

carnival 245
case grammar 140
cataphoric reference 158
categorisation 25–6
Chomsky 5–6, 28
closed-system 73, 75
co-operational principle 182–7
cohesive devices 222
cohesive features 157–66
collocation 123–9, 161
competence 28, 241
complement 137
complementaries 107
complementarity 104
complementary opposites 108
componential analysis 87–9
compound (words) 84, 86
compounding 85
connotation 14, 109–14
context 31–3
context-bound 75
context-free 75
contrastive stress 56, 65, 143
converse 107, 238

converseness 104
created opposition, opposites 150,
    151
Critical linguistics 224

dactylic 67
de Saussure 18, 19, 22, 87
deixis, deictic 76–7, 78–9
derivation 85
derivational morphemes 80, 81–4
dialect 49
dialogic, dialogism 243
directional opposition 105, 107
discourse 5

ellipsis 159
emblems 203
entailment(s) 151, 191–3

focus 142, 144
foregrounded 236
free morpheme(s) 79, 86
fricatives 41

gendered meanings 51
given information 141
gradable antonymy 102, 106
gradable opposite 107
(Grice's) maxims 182–7, 208

head 59
hierarchical model 9–11
hierarchy 6–8, 100–1, 106
homonymy 114
hyponym 100, 106, 108

iambic 65
icon 18, 26

iconic 19, 42, 67–8
ideologies 222, 224–8
illocutionary force 13
illustrators 203–4
implicature 195, 222–3, 226, 228
inclusiveness 101
index 19, 26
inflection 85
inflectional morphemes 80, 81
information 141–7
interruption 179
intertextual, intertextuality 234,
242, 243
intonation 59, 61, 63

langue 27–9, 108, 128, 150, 233,
236, 238, 247, 248
levels 4–5
lexical field theory 93
lexical field(s) 92, 93, 107
lexis 5
linearity 4
literary meaning 236–40
literature 236
metaphor 249–52

model 2–11, 19, 29, 64, 68, 81, 87,
93, 140, 182, 216–17, 241, 247
morpheme 37, 79–87
morphology 5
motivated 24–5
multiple meanings 114

nasal sounds 41
negotiation of meaning 220, 240–6
new information 141
non-literal meaning 12, 15–16
non-segmental 48–9, 55, 62
noun 130

Object 138
observer's paradox 27
omniscient narrator 188
onomatopoeia 37, 39–42, 45
open-classes 73
openings 172
oppositeness 102

paradigm, paradigmatic 19–22

parole 27–9, 108, 233, 247, 248
performance 28, 241
performative(s) 168–9
perlocutionary effect 168
phonology 5
pitch 49, 51, 62
plosive consonant 40
political correctness 219
polysemous meanings 115–19
polysemy 114
postural congruence 202
pragmatics 193
pre-sequences 174–5
prefixes 81
presuppositions 152–4, 155, 191–3,
195, 222–3, 226, 228
proposition(s) 151

referent 18
regulators 203–4
rhythm 63–7

segmental 48–9
selectional restrictions 122, 124,
127
semantic derogation 232–3
semantic features 87–9, 93, 96
Semantic Field Theory 91
semantic fields 91
semiotics 18
sense relations 98–9, 106, 108, 161
sentence stress 55–9
sign 18, 25
signified 18
signifier 18
sound-symbolism 37, 42–8
SPEAKING 210–15
speech act 173
speech act theory 166–70
speech communities 208–10
standard English 50
stress 55
stress-timed language 64
stressed syllables 64
Structuralism 22
Subject 138
substitution 158
suffixes 80
superordinate 100–1

syllabic /l/ 47
syllable-timed language 64
symbol 18, 26
symbolic system 17
synonyms 108
synonymy 99, 106
syntagma, syntagmatic 19–22, 30
syntax 5, 30
system 22–3, 28, 73, 98, 242

taboo 109, 218–22
three-part list 189
timbre 53
tone-unit 59, 61
tone-unit sequences 61–2
transformational grammar 122

turn-taking 177–82

unstressed syllables 64

verb 130
verbal function 137
volume 52, 62

Whorfian hypothesis 190, 229–36,
    246, 248
word order 30
word stress 55, 65
word-class 129

zero-derivation 83–4